CuR
500
McG
2002/1

~~LOURDES LIBRARY~~
CURRICULUM COLLECTION

 **W9-ABK-461**

McGRAW-HILL
SCIENCE

Macmillan/McGraw-Hill Edition
Teacher's Edition

Richard Moyer • **Lucy Daniel** • **Jay Hackett**
H. Prentice Baptiste • **Pamela Stryker** • **JoAnne Vasquez**

**NATIONAL
GEOGRAPHIC
SOCIETY**

On the Cover:
This black bear cub, native to North America, was born
in January or February and weighed less than a pound. An
adult male usually weighs between 90 and 135 kilograms
(200 and 300 pounds). But one weighed in at 236 kilograms
(520 pounds). Black bears fatten up on fruit and then
often sleep through the winter's coldest weather.

~~llege~~
P. O. Box 901
~~19437-0901~~

**Macmillan
McGraw-Hill**

New York   Farmington

PROGRAM AUTHORS

Dr. Lucy H. Daniel
Teacher, Consultant
Rutherford County Schools,
North Carolina

Dr. Jay Hackett
Professor Emeritus of Earth Sciences
University of Northern Colorado

Dr. Richard H. Moyer
Professor of Science Education
University of Michigan-Dearborn

Dr. H. Prentice Baptiste
Professor of Science and Multicultural Education
New Mexico State University
Las Cruces, New Mexico

Pamela Stryker, M.Ed.
Elementary Educator and Science Consultant
Eanes Independent School District
Austin, Texas

Dr. JoAnne Vasquez
Elementary Science Education Consultant
Mesa Public Schools, Arizona
NSTA Past President

NATIONAL
GEOGRAPHIC
SOCIETY
Washington, D.C

The features in this textbook entitled "Who's a Scientist?" "Amazing Stories," and "People in Science," as well as the unit openers, were developed in collaboration with the National Geographic Society's School Publishing Division. Copyright © 2002 National Geographic Society. All rights reserved.

The name "National Geographic" and the Yellow Border are registered trademarks of the National Geographic Society.

Macmillan/McGraw-Hill

*A Division of The **McGraw·Hill** Companies*

Copyright © 2002 Macmillan/McGraw-Hill,
a Division of the Educational and Professional
Publishing Group of The McGraw-Hill Companies, Inc.

All rights reserved. No part of this book may be reproduced or transmitted in any form
or by any means, electronic or mechanical, including photocopying, recording,
or by any information storage and retrieval system, without permission in writing from the publisher.

Macmillan/McGraw-Hill
Two Penn Plaza
New York, New York 10121-2298

Printed in the United States of America

ISBN 0-02-280085-9 / 1, Vol. 2

1 2 3 4 5 6 7 8 9 073/046 07 06 05 04 03 02 01

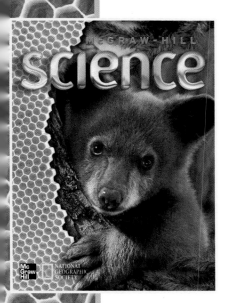

McGRAW-HILL SCIENCE

Macmillan/McGraw-Hill Edition
TEACHER'S EDITION

Table of Contents

Grade 4

LIFE SCIENCE

Unit A - *The World of Living Things*

1 The Cells in Living Things
2 Classifying Organisms
3 Organisms of the Past
4 Organisms and Where They Live
5 Changes in Ecosystems
6 Plant Parts
7 Plant Growth and Reproduction

Unit B - *Animals as Living Things*

1 Animal Characteristics
2 Animals Without Backbones
3 Animals with Backbones
4 Organ Systems
5 Development and Reproduction
6 Animal Survival

EARTH SCIENCE

Unit C - *Earth and Beyond*

1 What You Can Learn from Rocks
2 Clues from Fossils
3 Shaping Earth's Surface
4 The Story of Soil
5 Inside Earth
6 Earth, the Moon, and the Sun
7 The Solar System and Beyond

Unit D - *Water and Weather*

1 Water, Water Everywhere
2 Follow the Water (water cycle)
3 Motions in the Oceans
4 Go with the Flow (groundwater)
5 Water Please! (conservation)
6 Air, Wind, and the Atmosphere
7 Weather and Climate

PHYSICAL SCIENCE

Unit E - *Matter*

1 Matter (properties, states)
2 Measuring Matter
3 What Matter Is Made Of
4 Physical Changes
5 Chemical Changes

Unit F - *Energy*

1 Forces, Motion, and Energy
2 Energy and Tools
3 Heat
4 Light
5 Sound
6 Static Electricity
7 Current Electricity
8 Electricity and Magnetism

Grade 5

Unit A - *Structures of Plants and Animals*

1 Classifying Living Things
2 Roots, Stems, and Leaves
3 The Importance of Plants (photosynthesis)
4 Plants Without Seeds
5 Plants with Seeds
6 Flowers and Seeds
7 Plant Responses and Adaptations
8 Animal Structure and Function
9 Animal Adaptation

Unit B - *Interactions of Living Things*

1 Living Things and Their Environment
2 Food Chains and Food Webs
3 Cycles of Life
4 How Populations Survive
5 Biomes
6 How Ecosystems Change

Unit C - *Earth and Its Resources*

1 Earth and Its Neighbors
2 Earth's Changing Crust
3 Minerals of Earth's Crust
4 Earth's Rocks and Soil
5 Earth's Atmosphere
6 Earth's Fresh Water
7 Earth's Oceans
8 Energy Resources

Unit D - *Weather and Climate*

1 Atmosphere and Air Temperature
2 Water Vapor and Humidity
3 Clouds and Precipitation
4 Air Pressure and Wind
5 Air Masses and Fronts
6 Severe Storms
7 Climate

Unit E - *Properties of Matter and Energy*

1 Physical Properties
2 Elements and Compounds
3 Solids, Liquids, and Gases
4 Mixtures and Solutions
5 Chemical Changes
6 Acids and Bases
7 How Matter and Energy Interact

Unit F - *Motion and Energy*

1 Newton's First Law
2 Newton's Second and Third Laws
3 Newton's Law of Gravitation
4 Sound Waves
5 Pitch and Loudness
6 Reflection and Absorption
7 Light and Mirrors
8 Light and Lenses
9 Light and Color
10 Invisible Light

Grade 6

Unit A - *Classifying Living Things*

1 The Kingdoms of Life
2 Classifying Plants
3 Invertebrates
4 Vertebrates
5 Reproduction and Growth

Unit B - *Organization of Living Things*

1 From Cells to Ecosystems
2 Comparing Earth's Biomes
3 Parts of a Cell
4 Movement and Nutrition in Cells
5 Cells Divide and Grow
6 The History of Genetics
7 Predicting Traits
8 How DNA Controls Traits
9 Using Genetics

Unit C - *Observing the Sky*

1 The Tools of Astronomers
2 Earth and the Sun
3 The Moon in Motion
4 The Inner Solar System
5 The Outer Solar System
6 Stars
7 Galaxies and Beyond

Unit D - *The Restless Earth*

1 Moving Plates
2 Earthquakes
3 Volcanoes
4 Making Mountains and Soil
5 Erosion and Deposition
6 The Rock Cycle
7 Geologic Time

Unit E - *Interactions of Matter and Energy*

1 Physical Properties of Matter
2 Elements and Atoms
3 Chemical Changes
4 Temperature and Heat
5 How Heat Affects Matter
6 Sources of Energy
7 Static Electricity
8 Circuits
9 Electromagnets
10 Using Electricity

Unit F - *Motion, Work, and Machines*

1 Speed and Distance
2 Forces and Motion
3 Acceleration and Momentum
4 Energy and Work
5 How Levers Work
6 How Inclined Planes Work

Meeting National Science Standards

National Science Education Standards

The National Research Council set up a
National Committee on Science Education Standards and Assessment
to develop national standards in science education.
The Standards are summarized in these categories:

- Science as Inquiry
- Physical Science Content
- Life Science Content
- Earth and Space Science Content
- Science and Technology

- Science in Personal and Social Perspectives
- Nature and History of Science
- Unifying Concepts and Processes
- Fair, Consistent Assessment in a Variety of Contexts

Benchmarks for Science Literacy

The groundbreaking Project 2061 as presented in a report of the
American Association for the Advancement of Science,
the Benchmarks for Science Literacy,
provides teachers with common goals without requiring
uniform curricula and methods.

The Benchmarks can be summarized by:

- The Nature of Science
- The Nature of Technology
- The Physical Setting

- The Living Environment
- The Human Organism
- Common Themes

McGraw-Hill Science was developed to enable teachers to implement
these national science standards within the context of their
own state and local science criteria by focusing on three major aspects:

- **the tools and processes of inquiry in every lesson**
- **grade-level sequenced content**
  with life, earth, and physical sciences
  taught at each grade
- **assessment in a variety of contexts**

Pages TR2–TR3 in the Teacher Reference Section present a
correlation of the units of this grade level to both sets of these national standards.

Assessment in *McGraw-Hill Science*

McGraw-Hill Science provides a variety of contexts for assessment while students are learning and at ends of lessons, chapters, and units.

The assessment is student-centered, encompassing a four-fold assessment plan:

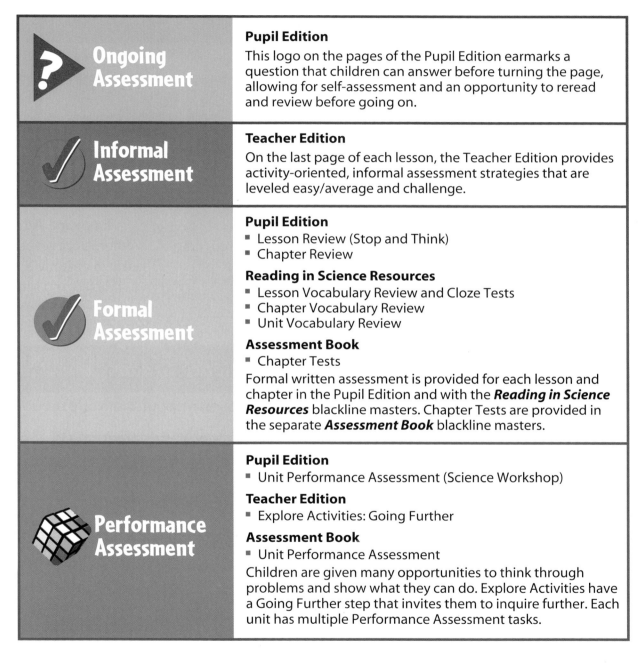

Ongoing Assessment

Pupil Edition
This logo on the pages of the Pupil Edition earmarks a question that children can answer before turning the page, allowing for self-assessment and an opportunity to reread and review before going on.

Informal Assessment

Teacher Edition
On the last page of each lesson, the Teacher Edition provides activity-oriented, informal assessment strategies that are leveled easy/average and challenge.

Formal Assessment

Pupil Edition
- Lesson Review (Stop and Think)
- Chapter Review

Reading in Science Resources
- Lesson Vocabulary Review and Cloze Tests
- Chapter Vocabulary Review
- Unit Vocabulary Review

Assessment Book
- Chapter Tests

Formal written assessment is provided for each lesson and chapter in the Pupil Edition and with the *Reading in Science Resources* blackline masters. Chapter Tests are provided in the separate *Assessment Book* blackline masters.

Performance Assessment

Pupil Edition
- Unit Performance Assessment (Science Workshop)

Teacher Edition
- Explore Activities: Going Further

Assessment Book
- Unit Performance Assessment

Children are given many opportunities to think through problems and show what they can do. Explore Activities have a Going Further step that invites them to inquire further. Each unit has multiple Performance Assessment tasks.

Portfolio Assessment

McGraw-Hill Science provides blackline masters *(Activity Resources)* to accompany all activities in the Pupil Editions, and Chapter Graphic Organizers *(Reading in Science Resources)* as well as *School to Home Activities* and *Cross Curricular Projects* blackline masters from which children can select items to build a portfolio.

Building Science Process Skills in McGraw-Hill Science

Building the skills of inquiry empowers children to solve problems, to evaluate their solutions, and to plan and implement their own investigations.

McGraw-Hill Science has a three-fold plan for building science process skills:

Introduction

Who's a Scientist?
Pupil Editions open with an introduction to all the process skills listed below.

Skill Instruction

Science Skill Builders
Special activities teach children how to use a process skill to accomplish a task.

Consistent Practice

Explore Activities
When children use a process skill in an activity, the step is labeled and highlighted.

The Process Skills taught in *McGraw-Hill Science Grades 1 and 2* are:

Observe	To see, hear, taste, touch, or smell to learn about the world around you
Measure	To find out how long, how much, or how warm something is
Compare	To tell how things are alike and different
Classify	To put things into groups to show how they are alike
Make a model	To make something to show a place or thing
Communicate	To write, draw, or tell to share ideas with others
Infer	To use what you know to figure something out
Put things in order	To tell or show what happens first, last, and in between
Predict	To use what you know to tell what will happen
Investigate	To make a plan and try it out
Draw a conclusion	To use what you observe to explain what happens

Developing Reading Skills in McGraw-Hill Science

Before– and After–Reading Questions

- **Before Reading**
  All Pupil Edition headings are questions that children can try to answer before reading.

- **After Reading**
  A corresponding question is provided at the end of each page or two-page spread to allow children to assess their comprehension.

Developing Vocabulary

- **Preview**
  The Teacher Edition provides a Chapter Vocabulary Preview on each Chapter Opener spread. The Pupil Edition previews vocabulary on the opening spread of each chapter.

- **Point of Instruction**
  Each vocabulary word is highlighted in yellow at the point where it is taught. At point of appearance the side column of the Teacher Edition provides a vocabulary teaching strategy for each vocabulary word.

SCIENCE Reading MiniLesson

Throughout the lessons, the Teacher Edition provides Reading Skill MiniLessons. Each MiniLesson is a brief tutorial and an activity for students to practice a specific reading skill for each chapter. One of the following skills is developed in each chapter:

- **Compare and Contrast**
- **Find the Main Idea**
- **Cause and Effect**
- **Draw Conclusions**
- **Sequence of Events**
- **Summarize (retell)**

SCIENCE Reading Strategy

The Teacher Edition provides additional opportunities for students to develop and apply reading skills. A listing on each Chapter Opener shows where the following skills are taught.

- **Cause and Effect**
- **Compare and Contrast**
- **Draw Conclusions**
- **Find the Main Idea**
- **Order of Events (act out or retell)**
- **Summarize (retell)**
- **Read Pictures**
- **Draw Visual Images Based on Text**
- **Ask Questions**
- **Follow Directions**
- **Build on Prior Knowledge**

BLACKLINE Reading in Science Resources

Throughout the Teacher Edition, reductions of blackline masters for:
- Lesson Outlines
- Reading Pictures

from the **Reading in Science Resources** are provided at point of use.

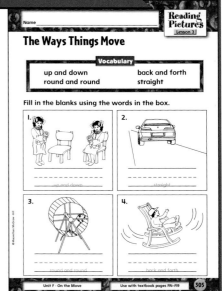

L·I·N·K·S
to Reading, Writing, Arithmetic, and More

McGraw-Hill Science is linked to all parts of your daily curriculum.
Children can integrate what they learn in science with what they learn throughout the day.

 CHAPTER LINKS At the end of each chapter, just before the Chapter Review, look for two pages earmarked with this logo.

You will find Links to:

READING LINK

Grade-Level Science Books

Three Grade-Level Science books for each unit, cross referenced in the Pupil Editions.

Cross Curricular Books

Books from the Reading and Social Studies curricula, 5 per unit, are pictured in the Teacher Edition at point of suggested use.

MUSIC/ART LINK

Children will find activities making pictures. In addition, opportunities to draw and create models are found in Explore Activities and Science Workshops.

HEALTH LINK

Children will find activities involving growing and staying healthy.

SOCIAL STUDIES LINK

Children will find activities involving neighborhoods, map skills, cultural perspectives, and more.

TECHNOLOGY LINK

In the Teacher Edition, options are provided for you and your children to use
- the Internet
- the Science Newsroom CD-ROMs

MATH LINK

Children will find activities involving graphs, measurements, basic operations and facts, and shapes.

LESSON LINKS

At the end of each lesson and in the Chapter Review, look for

CROSS CURRICULAR PROJECTS

This blackline master booklet provides cross curricular projects organized into easy to use activities for each unit, complete with a Unit Culminating Activity.

Materials

Consumable materials (based on six groups)

Materials	Quantity Needed per group	Kit Quantity	Unit/Lesson
Acorn	1	1	Science Center Card 5
Animal, Butterfly Garden Kit	1	1	A/2
Bag, plastic zip lip, 1 qt	2	50	A/8, Science Center Card 3
Balloon, 9"	1	35	D/4, E/1
Balloon, 15"	1	24	Science Center Card 36
Batteries, D-cell	2	12	C/2, Science Center Card 13
Bowl, Styrofoam, 12 oz	1	25	F/7
Can, coffee	1		Science Center Card 23, 36
Cotton balls		300	B/6
Crayons			A/3, 4, 5, B/6, C/6, E/3, Science Center Card 4, 7, 8, 12, 18, 21, 24
Cups, graduated, 30 ml	1	50	E/4
Cups, paper, 200 ml		100	F/1, 3, Science Center Card 20
Cups, plastic, 3.5 oz	1	25	Science Center Card 3
Cups, plastic, 300 ml	10	100	C/7, E/1, 3, Science Center Card 3, 19, 29
Detergent, household		14.7 oz	Science Center Card 28
Fasteners, brass	1	100	F/4, Science Center Card 8
Foil, aluminum, 12" x 25'		1 roll	F/8
Food coloring, blue, 30 ml		1 bottle	A/6
Food coloring, dark red, 30 ml		1 bottle	Science Center Card 29
Food, bean soup mix		20 oz	A/7
Food, bird seed			B/1
Food, peanut butter			B/1
Glue			A/7, B/6, Science Center Card 2, 4, 6, 8, 10, 15
Gloves, disposable		50 pair	Science Center Card 29
Ice			C/7, E/7, Science Center Card 30
Jelly, petroleum		4 oz	D/6
Lightstick, red	1	6	C/2
Newspaper			A/4, 5, B/7, D/7, E/6, Science Center Card 7
Notes, self-stick			D/5
Objects, old; e.g. soda cans, newspaper, bottles, jars, etc.			Science Center Card 24
Objects, old; e.g. yogurt container, milk container, paper towel and toilet paper tubes, shoebox, empty egg carton, plastic water bottle, coffee can			D/7
Paint			D/7
Paper			E/3, Science Center Card 6, 12
Paper towels			A/8
Paper, black			Science Center Card 8
Paper, construction			B/3, 6, E/5, Science Center Card 4, 15
Paper, construction, yellow and white			B/7
Paper, crepe streamer	1	81 ft	C/4
Paper, drawing			A/3, 4, 5, C/6
Paper, tissue	1		E/4
Paper, tissue, assorted colors		20 sheets	Science Center Card 15
Paper, wax, 75 sq ft		1 roll	B/1
Pencil	1		E/2
Pencil, w/eraser	1		Science Center Card 22
Plant, branch, large tree	1		Science Center Card 23
Plant, carnation, white	1		A/6
Plant, marigold, potted	1		A/5
Plants, identical, potted	2		A/3
Plants, radish, petunia, unpotted	1 each		A/4
Plate, paper	8	100	A/7, D/2, E/7, Science Center Card 8, 30
Rubber bands, assorted	1	4 oz	F/7, Science Center Card 36
Salt		737 g	E/6
Sand, fine		10 kg	D/3, F/8, Science Center Card 23
Seeds, corn		30 g	A/7, Science Center Card 5
Seeds, grass		30 g	A/7, Science Center Card 5
Seeds, Oriental Mung bean		60g, 2 pkgs	A/8, Science Center Card 5, 19
Seeds, red maple		10	A/7, Science Center Card 5
Seeds, sunflower		30 g	A/7, Science Center Card 5
Seeds, wheat		30 g	A/7, Science Center Card 5
Shoebox	1		B/6
Soil, clay		5 kg	D/2, Science Center Card 19, 20
Soil, loam		2.5 kg	D/2
Soil, potting		16 lbs	Science Center Card 3, 19, 20
Soil, sandy		2.5 kg	D/2
Spoons, plastic	1	24	E/1, 6, Science Center Card 3

Materials

Consumable materials (based on six groups)

Materials	Quantity Needed per group	Kit Quantity	Unit/Lesson
Sticks, craft		50	B/1, C/4
Straws, plastic, wrapped		100	D/4, Science Center Card 5, 28, 34
String		200 ft	B/1, Science Center Card 23
Tape			C/3, 4, D/4, Science Center Card 12, 23
Tube, cardboard	1	6	B/1
Yarn, red		1 skein	Science Center Card 15
Yarn, yellow		1 skein	Science Center Card 15

Non-consumable materials (based on six groups)

Materials	Quantity Needed per group	Kit Quantity	Unit/Lesson
Balance	1	2	E/2
Ball, multicolored hard rubber	1	6	A/1, C/2, F/1, 3
Block, wood	1	6	E/1, F/1, 4
Bolt	1	6	F/4
Book	1		E/2
Bowl, plastic clear, 12 oz	1	7	E/3, Science Center Card 5
Canister, film type	8	48	F/8
Clock	1		Science Center Card 30
Coin, pennies	7		E/6, Science Center Card 26
Coin, quarters	3		Science Center Card 26
Container, clear plastic, w/lid	3	6	E/3, 4, 6
Cork	1	6	E/6
Cup, plastic measuring, 500 ml	1	6	D/3, Science Center Card 20
Droppers	1	2	Science Center Card 7, 29
Eraser, chalk	1		E/2
Eraser	1	6	F/2, 4
Flashlight	1	6	C/2, Science Center Card 13
Goggles			Science Center Card 28, 29
Glove	1		C/7
Hand lens	1	6	A/2, 4, 5, 7, 8, D/1, 2, 6
Jar, tall, w/lid	1	6	A/6
Labels, "Earth" and "Sun"	1 of each		C/3
Magnet, bar	2	6	F/4, 5, 6, Science Center Card 35
Nut, hex	1	6	F/4

Materials	Quantity Needed per group	Kit Quantity	Unit/Lesson
Pan, aluminum foil, 13" x 10" x 2"	1	6	D/3
Pan, aluminum foil, 31 cm x 22 cm x 3 cm	1	1	Science Center Card 28
Paper clips		200	F/4, 5, 6, 8
Pencil	1		Science Center Card 25
Picture Cards, set, #1-6		1	B/4
Picture Card, set, #7-12		1	B/5
Pin, straight	1	150	Science Center Card 22
Rock	1		A/2
Rock, basalt specimen pack	1	1	D/1
Rock, limestone specimen pack	1	1	D/1
Rock, obsidian specimen pack	1	1	D/1
Rock, sandstone specimen pack	1	1	D/1
Rock, schist specimen pack	1	1	D/1
Ruler	1		Science Center Card 19
Scissors	8		B/6, E/5, Science Center Card 1, 4, 6, 8, 10, 12
Shoebox	1		C/2
Socks, cotton	1	2	Science Center Card 5
Sponge	1	6	A/1
Thermometer	2	12	C/1, 4, 5, Science Center Card 18
Toy, bee	1		B/3
Toy, bird		6	B/3
Toy, butterflies	1	6	B/3
Toy, cat		6	B/3
Toy, dog		6	B/3
Toy, fish	1	12	B/3
Toy, frog	1	6	B/3
Toy, game chips		100	Science Center Card 31
Toy, horse		6	B/3
Toy, lizard		6	B/3
Toy, penguin	1		B/3
Toy, shark	1		B/3
Toy, Slinky	1	6	F/3
Toy, snake	1	6	B/3

Consultants

LIFE SCIENCES

Dr. Carol Baskin
University of Kentucky, Lexington, KY

Dr. Joe W. Crim
University of Georgia, Athens, GA

Dr. Marie DiBerardino
Allegheny University of Health Sciences
Philadelphia, PA

Dr. R. E. Duhrkopf
Baylor University, Waco, TX

Dr. Dennis L. Nelson
Montana State University, Bozeman, MT

Dr. Fred Sack
Ohio State University, Columbus, OH

Dr. Martin VanDyke
Denver, CO

Dr. E. Peter Volpe
Mercer University, Macon, GA

EARTH SCIENCES

Dr. Clarke Alexander
Skidaway Institute of Oceanography,
Savannah, GA

Dr. Suellen Cabe
Pembroke State University, Pembroke, NC

Dr. Thomas A. Davies
Texas A & M University, College Station, TX

Dr. Ed Geary
Geological Society of America, Boulder, CO

Dr. David C. Kopaska-Merkel
Geological Survey of Alabama, Tuscaloosa, AL

PHYSICAL SCIENCES

Dr. Bonnie Buratti
Jet Propulsion Lab, Pasadena, CA

Dr. Shawn Carlson
Society of Amateur Scientists, San Diego, CA

Dr. Karen Kwitter
Williams College, Williamstown, MA

Dr. Steven Souza
Williamstown, MA

Dr. Joseph P. Straley
University of Kentucky, Lexington, KY

Dr. Thomas Troland
University of Kentucky , Lexington, KY

Dr. Josephine Davis Wallace
University of North Carolina, Charlotte, NC

CONSULTANT FOR PRIMARY GRADES
Donna Harrell Lubcker
East Texas Baptist University, Marshall, TX

• TEACHER PANELISTS

Newark, NJ
First Avenue School
Jorge Alameda
Concetta Cioci
Neva Galasso
Bernadette Kazanjian - reviewer
Janet Mayer - reviewer
Toby Marks
Maria Tutela

Brooklyn, NY
P.S. 31
Paige McGlone
Janet Mantel
Madeline Pappas
Maria Puma - reviewer

P.S. 217
Rosemary Ahern
Charles Brown
Claudia Deeb - reviewer
Wendy Lerner

P.S. 225
Christine Calafiore
Annette Fisher - reviewer

P.S. 250
Melissa Kane

P.S. 277
Erica Cohen
Helena Conti
Anne Marie Corrado
Deborah Scott-DiClemente
Jeanne Fish
Diane Fromhartz
Tricia Hinz
Lisa Iside
Susan Malament
Joyce Menkes-reviewer
Elaine Noto
Jean Pennacchio

Jeffrey Hampton
Mwaka Yavana

Elmont, NY
Covert Avenue School
Arlene Connelly

Mt. Vernon, NY
Holmes School
Jennifer Cavallaro
Lou Ciofi
George DiFiore
Brenda Durante
Jennifer Hawkins - reviewer
Michelle Mazzotta
Catherine Moringiello
Mary Jane Oria - reviewer
Lucille Pierotti
Pia Vicario - reviewer

Ozone Park, NY
St. Elizabeth School
Joanne Cocchiola - Reviewer
Helen DiPietra - Reviewer
Barbara Kingston
Madeline Visco

St. Albans, NY
Orvia Williams

• TEACHER REVIEWERS

Peoria, IL
Rolling Acres Middle School
Gail Truho

Rockford, IL
Rockford Public Schools
Dr. Sharon Wynstra
Science Coordinator

Newark, NJ
Alexander Street School
Cheryl Simeonidis

Albuquerque, NM
Jackie Costales
Science Coordinator,
Montgomery Complex

Poughkeepsie, NY
St. Peter's School
Monica Crolius

Columbus, OH
St. Mary's School
Linda Cotter
Joby Easley

Keizer, OR
Cummings Elementary
Deanna Havel

McMinnville, OR
McMinnville School District
Kristin Ward

Salem, OR
Fruitland Elementary
Mike Knudson

Four Corners Elementary
Bethany Ayers
Sivhong Hanson
Cheryl Kirkelie
Julie Wells

Salem-Keizer Public Schools
Rachael Harms
Sue Smith,
Science Specialist

Yoshikai Elementary
Joyce Davenport

Norristown, PA
St. Teresa of Avila
Fran Fiordimondo

Pittsburgh, PA
Chartiers Valley
Intermediate School
Rosemary Hutter

Memphis, TN
Memphis City Schools
Quincy Hathorn
District Science Facilitator

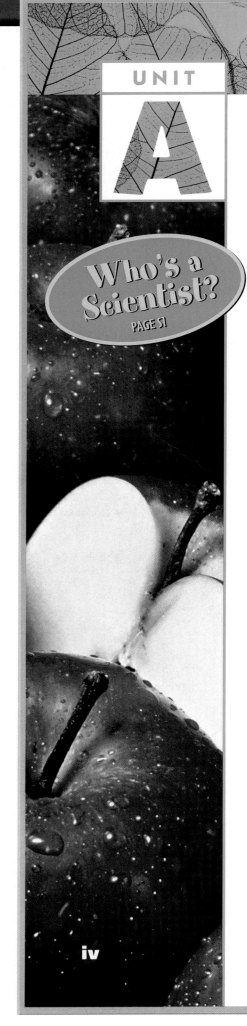

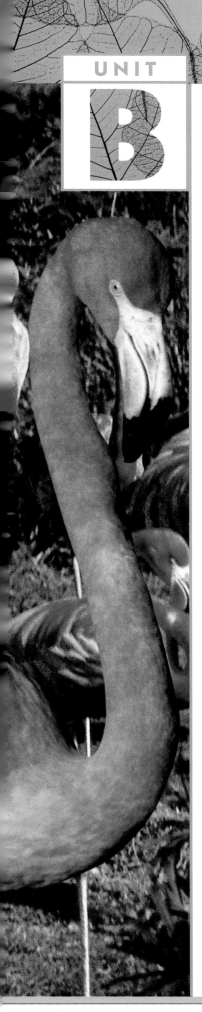

Animals Are Living Things PAGE B1

The Sky and Weather PAGE C1

Caring for Earth PAGE D1

Physical Science

On the Move PAGE F1

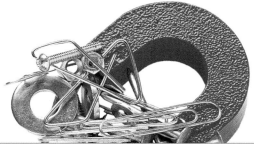

Read these pages. They will help you understand this book.

This is the name of the lesson.

Get Ready asks a question to get you started. You can answer the question from the picture.

This Science Skill is used in the Explore Activity.

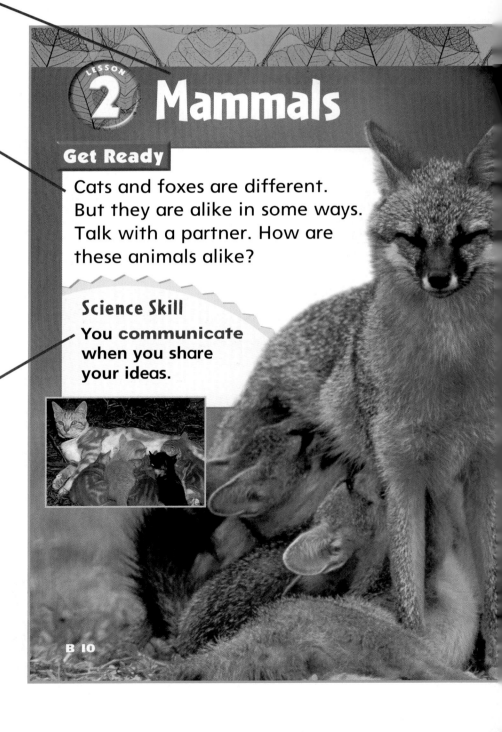

LESSON
2 Mammals

Get Ready

Cats and foxes are different. But they are alike in some ways. Talk with a partner. How are these animals alike?

Science Skill

You **communicate** when you share your ideas.

B 10

You can try the **Explore Activity** before you read the lesson.

The **Explore Activity** helps you answer a question.

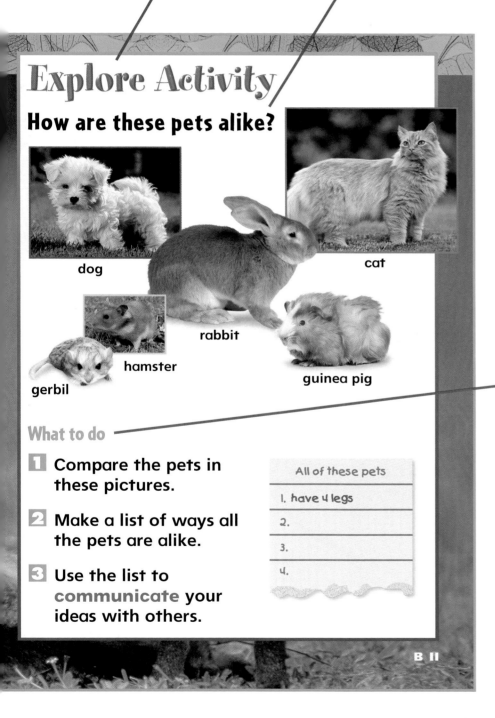

Explore Activity

How are these pets alike?

dog

cat

rabbit

hamster

gerbil

guinea pig

What to do

What to do are the steps you follow.

1 Compare the pets in these pictures.

2 Make a list of ways all the pets are alike.

3 Use the list to **communicate** your ideas with others.

All of these pets
1. have 4 legs
2.
3.
4.

B 11

xi

Now you are ready to read

Before You Read
Read the red question at the top of the page. It will help you find the main idea.

Dark words with yellow around them are new words to learn.

Read
As you read, look for the answer.

Read to Learn

What are mammals?

Mammals are a group of animals with hair or fur. All mother mammals feed milk to their young. All mammals can move. Some mammals may walk, run, or fly. Some hop or swim.

bat

cougar

kangaroo

B 12

This label tells you what the picture is. Pictures and words work together.

seal

Bats, cats, and seals are mammals. You know another mammal—you! That's right, people are mammals, too.

human

▷ **How are mammals alike?**
They have hair or fur, they get milk from their mothers, and they move.

After You Read
This question helps you check what you just read.

These questions check what you learned in the lesson.

Stop and Think

1. What do mammals feed their young?
2. What makes people mammals?

MORE TO READ Read **Baby Whales Drink Milk** by Barbara Juster Esbensen.

Fun activities help you learn more.

B 13

Science Safety
The Classroom

- Learn safety procedures for classroom activities.
- Learn safety procedures for outdoor activities.

Build on Prior Knowledge

Invite children to share their experiences with using protective clothing. Ask:

- **When might people wear safety gloves?** (Safety gloves might be worn when working with hot items, using hazardous chemicals, and handling sharp objects.)

- **What other protective clothing might people wear?** (Possible responses: aprons, protective face masks, heat-resistant suits, steel-tipped boots)

- **When do people wear safety goggles?** (When they use dangerous machinery or when they work with something that might splash into their eyes.)

Developing the Main Idea

Read aloud the classroom safety tips on pages xiv–xv as children follow along. Pause after each safety tip to discuss why it is important and what can happen when someone does not follow the tip.

Using the Illustrations

Point out the "Be Careful" logo. Explain to children that when they see the safety logo, a safety tip follows.

Demonstrate how to use safety goggles and have children practice putting them on.

- **When would it be a good idea to wear safety goggles in the classroom?** (Wear safety glasses whenever an activity might injure the eyes.)

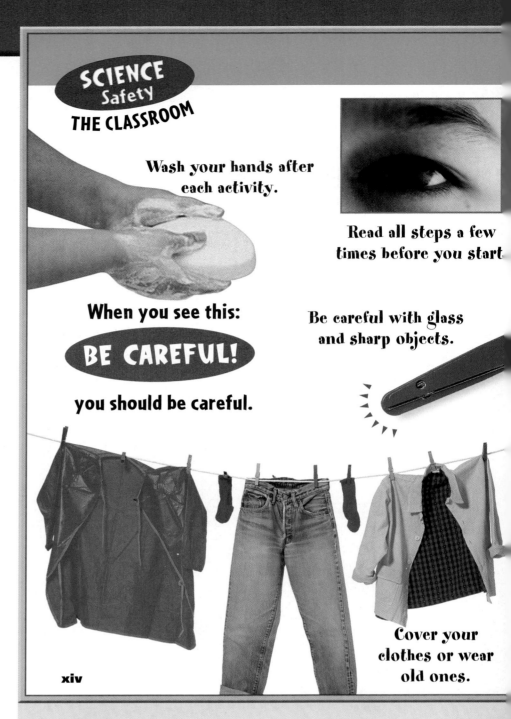

SCIENCE Safety
THE CLASSROOM

Wash your hands after each activity.

Read all steps a few times before you start.

When you see this:

BE CAREFUL!

you should be careful.

Be careful with glass and sharp objects.

Cover your clothes or wear old ones.

xiv

Science Background

Important Precautions

Children should wash hands with soap and water after handling chemicals, natural materials, or organisms, and before using science equipment. Generally, children should wash hands with soap and water *before* and *after* an activity.

Children should wear splash-proof goggles when working with liquids, or when using equipment or materials that can pop off or fly through the air.

listen to the teacher.

Never taste or smell anything unless your teacher tells you to.

Keep your workplace neat. Clean up after you are done.

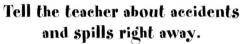

Tell the teacher about accidents and spills right away.

Wear goggles when you are told to.

xv

Thinking Further: *Drawing Conclusions*

■ **You take worms from a terrarium and examine them. What safety tip would you follow after you put the worms back?** (Wash your hands with soap and water.)

■ **While watering the plants for a science experiment, you spill water on the floor. What safety tip would you follow?** (Clean up spills right away.)

■ **You need seeds, water, sand, soil, clay, and pots for a science activity. What safety tips would you follow?** (Possible responses: Read all the steps before you start; listen to the teacher; clean up when you are done; wash your hands with soap and water.)

Exploring the Main Idea

Encourage children to suggest classroom activities in which they follow safety tips or rules. Children may say they follow safety tips when using sharp or pointed objects, working with glass containers, handling the class pets, watering plants, and using a flashlight as examples. Emphasize that by following safety tips or rules, they can help prevent accidents and stay safe.

SCIENCE Reading Strategy

Sequence of Events

Developing Reading Skills

Discuss with children which of the *Classroom Safety Tips* should be done at the start of an activity. Read all the steps before you start.

Ask children why they think this tip comes first. (Knowing exactly what to do before you start an activity can help you stay safe throughout it.)

Science Safety
Outdoors

Developing the Main Idea
Tell children that page xvi shows safety tips for outdoor activities. Read aloud the page as children follow along. Pause after each safety tip to discuss why it is important and what can happen when someone does not follow the tip.

- **Why is it important to stay with your group when you go outside or on a field trip?** (to stay out of dangerous situations; to keep from getting lost)

- **What should you do if an accident happens?** (Tell the teacher right away.)

- **Why shouldn't you touch plants or animals unless your teacher tells you?** (Possible answers: Animals might bite; you might injure plants and animals; and so on.)

Children may write about or discuss appropriate safety procedures for classroom activities, outside activities, and for field trips.

Retelling
Check children's understanding by asking them why safety tips are important and what can happen if safety tips aren't followed.

SCIENCE Safety OUTDOORS

Don't touch plants or animals unless your teacher tells you to.

Tell the teacher about accidents right away.

Listen to the teacher.

Stay with your group.

Never taste or smell anything unless your teacher tells you to.

Never throw your trash on the ground.

Put living things back where you found them.

xvi

English Language Learners

Safety Demonstrations
Invite children to show their understanding of the safety tips by demonstrating how to handle a sharp object, carry a jar, clean up a spill, tell about an accident, put on goggles when told, put materials where they belong after an activity, and so on.

NATIONAL GEOGRAPHIC

Who's a Scientist?

Look and see.

Who's a Scientist?

There are many kinds of scientists.
You can be one, too.

A Scientist:

- observes
- compares
- measures
- classifies things
- makes a model
- communicates
- infers
- puts things in order
- predicts
- investigates
- draws a conclusion

Scientists observe.

Look for a red rock. Tell what you might hear at this pond.

S1

 Science Background

Scientific Process
Scientists use many different tools to observe, including measuring instruments, hand lenses, computers, microscopes, telescopes, X rays, and satellites. They take photographs, make charts and models, and write about their observations. They question their observations, construct explanations, perform experiments to test their explanations, and draw conclusions.

Who's a Scientist?

Objective

■ Explore the skills that scientists use in their work.

Scientists observe.

Build on Prior Knowledge
Direct children's attention to the front of the *Who's a Scientist?* divider. Ask:

■ **Which person is a scientist?** Encourage children to describe what each of the four scientists pictured is studying.

■ **What are some other things scientists study?** (Possible responses: plants; people that lived long ago; human body; rocks and minerals; Sun, Moon, planets, and stars; weather)

■ **How do scientists study things?** Read the list of skills scientists use on the back of the divider.

Using the Illustrations

Ask:

■ **What do you see in the pond?** (water, frog, red rock, gravel, bubbles)

■ **What sound does the frog make?** (plop)

Developing the Main Idea

Ask:

■ **Suppose you are at this pond. What senses would you use to observe the pond?** (seeing; hearing)

■ **What other senses can you name?** (tasting, smelling, touching, or feeling)

■ **Which sense did you use to find a red rock?** (seeing)

■ **How did you just act like a scientist?** (I used my senses to observe things.)

See Science Skill Builder, p. R2.

 Technology

■ Skills and Handbook Transparencies S1–S8: *Who's a Scientist?*

S1

Scientists compare and measure.

Using the Illustrations
- **What might a scientist measure?** (Possible responses: how long or short something is, how fast or slow something is; how warm or cold something is)

Developing the Main Idea
Read page S2 aloud as children follow along in their books. To make sure children understand what they should do, ask:

- **Which line do you think is the longest?** (Children might mention any one of the three lines.)

- **What tool will you use to measure the lines?** (a ruler) Remind children to line up the end of line with zero on the ruler.

- **After you measure each line, what will you do?** (Compare the measurements to see if one line is longer than the other two lines.)

- **What did you find out about the length of the lines?** (All three lines are the same length.) Explain to children that this is called an optical illusion.

- **How did you just act like a scientist?** (I measured and compared the length of lines.)

See Science Skill Builders, pp. R3–R4.

Scientists compare and measure.

Compare these lines.
Measure them.
Which one is longest?

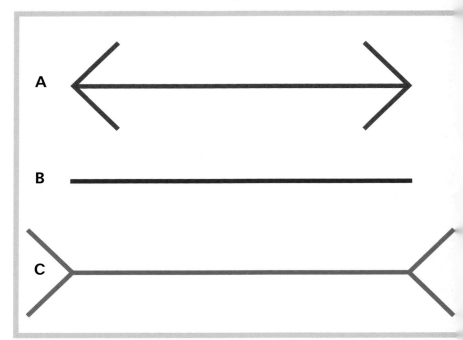

S 2

 Advanced Learners

Optical Illusions
Tell children it is the direction and angles of the lines at the end of each arrow pictured on page S2 that cause one line to appear longer or shorter than the others, creating an optical illusion. Have children look for other examples of optical illusions in books or on the Internet. Encourage students to explain what creates these optical illusions.

cientists classify things.

which group does this belong?
ow do you know?
ee! You are a scientist, too!

S 3

Scientists classify things.

Using the Illustrations

Read the sentence at the top of page S3 aloud. Then discuss the two groupings pictured on this page. Point to the group of fruits and ask:

- **How are all the things in this group alike?** (They are all fruits.)

Encourage children to identify and describe the fruits.

Point to the group of blocks next, and ask:

- **How are all the things in this group alike?** (They are all blocks made out of wood.)

- **How are they different?** (The blocks are different shapes and sizes.) Encourage children to describe the different blocks they see.

Developing the Main Idea

Point to the strawberry. Have children identify and describe the strawberry. Then ask:

- **In which group does the strawberry belong: the fruits or the blocks?** (the fruits)

Conclude by asking:

- **What do you do when you classify things?** (You group things that are alike.)

- **How did you just act like a scientist?** (I classified the strawberry by grouping it with the fruits.)

See Science Skill Builder, p. R5.

SCIENCE FOR ALL
Inclusion

Classifying

Divide a bulletin board into two sections. Attach pictures of three vegetables on one half and 3 four-legged animals on the other. Have children identify the things in each group, tell how they are alike, and suggest a label for each group (vegetables, animals with four legs). Then invite children to find and cut out magazine pictures to add to each group.

Scientists make models.

Using the Illustrations

Ask:

- **What kind of a model is being shown here?** (a model of an airplane.)
- **What can you use to make this model?** (paper)
- **How could you see if the model airplane works?** (test the model to see if it will fly)

Exploring the Main Idea

Invite children to make similar paper airplanes. Demonstrate the following directions:

1 Fold the paper in half lengthwise. Unfold the paper. Next fold the two corners at the top of the paper to the fold line.

2 Then bring in the outer edge of one half to the fold line and fold. Repeat with the other half.

3 Fold the two halves together as shown.

4 Then fold the two short sides down.

Have children write their names on their models. Children can then stand in a line at back of the room or outside and then test fly their models. Have children share the results. Then ask:

- **What is a model?** (A model is something you make to show a thing.)
- **How did you just act like a scientist?** (I made a model of an airplane.)

See Science Skill Builder, p. R9.

Scientists make models.

Make a model airplane.
How well did it fly?

S 4

Math MiniLesson

Measurement

Develop Display a ruler, meter stick or yardstick, and a measuring tape. Explain that all three can be used to measure distance. As children examine the tools, point out the units of measurement on each one as well as how to use each tool.

Activity Mark a starting line at the back of the classroom or outside on a playing field. Invite several children one at a time to stand on the line and then fly the paper airplanes they made. Help children use the measuring tools to determine the distance of each flight. Record each distance and child's name. Then compare all the distances to see which plane made the longest flight.

Scientists communicate.

What is missing from this picture? Tell others your answer.

S 5

Scientists communicate.

Using the Illustrations

Ask:

- **What kind of a day is it?** (rainy day) **How can you tell?** (Possible responses: The child has an umbrella; I see raindrops; the umbrella is wet.)

Developing the Main Idea

Read aloud the question above the illustration. Tell children that they must look for a clue—something in the picture that will help them to answer the question. Give children a minute to determine that part of the umbrella handle is missing. Encourage children to explain how they looked for clues. Did they look at one thing at a time? Did they start at the top (bottom, left, right) and work down (up, right, left)? Did they think about all the parts of an umbrella and then look for each part? Then ask:

- **What does it mean to communicate?** (possible response: to talk, write, or draw to share your ideas)

- **Did you communicate?** (yes) **How?** (by telling my ideas to others)

- **How did you just act like a scientist?** (I looked for clues and communicated my ideas.)

See Science Skill Builder, p. R6.

Inclusion

What's Missing?

Tell children to draw a person, place, or thing, but to leave out a part of it. For example, if they draw the front of the house, they might omit the front door. Have children then trade drawings, look for clues, and then draw in what is missing. Explain that by drawing, they are also communicating. Display the drawings for children to see and discuss.

Scientists infer.

Using the Illustrations
Have children focus their attention on the illustration. Explain that they can infer or figure out where the children have been by using what they know and see.

Ask:

- **What season of the year is it?** (summer) **Why do you think so? Tell what you know or what you see.** (Possible response: It is hot in the summer; the children are wearing swimsuits; the children wouldn't be outside in swimsuits if it were cold outside.)

- **Do you think the children have just been in the bathtub?** (No.) **Why do you think so? Tell what you know or what you see.** (Possible responses: I know that people don't usually wear a swimsuit in the bathtub; the children have a beach ball and pail; the children are outside, not inside.)

- **Where have the children been?** (swimming in a pool or at the beach) **Why do you think so? Tell what you know or what you see.** (Possible response: The children are wearing swimsuits, carrying beach gear, and standing outside, so I know they have been swimming at a pool or beach.)

- **How did you just act like a scientist?** (I used what I know and what I saw to infer where the children were.)

See Science Skill Builder, p. R8.

Scientists infer.

Where have these children been?
What clues help you know?

S 6

 English Language Learners

Infer
Have children take turns acting out scenes such as the following: getting up in the morning, ice skating for the first time, making and eating a sandwich, getting ready to go out in the snow, loading up a wagon and pulling it, walking a big dog. Have the "audience" use what they know and see to infer what each "actor" is doing.

Scientists put things in order.

Put these pictures in order.

Scientists predict.

Predict what will happen next.
You are a scientist, too.

S 7

Scientists put things in order and predict.

Using the Illustrations

Focus attention on the balloon sequence. Have children describe each picture. Ask:

■ **Are the pictures in order?** (No.) **How can you tell?** (Possible response: The first picture should not show a big balloon because when you start to blow up a balloon there is very little air in it.)

Developing the Main Idea

Ask:

■ **Which picture comes first?** (bottom right) **Which picture comes next?** (top right) **Which picture comes last?** (middle left)

■ **What do you think will happen next? Make a prediction.** (The balloon will burst.) **Why do you think so?** (Possible response: If you keep blowing air into the balloon, it will stretch and stretch until it can't stretch anymore and then burst.)

After completing the activity, ask:

■ **How did you just act like a scientist?** (I put the pictures in order and then predicted that the balloon would burst.)

See Science Skill Builders, pp. R7 and R10.

Inclusion

Putting Things in Order

Randomly display pictures of spring, summer, and fall. Have children identify the summer scene. Next have children identify the season that comes before and the season that comes after. Ask a volunteer to order the pictures. Then have children draw and label a picture to show the season that comes before spring and after fall. (winter)

Scientists investigate and draw conclusions.

Using the Illustrations
As you read aloud the sentences at the top of page S8, have children follow along. Then ask:

- **What is the picture on the left?** (footprints) Have children identify the animals on the right. (bird, bear, rabbit)

Developing the Main Idea
Focus children's attention on the footprints. Explain that one of the animals on the right made them.

- **What is your plan to find out what made the footprints?** (Possible response: compare the footprints with the feet of each animal.)

- **Which animal do you think made the footprints? Why?** (the bear because the footprints are big and have toes)

- **How did you just act like a scientist?** (I made a plan to investigate, tried it, and then drew a conclusion.)

Retelling
Have children summarize what they have learned. Ask:

- **What do scientists try to find answers for?** (questions they have about things around them)

- **What do scientists do to find answers?** (observe, compare, measure, classify, communicate, put things in order, infer, make a model, predict, investigate, draw a conclusion)

Have children turn to the list of skills on the divider page. As they read each skill, have children tell what each skill is and how they used it, just like a scientist does.

See Science Skill Builders, pp. R11–R12.

Scientists investigate and draw conclusions.

Investigate these tracks.
Which animal made them?

S 8

Inclusion

Scientists at Work
Have children draw and label a picture to show how they use one of the skills scientists use in their work. Then have them write a sentence that tells about it.

Advanced Learners

What Skill Did I Use?
Have children play a game in which clues are given, for example: I made a plan and tested it out. What skill did I use? (investigate)

Earth Science

UNIT C
The Sky and Weather

NATIONAL GEOGRAPHIC

The Sky and Weather

Main Idea: The Sun provides Earth with heat and light. Other objects in the sky include the Moon, stars, and planets. Weather and how it affects living things can be described according to the seasons.

Unit Organizer

CHAPTER 5 The Sky,
pp. C2–C23

Main Idea: Earth revolves around the Sun, which provides Earth with heat and light and causes night and day. Objects in the night sky include the Moon, which gets its light from the Sun; stars, which are grouped in constellations; and planets.

LESSON 1 The Sun, *pp. C4–C9*

Main Idea: The Sun is the source of heat, which can be measured by temperature, and light, which makes day and night.

LESSON 2 The Moon and Stars, *pp. C10–C15*

Main Idea: The Moon gets its light from the Sun. Stars are grouped in constellations.

LESSON 3 The Planets, *pp. C16–C19*

Main Idea: Earth moves around the Sun. Other planets also move around the Sun.

CHAPTER 6 Weather and Seasons,
pp. C24–C53

Main Idea: Weather, such as winds, rain, and snow, affects living things. The seasons help us understand how weather changes throughout the year.

LESSON 4 Weather, *pp. C26–C31*

Main Idea: Weather describes the air outside. Rain and snow fall from clouds.

LESSON 5 Weather Changes, *pp. C32–C37*

Main Idea: You can use weather-related instruments to measure weather and a chart to describe changes. Some weather events are harmful to living things.

LESSON 6 Spring and Summer, *pp. C38–C43*

Main Idea: Each spring and summer, the weather gets warmer and living things are more active.

LESSON 7 Fall and Winter, *pp. C44–A49*

Main Idea: In the fall and winter, the weather is cooler. Many plants stop growing and animals get less active. Some animals move to warmer areas during winter.

Grade-Level Science Books

EASY

Rosita gets wet when she slips in a puddle walking in the rain.

CHALLENGE

Fall is one of the four seasons of the year. Children can entertain themselves during the fall, especially when the leaves change color and fall.

EASY

While camping with his family each summer, a young boy especially loves night-time when he can gaze at the Moon and the stars. He watches and dreams each night as the Moon seems to change positions.

To order from Macmillan/McGraw-Hill, call 800-442-9685.

Cross Curricular Books from Macmillan/McGraw-Hill

Debbie's Good Night Pals by Jeanne Argente

Sheep Station by Shirley Frederick

Rain, Rain by Marilyn Greco

The Big Sun by Michael Maia

Night and Day by Robin Martell Zane

To order, call 800-442-9685.

Student Bibliography

Anholt, Catherine and Lawrence. **Sun Snow Stars Sky.** New York: Viking, 1995.

Asch, Frank. **Moondance.** New York: Scholastic, 1994.

Branley, Franklyn M. **The Moon Seems to Change.** New York: HarperCollins Publishers, 1987.

Hiscock, Bruce. **The Big Storm.** New York: Aladdin Paperbacks, 2000.

Keats, Ezra Jack. **The Snowy Day.** New York: Viking, Penguin, 1962, 1981.

Zolotow, Charlotte. **When the Wind Blows.** New York: Harper Trophy/HarperCollins Publishers, 1995.

Reading in Science

McGraw-Hill Science

Teacher Editions provide point-of-use strategies and resource support for students to practice reading skills as they read their science texts.

- **Reading MiniLessons**
- **Reduced Blackline Masters** from *Reading in Science Resources*
- **Additional Reading Strategies**

Reading in Science Resources

Boxes beneath the reduced Pupil Edition pages identify specific places in a lesson where students can complete worksheets from the *Reading in Science* Resources blackline masters. Reduced worksheets for this unit are found on the following pages of this Teacher Edition.

Lesson Outlines: C6, C12, C18, C28, C34, C40, C46

Interpret Illustrations (Reading Pictures): C8, C12, C18, C30, C35, C40, C46

Reading in Science Resources, p. 125

Reading MiniLesson

Reading MiniLessons provide a brief tutorial and an activity for children to practice a specific reading skill for each chapter. In this unit, the chapter reading skills are:

Cause and Effect: C8, C13

Sequence of Events: C30, C34, C41, C48

Reading Skills

Additional opportunities for students to develop and apply reading skills are provided in this unit as follows:

- ○ **Cause and effect**
- ◉ **Compare and contrast:** C29, C32, C38
- ○ **Draw conclusions**
- ○ **Find the main idea**
- ◉ **Order of events (act out or retell):** C13
- ◉ **Summarize (retell):** C9, C15, C19, C31, C37, C43, C49
- ◉ **Read pictures:** C8, C12, C18, C30, C35, C40, C46
- ◉ **Draw visual images based on text:** C31, C39, C50, C56
- ◉ **Ask questions:** C4, C10, C16, C26, C32, C38, C44
- ◉ **Follow directions:** C5, C11, C12, C27, C33, C39, C45
- ◉ **Build on Prior Knowledge:** C4, C10, C16, C26, C32, C38, C44

CROSS CURRICULUM IDEAS for integrating science

L·I·N·K·S

Meeting Individual Needs

McGraw-Hill Science **includes all children in the learning process by providing a variety of strategies in this unit.**

 English Language Learners

Season Game

Write one of these entries in each box of a tic-tac-toe grid: *seasons, summer, winter, spring, fall, hot, cold, warm, cool.* Other words may include *snowy, rainy, store food, build a nest, pick fruits.* Call out an entry. Before pairs of children can mark an *X* or *O* on their grids, they must explain the entry's meaning using gestures and by using it in a sentence. **Kinesthetic; Linguistic; Spatial**

 Advanced Learners

Black or White

Have children place a white cloth over one thermometer in a sunny spot, a black cloth of the same fabric over another and read the thermometers every 5 minutes for 20 minutes. Ask: **Does the thermometer rise higher and faster under the black or white cloth?** (black) **Which color clothing will keep you cooler in summer?** (white) **Logical; Spatial**

 Inclusion

Feeling Like the Weather

Have children look at pages C26 and C28–C29. Invite them to tell how different weather makes them feel. Ask: **Do rainy days make you sad or sleepy? Do cold snowy days make you happy or just cold? How do foggy days make you feel?** Encourage children to share their feelings and discover that others may have the same feelings. **Spatial; Linguistic**

For additional support, see pp. C4, C14, C16, C26, C29, C42, C47.

Learning Styles

Children acquire knowledge in a variety of ways that reflect different, often distinct, learning styles. The seven learning styles are:

- ◉ Kinesthetic pp. C4, C5
- ◉ Social C29
- ○ Intrapersonal
- ◉ Linguistic pp. C4, C8, C16, C26, C29, C47

- ◉ Logical/Mathematical pp. C36, C42
- ○ Auditory/Musical
- ◉ Visual/Spatial pp. C8, C14, C16, C26, C36, C42

Technology for McGRAW-HILL SCIENCE

CD-ROMs

Science Newsroom CD-ROM

Science Newsroom CD-ROM, Primary Edition, is available on the Web site.

Chapter 5: The Sky Constellations
Children identify and recognize constellations in the night sky.

Join me in the Science Newsroom

Videotapes

Explore Activity Videos

All Explore Activities are available on video. Introduce lessons with these Explore Activities on Video.

Lesson 1: Where will it be warmer?

Lesson 2: What can you see in the dark?

Lesson 3: How does Earth move around the Sun?

Lesson 4: What can you observe about the air?

Lesson 5: How does the weather change in a week?

Lesson 6: Is the weather the same all year?

Lesson 7: How can you stay warm when it is cold outside?

Science Experiences Videotapes

Chapter 6:

Lesson 2 The Moon and Stars
The Moon and Stars (Package 5)

Lesson 4 The Moon and Stars
Space Camp: A Week of Surprises (Package 5)

Lesson 5 Weather Changes
Sky Watch: Tracking a Winter Storm (Package 6)

Science Music CDs

Lesson 1: Twinkle, Twinkle, Little Star; Star Light, Star Bright

Lesson 3: The Arrival of Winter

Lesson 5–6: What Shall We Do on a Rainy Day?; The Arrival of Winter; Rain, Rain, Go Away

Lesson 7: The Arrival of Winter; Is That the Sweet Sound?

Transparencies

Visual Aid Transparencies

- **13** The thermometer
- **14** Sun in the morning and afternoon
- **15** The moon cycle (part 1)
- **16** The moon cycle (part 2)
- **17** What kinds of weather do you see?
- **18** Pond in spring
- **19** Pond in winter

Reading Aid Transparencies

- C1–C7

Science Skills and Handbook Transparencies

- Who's a Scientist?
- Science Handbook

Internet Resources

McGRAW-HILL SCIENCE is online at *www.mhscience02.com* with projects and activities for students, teachers, and parents.

At the Computer PE pp. C19, C43, C49, C55

Chapter Review TE pp. C22-C23, C52-C53

National Geographic pp. C54-C55

Glossary Preview Vocabulary TE pp. C3, C25, Glossary PE pp. R35–R48 also online

NATIONAL GEOGRAPHIC

* To order National Geographic Society Products, visit us online at *www.nationalgeographic.com/education* or call 1-800-368-2728. To order NGS PictureShow and NGS PicturePack, call McGraw-Hill at 1-800-442-9685.

Posters

- **The Earth's Moon; The Heavens**
- **The Solar System/Celestial Family**

NGS PicturePack Transparencies

- **Introduction to Weather**
- **Solar System; Stars and Galaxies**

Process Skills

Science Process Skills	Explore Activities (Pupil Edition)	Science Skill Builders
Observe	pp. C11, C27, C45	Pupil Edition, p. R2 Teacher Edition, p. R2 Activity Resources, pp. 175-176
Compare		Pupil Edition, p. R3 Teacher Edition, p. R3 Activity Resources, pp. 177-178
Measure		Pupil Edition, p. R4 Teacher Edition, p. R4 Activity Resources, pp. 179-180
Classify		Pupil Edition, p. R5 Teacher Edition, p. R5 Activity Resources, pp. 181-182
Communicate	pp. C33, C39	Pupil Edition, p. R6 Teacher Edition, p. R6 Activity Resources, pp. 183-184
Put Things in Order		Pupil Edition, p. R7 Teacher Edition, p. R7 Activity Resources, pp. 185-186
Infer		Pupil Edition, p. R8 Teacher Edition, p. R8 Activity Resources, pp. 187-188
Make a Model	p. C17	Pupil Edition, p. R9 Teacher Edition, p. R9 Activity Resources, pp. 189-190
Predict	p. C5	Pupil Edition, p. R10 Teacher Edition, p. R10 Activity Resources, pp. 191-192
Investigate		Pupil Edition, p. R11 Teacher Edition, p. R11 Activity Resources, pp. 193-194
Draw a Conclusion		Pupil Edition, p. R12 Teacher Edition, p. R12 Activity Resources, pp. 195-196

Science Center Cards

The six *Science Center Cards* for this unit on the sky and weather reinforce objectives and skills presented in the unit lessons. Each card is a hands-on activity that children can do independently in your classroom Science Center. Companion worksheets are available as blackline masters in *Activity Resources*. See pages C56•a–C56•f for instructions on using these cards.

Science Center Card 13

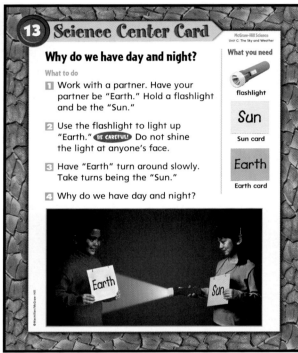

13 Science Center Card
McGraw-Hill Science
Unit C: The Sky and Weather

Why do we have day and night?

What to do

1. Work with a partner. Have your partner be "Earth." Hold a flashlight and be the "Sun."

2. Use the flashlight to light up "Earth." **BE CAREFUL!** Do not shine the light at anyone's face.

3. Have "Earth" turn around slowly. Take turns being the "Sun."

4. Why do we have day and night?

What you need

flashlight

Sun
Sun card

Earth
Earth card

Why do we have day and night?
Children shine a flashlight on their partners and have their partners rotate to learn why we have day and night. *(Use after Lesson 1.)*

Science Center Card 14

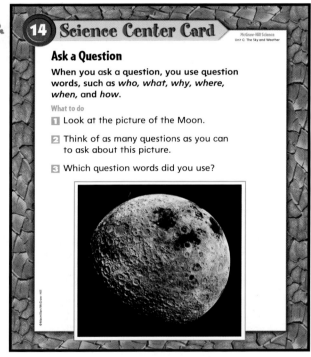

14 Science Center Card
McGraw-Hill Science
Unit C: The Sky and Weather

Ask a Question

When you ask a question, you use question words, such as *who, what, why, where, when,* and *how.*

What to do

1. Look at the picture of the Moon.

2. Think of as many questions as you can to ask about this picture.

3. Which question words did you use?

Ask a Question
Children ask questions about a picture of the moon. *(Use after Lesson 2.)*

15 Science Center Card

McGraw-Hill Science
Unit C: The Sky and Weather

Follow Directions

When you follow directions, you can make things correctly.

What to do

1. Glue the paper together like a tube to make a windsock. Glue tissue paper strips inside one end of the windsock.

2. Your teacher will punch 4 holes in the other end of the tube. Thread a string through each hole. Tie a knot to hold each string in place.

3. Tie the 4 strings together to the fifth string.

4. Use your windsock for the activity "Watch the Wind Blow."

What you need

- construction paper
- tissue paper
- 5 pieces of string
- glue stick

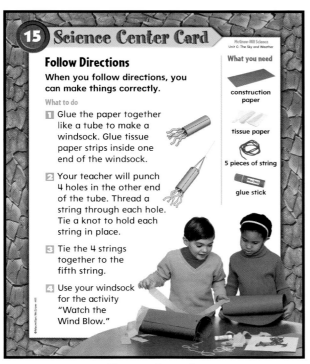

Follow Directions
Children follow directions to make a windsock.
(Use after Lesson 4.)

16 Science Center Card

McGraw-Hill Science
Unit C: The Sky and Weather

Watch the Wind Blow

What to do

1. Tie the windsock outside. Observe the windsock for 5 days. Record on the chart what you observe.

2. Which day had the least wind? Which had the most wind?

3. Which day had no wind?

4. What did you observe about the wind?

What you need

- windsock
- wind chart

Watch the Wind Blow
Children observe a windsock for 5 days and observe how the wind changes from day to day.
(Use after Lesson 5.)

17 Science Center Card

McGraw-Hill Science
Unit C: The Sky and Weather

Use a Pattern

A pattern repeats things in an order. Use a pattern to predict what comes next.

What to do

1. The pictures below show a pattern. Talk about the pattern. What do you see?

2. Look at the last picture. What comes next in the pattern?

3. What comes after ?

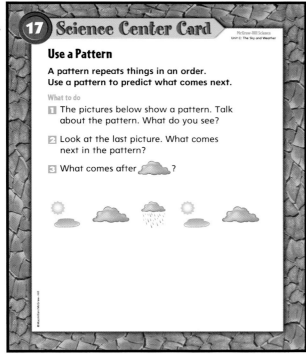

Use a Pattern
Children observe a pattern of rainfall from clouds and predict what comes next. *(Use after Lesson 4.)*

18 Science Center Card

McGraw-Hill Science
Unit C: The Sky and Weather

Be a Weather Tracker

What to do

1. During the fall, keep track of the weather. Fill in a weather chart.

2. Fill in weather charts in the winter and the spring.

3. How was the weather the same in each season? How was it different?

What you need

- 3 weather charts
- crayons
- thermometer
- weather tool

Be a Weather Tracker
Children track how the weather changes from fall to spring. *(Use after Lesson 7.)*

Materials

Consumable materials (based on six groups)

Materials	Quantity	Kit Quantity	Lessons
Batteries, D-cell	2	12	2 Science Center Card 13
Crayons			6, Science Center Card 18
Cups, plastic, 300 mL	1	100	7
Glue			Science Center Card 15
Ice			7
Lightstick, red	1	6	2
Paper, drawing			6
Paper, construction			Science Center Card 15
Paper, crepe streamer		81 ft	4
Paper, tissue, assorted colors		20 sheets	Science Center Card 15
Stick, craft	1	50	4
Tape			3, 4
Yarn, red		1 skein	Science Center Card 15
Yarn, yellow		1 skein	Science Center Card 15

Non-consumable materials (based on six groups)

Materials	Quantity	Kit Quantity	Lessons
Balls, multicolored hard rubber	1	6	2
Flashlight	1	6	2, Science Center Card 13
Glove	1		7
Labels, "Earth" and "Sun"	1 of each		3
Shoebox	1		2
Thermometer	5	12	1, 4, 5, Science Center Card 18

The Sky and Weather

LOOK!

What covers the trees and
the ground here? Where do
you think it came from?

C 1

Resources

- Reading in Science Resources, Unit Vocabulary, pp. 173–175
- School to Home Activities, pp. 15-22
- Cross Curricular Projects, pp. 15-20

LOOK!

Snow is covering the trees
and ground. The snow
came from clouds in the
sky.

Assessment Strand

McGraw-Hill Science provides a variety of strategies for assessing students' learning and progress, including ongoing assessment, informal assessment, formal assessment, and performance assessment.

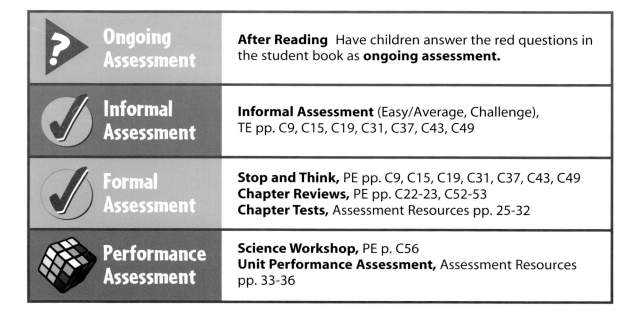

?	**Ongoing Assessment**	**After Reading** Have children answer the red questions in the student book as **ongoing assessment.**
✓	**Informal Assessment**	**Informal Assessment** (Easy/Average, Challenge), TE pp. C9, C15, C19, C31, C37, C43, C49
✓	**Formal Assessment**	**Stop and Think,** PE pp. C9, C15, C19, C31, C37, C43, C49 **Chapter Reviews,** PE pp. C22-23, C52-53 **Chapter Tests,** Assessment Resources pp. 25-32
▦	**Performance Assessment**	**Science Workshop,** PE p. C56 **Unit Performance Assessment,** Assessment Resources pp. 33-36

Lesson Planner

Lesson	Objectives	Vocabulary	Pacing	Resources and Technology
LESSON 1 **The Sun** pp. C4-C9	■ Explore and predict warm places using a thermometer. ■ Recognize that the Sun provides Earth with light and heat. ■ Recognize the pattern of the Sun's position in the sky. ■ Explain why we have day and night.	**star** **temperature**	3 days	■ Big Book, pp. C4–C9 ■ Activity Resources, pp. 60-62, 81 ■ Reading in Science Resources, pp. 123-128 ■ School to Home Activities, pp. 16-18 ■ Vocabulary Cards ■ Reading Aid Transparency C1 ■ Visual Aid Transparencies 13, 14 ■ **Explore Activity Video**
LESSON 2 **The Moon and Stars** pp. C10-C15	■ Explore and observe objects in the dark. ■ Recognize that the Moon gets its light from the Sun. ■ Explain that groups of stars form constellations.	**constellation**	3 days	■ Big Book, pp. C10–C15 ■ Activity Resources, pp. 63-65, 82 ■ Reading in Science Resources, pp. 129-134 ■ School to Home Activities, p. 19 ■ Vocabulary Cards ■ Science Center Card 14 ■ Reading Aid Transparency C2 ■ Visual Aid Transparency 15 ■ **Explore Activity Video** ■ **Science Experiences Videotapes**
LESSON 3 **The Planets** pp. C16-C19	■ Explore by modeling how the Earth moves around the Sun. ■ Discuss likenesses and differences among the planets.	**planet**	2 days	■ Big Book, pp. C16–C19 ■ Activity Resources, pp. 66-68 ■ Reading in Science Resources, pp. 135-140 ■ Vocabulary Cards ■ Reading Aid Transparency C3 ■ **Explore Activity Video**

Activity Planner

Activity	Process Skills	Materials	Plan Ahead
1 Explore Activity **Where will it be warmer?** p. C5	predict	two thermometers with primary scale	Plan to do this activity on a sunny day. Use the Primary Thermometer Teacher Aid on page TR6 to modify the thermometers children will use. Introduce or review how to use thermometers. Refer to Handbook p. R20.
2 Explore Activity **What can you see in the dark?** p. C11	observe	shoebox, soft ball, glowstick, flashlight	In each shoebox, cut a small viewing hole at one end. Cut another larger hole on the side of the box through which children will shine the flashlight.
3 Explore Activity **How does Earth move around the Sun?** p. C17	make a model	two labels, string	Cut 8 1/2 x 11 inch sheets of paper into thirds. Draw write-on-lines as needed to help guide children as they make their labels.

For additional activities, see Science Center Cards, pp. C56•a–C56•f.

Reading in Science Resources

McGraw-Hill Science **Reading in Science Resources** provides the following **Blackline Master** worksheets for this chapter.

Chapter Graphic Organizer

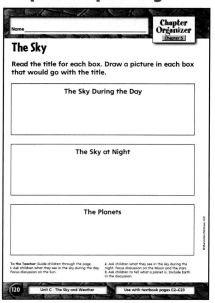

Reading in Science Resources,
p. 120

Chapter Reading Skill

Reading in Science Resources,
pp. 121-122

Chapter Vocabulary

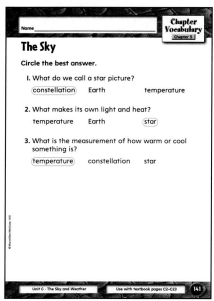

Reading in Science Resources,
pp. 141-142

McGraw-Hill Science **Reading in Science Resources** provides the following **Blackline Master** worksheets for every lesson in this chapter.

Lesson Outline

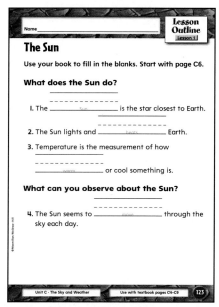

Reading in Science Resources,
pp. 123-124, 129-130, 135-136

Interpret Illustrations

Reading in Science Resources,
pp. 125-126, 131-132, 137-138

Lesson Vocabulary and Cloze Test

Reading in Science Resources,
pp. 127-128, 133-134, 139-140

Activities and Assessment

McGraw-Hill Science **Activity Resources** provides the following **Blackline Master** worksheets for every lesson in this chapter.

Explore Activity and Alternative Explore Activity

Activity Resources,
pp. 60-62, 63-65, 66-68

Science Center Card

Activity Resources,
pp. 81-82

Science Skill Builder

Activity Resources, pp. 183-184

All Science Skill Builders are found at the back of the Student Book.

McGraw-Hill Science **Assessment Book** provides the following **Blackline Master** worksheets for this chapter.

Chapter Test

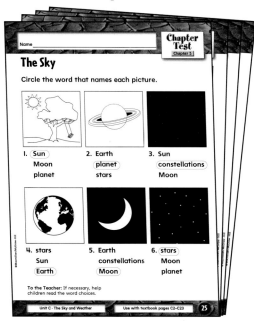

Assessment Resources, pp. 25-28

CHAPTER

5 The Sky

Resources

- Big Book, pp. C2–C3
- Reading in Science Resources, pp. 120–142

Did You Ever Wonder?

Invite children to look at the chapter opener photograph and describe the scene. Ask when they have observed a sky like the one in the photograph. Discuss whether children think the Sun is coming up or going down and why. Read aloud the paragraph on page C3 and have children answer the questions. (The Sun seems low in the eastern sky in the morning and then rises.)

Tell children that in this chapter, they will discover why they cannot see the Sun at night.

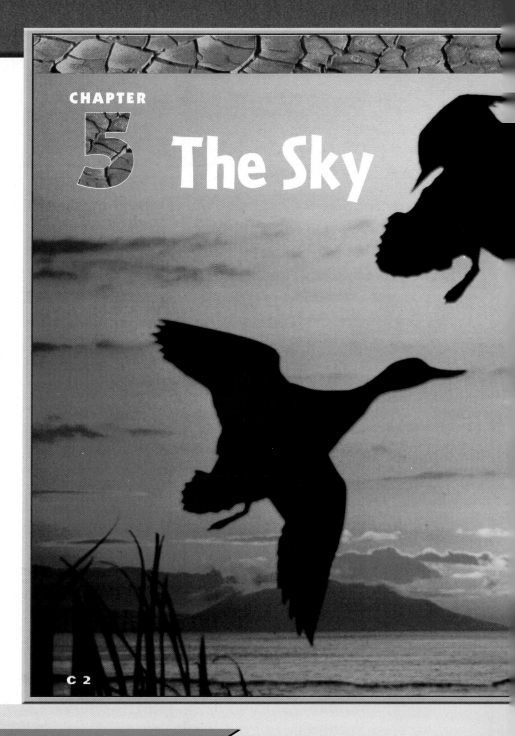

CHAPTER **5** The Sky

C 2

Reading Skills

This chapter provides MiniLessons and other strategies for developing, practicing, and applying the following reading skills.

- ◉ **Cause and Effect:** pp. C8, C13
- ○ **Compare and Contrast**
- ○ **Draw Conclusions**
- ○ **Find the Main Idea**
- ◉ **Order of Events (act out or retell):** pp. C13, C21
- ◉ **Summarize (retell):** pp. C9,C15, C19

- ◉ **Read pictues:** pp. C8, C12, C18
- ◉ **Draw visual images based on text:** pp. C9, C20, C21, C56
- ◉ **Ask questions:** pp. C4, C10, C16
- ◉ **Follow directions:** pp. C5, C11, C17
- ◉ **Build on prior knowledge:** pp. C4, C10, C16

Vocabulary

star

temperature

constellation

planet

Did You Ever Wonder?

Where does the Sun go at night? The Sun seems to disappear at night. But it does not. You just can not see it. Where is the Sun in the morning?

Preview vocabulary by having children pronounce and spell each word. Encourage children to look up these words and their definitions in their Glossary beginning on page R35.

star object in the sky that glows and makes its own light, C6

temperature how warm or cool something is, C7

constellation a group of stars that makes a picture, C15

planet Earth is a planet that moves around the Sun, C18

Technology

Visit **www.mhscience02.com** for an online glossary.

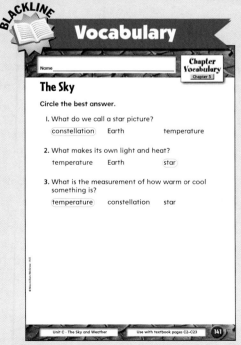

Reading in Science Resources, pp. 141-142

Reading in Science Resources, p. 120

LESSON 1 The Sun

Objectives

- Explore and predict warm places using a thermometer.
- Recognize that the Sun provides Earth with light and heat.
- Recognize the pattern of the Sun's position in the sky.
- Explain why we have day and night.

Resources

- Big Book, pp. C4–C9
- Activity Resources, pp. 60–62, 81
- Reading in Science Resources, pp. 123–128
- Vocabulary Cards
- Reading Aid Transparency C1
- Visual Aid Transparencies 13, 14
- Science Center Card 13
- School to Home Activities, pp. 16–18

Build on Prior Knowledge

Before class, put a small bowl of water in a sunny place and another in the shade. Have students touch the water in each bowl. Then have children discuss why they think the Sun is important to us.

1 Get Ready

Using the Illustrations
Ask:

- **Where will it be cooler, in the Sun or in shade?** (It is cooler in shade.)

See Science Skill Builder **Predict,** p. R10.

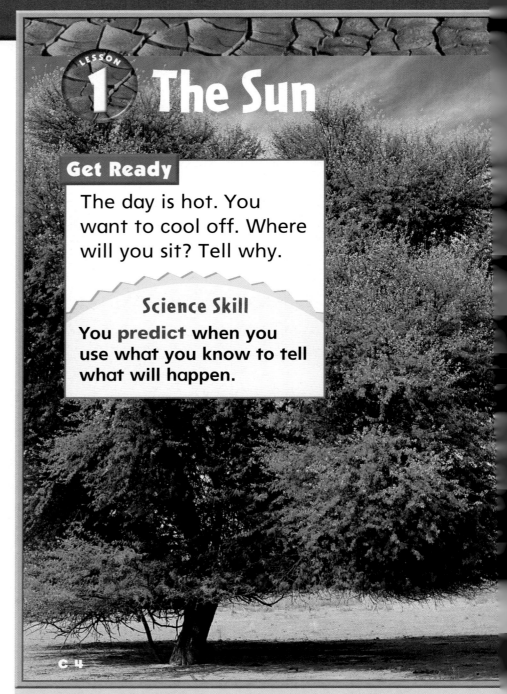

LESSON 1 The Sun

Get Ready

The day is hot. You want to cool off. Where will you sit? Tell why.

Science Skill

You **predict** when you use what you know to tell what will happen.

C 4

Cross Curricular Books

Additional Outside Reading

The Big Sun

written by Michael Maia
illustrated by Fran Lee

To order, see page C1·b.

Inclusion

A Sunny Spot, A Shady Spot
Reinforce the concepts of *sunny* and *shady*. Find a schoolyard location with sunny and shady spots. Have children form a circle and move clockwise to a rhythm that you clap. Explain that when you stop clapping you will call out a *sunny spot* or a *shady spot,* and children are to move to the type of spot you identify. Allow children to take turns being the caller. **Kinesthetic; Linguistic**

Explore Activity

Where will it be warmer?

What you need

2
thermometers

What to do

1 Will it be warmer in the Sun or in the shade? Tell what you **predict**.

2 Put one thermometer in a sunny place. Put the other in shade. Wait a few minutes.

3 Compare the thermometers. Where is it warmer? Why do you think so? Did you predict this?

sunlight

shade

C 5

Alternative Explore Activity

Materials piece of ice, plastic plate

Hot Stuff Have children use the sense of touch to determine if it is warmer in the Sun or in the shade. As a group, decide on a sunny spot and a shady spot. Place one ice cube in each location. Have children predict which will melt faster. Have children check the ice cubes every five minutes to determine which melts faster. Discuss why.
Kinesthetic

Name_____

Alternative Explore Lesson 1

Hot stuff

In this activity, you will use your sense of touch to figure out if it's warmer in the Sun or in the shade.

What you need
- piece of ice
- plastic plate

What to do

1. Place one ice cube in a sunny spot. Place another ice cube in a shady spot.

2. Which ice cube do you think will melt faster?
_ _
The one in the sun.

3. Check both ice cubes every five minutes. What made one ice cube melt faster than the other?
_ _
The heat from the sunlight.

62 Unit C - The Sky and Weather   Use with TE textbook page C5

Activity Resources, p. 62

Explore Activity

Where will it be warmer?

Science Process Skills *predict*

Resources Activity Resources, pp. 60–61

Pacing 15–20 minutes

Grouping small groups

Plan Ahead

This activity should be done on a sunny day. Use the Primary Thermometer Teacher Aid on page TR6 to modify the thermometers from the kit. To review how to use thermometers, see p. R20 in the back of the student book.

What to do

Read and discuss the activity with the class before they begin.

1 Have each group agree on a prediction. Record each group's prediction.

2 Help children to identify a sunny spot and a shady spot.

3 Have children keep their thermometers in place for five minutes. If necessary, help children read the modified thermometers, and then how to compare the results. (Children should verify their predictions and conclude that the heat from sunlight made one temperature higher.)

Going Further

Ask children what the temperatures might be in the same places later in the day. Discuss whether the sunny and shady spots might change and how this might affect temperatures.

For an additional activity, see Science Center Card 13, p C56•a.

Technology

- When time is short, preview the activity with the **Explore Activity Video.**

2 Read to Learn

What does the Sun do?

Before Reading
Have children try to answer the red question at the top of the page.

Developing the Main Idea
Explain that there are many, many stars (billions), some larger than the Sun, others smaller than Earth, and all separated by very great distances. Ask:

- **How is the Sun different from the other stars?**
  (We see the Sun only during the day and the other stars only at night when the sky is clear.) Mention that stars glow day and night, but we cannot see them during the day because the light from the Sun is so bright.

- **Of all the stars, which one is most important to us?** (the Sun) **Why?** (The Sun gives us heat and light.) Mention that there would be no life on Earth without the Sun. Recall with children how plants, for example, use sunlight to make food.

Read to Learn

What does the Sun do?

The Sun is a **star**. Stars glow. They make their own light and heat. The Sun is the star closest to Earth. It is the only star you see during the day.

C 6

Cultural Perspective

Sun Worship

Many early cultures, including the Greeks, Egyptians, and Aztec Indians, worshipped the Sun as a god. Some believed that a solar eclipse was the Sun god showing his anger. Others explained the Sun's east to west movement as the Sun god driving a chariot or sailing a ship across the sky. Invite children to pretend they know nothing about the Sun and write a story about what it is and what it does.

BLACKLINE Lesson Outline

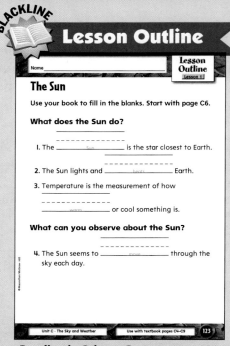

Name _____ Lesson Outline Lesson 1

The Sun

Use your book to fill in the blanks. Start with page C6.

What does the Sun do?

1. The _____ Sun _____ is the star closest to Earth.

2. The Sun lights and _____ heats _____ Earth.

3. Temperature is the measurement of how

_____ warm _____ or cool something is.

What can you observe about the Sun?

4. The Sun seems to _____ move _____ through the sky each day.

Unit C · The Sky and Weather   Use with textbook pages C4–C9   123

Reading in Science Resources, p.123

he Sun lights and heats Earth. Its heat warms Earth's land, water, and air.

ou can measure how much the Sun eats things on Earth. **Temperature** is ow warm or cool something is.

▷ **What does the Sun do here?**

The Sun heats the water, air, land, plants, and animals.

C 7

- **Is the air more likely to be warm or cool here?** (warm) **Why?** (The Sun is shining brightly. A turtle is sunning itself.)

- **What is warming the living and nonliving things here?** (heat from sunlight)

- **If we were at the pond, how could we find out how warm or cool the air really is?** (measure the temperature with a thermometer)

▶ **After Reading**
Ask the red question in the student book as **ongoing assessment.**

Technology

- Visual Aid Transparency 13:

  The Thermometer

Developing Vocabulary

star, temperature Display photographs of a sunny sky and a starlit nighttime sky. Ask: **What is similar about both pictures?** (Stars are shining in both.) **What is the only star we can see during the day?** (the Sun)
Display a thermometer. Ask: **What can we find out with a thermometer?** (the temperature of something, or how warm or cool something is) Fill one container with cold water and another with very warm water. Place a thermometer from the Explore activity in each. After several minutes, have children read the thermometers and identify which water is warmer.

Introduce the Vocabulary Cards for the word *star* and *temperature*. Place them on the word wall.

 Math | **MiniLesson**

Temperature

Develop Use Visual Aid Transparency19 to help children learn how to read a thermometer. Then have children find the air temperature of the room.

Activity First thing in the morning, have children put a thermometer into a jar of water, then place the jar in a sunny spot. Have children predict what will happen to the water temperature as the day goes on. Record the temperature at one-hour intervals throughout the day. Compare predictions with actual results.

What can you observe about the Sun?

Before Reading
Have children try to answer the red question at the top of the page.

Using the Illustrations
Ask:

- **Why is the girl wearing a jacket in the morning?** (It is cool.)
- **Is it warmer or cooler by noon?** (warmer) **How can you tell?** (The girl has taken off her jacket.) **Where is the Sun at noon?** (high in the sky)
- **Is it warmer or cooler at night than at noon?** (cooler) **How can you tell?** (The girl is wearing her jacket again.) **What seems to happen to the Sun in the sky between noon and night?** (The Sun gets lower and then finally sets.)

Exploring the Main Idea
Use a globe, a self-stick note, and a flashlight to demonstrate the pattern of day and night as Earth rotates. Place the note on the globe to indicate where you live. Darken the room. Tell children that the flashlight represents the Sun. Emphasize that the Sun stays in the same place in space. As you turn the globe, have children tell whether it is day or night. Ask:

- **Where is our side of Earth at night?** (away from the Sun) **Where is our side of Earth during the day?** (facing the Sun) **What causes day and night?** (Earth turns.)

What can you observe about the Sun?

The Sun seems to move through the sky each day. But the Sun does not really move. Our Earth moves and turns. Each time Earth turns, we have one day and one night.

Morning
When the Sun rises, it looks low in the sky. All morning the Sun gets higher. It warms Earth.

C 8

Reading **MiniLesson**

Cause and Effect

Develop Explain that an *effect* is something that happens, and a *cause* is why it happened. Refer to the picture on C8. Write and ask: **Why did the girl put on her jacket?** (It is cool outside.) Write the response and label it *Cause*. Draw an arrow to "the girl put on her jacket" and label it *Effect*.

Practice Repeat the activity for the other pictures. Record responses. Identify each cause and effect. **Spatial; Linguistic**

Reading in Science Resources, pp. 125-126

Noon
At noon, the Sun looks high in the sky. On most days, it is warmer than morning. After noon, the Sun gets lower in the sky.

When the Sun rises, it looks low in the sky. It seems to get higher in the sky, then lower. It seems to disappear when the Sun sets.

▶ **Tell how the Sun moves through the sky each day.**
See annotation at right.

Evening
When the Sun sets, it looks low in the sky. The air starts to cool. Soon it is night.

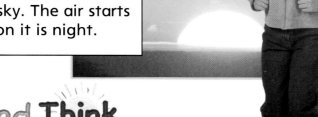

Stop and Think

1. What does Earth get from the Sun?
2. Why do we have day and night?

HOME ACTIVITY   Draw what you like to do at different times of day.

C 9

▶**After Reading**
Ask the red question in the student book as **ongoing assessment.**

3 | Lesson Review

Answers to Stop and Think

1. Earth gets light and heat from the Sun. (pp. C6–C7)

2. We have day and night because Earth turns. (pp. C8–C9)

Retelling
Write the following scaffolding for summarizing the lesson on the board. Have children retell the lesson by filling in the blanks. Ask:

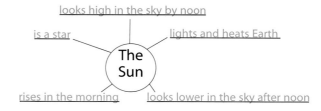

looks high in the sky by noon

is a star   lights and heats Earth

The Sun

rises in the morning   looks lower in the sky after noon

Technology

- Science Music CD
  Twinkle, Twinkle, Little Star
  Star Light, Star Bright

- Visual Aid Transparency 14:
  Sun in the Morning and Afternoon

✔ Informal Assessment

Easy/Average Have children form groups of three. Ask each group to stand in a line. Provide each group with a large yellow construction-paper circle to represent the Sun. Have the child on the left hold up the circle to show where the Sun is as the day begins (sunrise). Have the next child show where the Sun is at noon. Have the last child take the circle and show where the Sun is at the end of the day (sunset). **Kinesthetic**

Challenge Have each child make a timeline on a large sheet of drawing paper. Help them to mark off and label *sunrise, morning, noon, afternoon,* and *sunset*. Then challenge children to draw the position of the Sun above each label on the timeline. Encourage children to use the timeline to describe how the Sun appears to move across the sky each day. **Kinesthetic; Linguistic**

LESSON 2 — The Moon and Stars

Objectives

- Explore and observe objects in the dark.
- Recognize that the Moon gets its light from the Sun.
- Explain that groups of stars form constellations.

Resources

- Big Book, pp. C10–C15
- Activity Resources, pp. 63–65, 82
- Reading in Science Resources, pp. 129–134
- Vocabulary Cards
- Reading Aid Transparency C2
- Visual Aid Transparency 15
- Science Center Card 14
- School to Home Activity, p. 19

Build on Prior Knowledge

Have children look out at the sky, and then discuss how the sky will change as night falls. Ask:

- **What do you see at night that you cannot see during the day, if the sky is clear?** (stars)
- **What else might you see?** (the Moon)

1 Get Ready

Using the Illustrations
Ask:

- **How do you know that it is nighttime?** (The sky is dark and you can see stars and the Moon.)
- **What is the Moon's shape here?** (like a circle)

See Science Skill Builder **Observe**, p. R2.

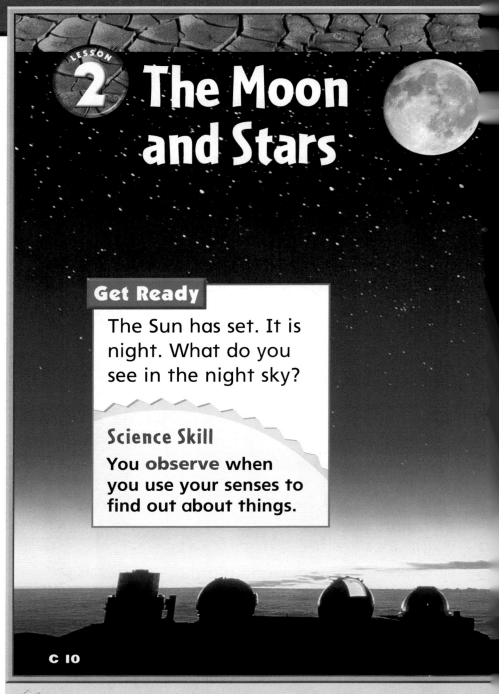

LESSON 2 — The Moon and Stars

Get Ready

The Sun has set. It is night. What do you see in the night sky?

Science Skill

You **observe** when you use your senses to find out about things.

C 10

 Cross Curricular Books

Additional Outside Reading

Night and Day

retold by Robyn Martell Zane
illustrated by Mariano Gil

To order, see page C1·b.

Cultural Perspective

Moon Myths

Share these Moon myths, then invite children to create their own.

- The Iroquois Indians said the Moon was a weaving and the marks on it were the weaver and her cat.
- An Aborigine tribe said the Moon was Baloo, a man who hides himself when he remembers being embarrassed by falling out of his boat. He grows full and bright when he feels courageous.

Explore Activity

What can you see in the dark?

What to do

What you need

shoebox

ball

glowstick

flashlight

1 Make the room dark. Put the glowstick in the box. Cover the box. Look in the end hole. What do you **observe**?

2 Take out the glowstick. Put the ball in the box. Cover it. What do you observe in the box?

3 Now shine the flashlight in the side hole. What do you observe? Which things could you see? Why?

C 11

Alternative Explore Activity

Materials objects that make their own light, objects that don't make their own light

Night Sight Display objects that give off light and objects that do not. Have children predict which items they can and cannot see in the dark, then sort them. Turn out the light and have children test their ideas. Ask which objects were easy to see and why, and which objects were hard to see and why.

Alternative Explore
Lesson 2

Night sight

In this activity, you will discover which objects you can see in the dark and which you cannot.

What to do

1. Look at the objects. Guess which ones you can see in the dark and which ones you cannot.

2. Fill in the chart.

What you need

- objects that give off light, such as flashlight and glowstick

- objects that do not give off light, such as a ball and crayon

can see in dark	cannot see in dark

3. Test your guesses. Draw a circle around the correct guesses. Draw an X through the wrong guesses.

Unit C · The Sky and Weather   Use with TE textbook page CII   65

Activity Resources, p. 65

Explore Activity

What can you see in the dark?

Science Process Skills *observe*

Resources Activity Resources, pp. 63–64

Pacing 15–20 minutes

Grouping small groups

Plan Ahead In each shoebox, cut a small viewing hole at one end and a larger hole on the side of the box through which children will shine the flashlight.

Safety Note For step 3, remind children not to shine their flashlights in anyone's eyes.

What to do

Read and discuss the activity with the class before they begin. Before children make their observations, suggest that they predict which objects they will see clearly in the dark without using the flashlight.

1 Have children follow the directions. (Children should observe the glowstick in the box.)

2 Have children follow the directions. (Children will not be able to see the ball in the box.)

3 Have children follow the directions. (Children will see the ball. They could see the glowstick because it made its own light. They could see the ball because they shined the light on it.)

Going Further

Ask: **When can't you see stars at night?** (When it is cloudy.) **Why?** (Clouds can block their light.)

For an additional activity, see Science Center Card 14, p. C56·b.

Technology

■ When time is short, preview the activity with the **Explore Activity Video.**

2 Read to Learn

What can you observe about the Moon?

Before Reading
Have children try to answer the red question at the top of the page.

Using the Illustrations
Ask:

- **What pattern do you see in these shapes?** (Children describe the shapes as getting bigger and then smaller.)

- **Do you think the Moon actually changes shape?** (Children may answer yes.) Explain that the Moon does not change shape. What changes is how much of the lighted part we see from Earth.

Read to Learn

What can you observe about the Moon?

You can see the Moon on many nights. But the Moon does not make its own light. The Sun lights the Moon.

C 12

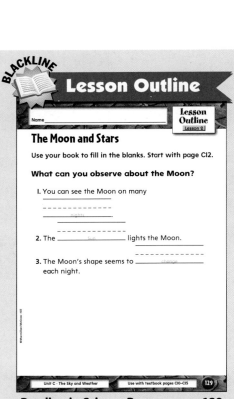

Reading in Science Resources, p. 129

Reading in Science Resources, pp. 131-132

The Moon's shape seems to change each night. But the Moon does not really change shape.

The Moon starts out thin and gets wider until it is a circle. Then it gets thinner again.

▷ **Tell how the Moon's shape seems to change here.**

C 13

If possible, have children view the Moon when it is visible during the day. Demonstrate how the Sun lights the Moon. Shine a very bright flashlight on white posterboard. Explain to children that the Sun's light shines on the Moon, just as the flashlight shines on the posterboard. The light bounces back to Earth, just as the light bounces off the posterboard. Because the Sun's light is so bright, we are able to see this reflected light, even in the daytime.

You may wish to demonstrate the Moon's phases, but do not expect full understanding of the concept. Place a large ball on a table in front of the room that is in line with a projector several feet away. Have children sit on the floor facing the ball between the projector and ball. Tell children that the light represents the Sun, the ball represents the Moon, and they represent Earth. Focus the light on the ball. Ask:

■ **What is the shape of the lit part?** (circle)

Continue by leaving the projector as it is and moving the ball to model other phases of the Moon. For each phase modeled, repeat the question above. Tell children that the Moon travels around Earth, and that as it does, our view of it changes. This pattern repeats every month.

▶**After Reading**
Ask the red question in the student book as **ongoing assessment.**

Technology

■ **Science Experiences Videotapes**
Space Camp: A Week of Surprises (Package 5)

■ Visual Aid Transparencies 15, 16: *The Moon Cycle* (parts 1 and 2)

Reading MiniLesson

Cause and Effect

Develop Review the meaning of cause and effect with children. Write *effect* and *cause* on the board. Under effect, write "We can see the moon…". Then ask: **Why can we see the moon?** (…because the Sun lights the Moon) Write this phrase under *CAUSE* to complete the sentence.

Practice Ask children to recall the Explore Activity as you write "The glowstick was easy to see in the box…" on the board under *EFFECT*. Have children tell why. (…because it makes its own light) Write this phrase under *CAUSE* to complete the sentence. Have children find other examples of cause and effect.

What can you observe about the stars?

Before Reading
Have children try to answer the red question at the top of the page.

Developing the Main Idea
Ask:

- **What are stars?** (glowing objects seen in the night sky)
- **Where do stars get their light?** (They make their own light.)
- **Why can't we feel the heat of most stars?** (They are too far away.)
- **What is a constellation?** (a group of stars that makes a picture)

Using the Illustrations
Ask:

- **What do the Big and Little Dippers look like?** (spoons) Tell children the Big Dipper is part of a larger constellation called Big Bear (Ursa Major) and the Little Dipper makes up most of the constellation Little Bear (Ursa Minor).
- **What does the constellation Orion look like?** (a hunter) Explain that it was named for a great mythological hunter.

Developing Vocabulary

constellation Explain that a constellation is a group of stars that seems to form a picture. Draw the stars of the Big Dipper or Little Dipper on the board. Then draw the lines to connect them to show that it looks like a dipper, or ladle. Introduce the Vocabulary Card for the word *constellation*. Place it on the word wall.

What can you observe about the stars?

You can see the stars glow at night. Stars make their own light and heat. But you can not feel their heat. They are too far away.

Big Dipper

Little Dipper

C 14

 Cross Curricular Books

Additional Outside Reading

DEBBIE'S GOOD NIGHT PALS

written by Jeanne Argente
illustrated by Diane Paterson

To order, see page C1•b.

Advanced Learners

Star Light
Have children use flashlights to represent stars and overhead lights to represent the Sun to model why most stars are seen only at night. Children should place lighted flashlight "stars" throughout the room while the overhead lights are on. Children should then turn out the lights and compare. Ask: Why can't you see most stars during the day? (The sunlight is too bright.) **Spatial**

roups of stars seem to make pictures the sky. A star picture is called a onstellation . Constellations can look e people, animals, or things.

 What does the Big Dipper constellation look like?

It looks like a big spoon.

Stop and Think

1. Why can we see the Moon at night?

2. What is a constellation?

 Read **Moondance** by Frank Asch.

C 15

Informal Assessment

Easy/Average Help children fold a sheet of paper in half. Have them draw a daytime scene on one half and the same scene at night on the other. Have children share their drawings and tell how the skies are alike and different. Ask: **What do you see at night that you don't usually see during the day?** (stars and Moon) **What star do you see during the day that you don't see at night?** (Sun) **Kinesthetic; Social**

Challenge Have children keep a pictorial record of the Moon's shapes each day for 35 days. Remind children to face south and stand in the same place each time. Point out that the drawings should be made at the same time every day. When children's records are complete, have them compare the pictures with the ones on pages C12–C13 and try to predict what will happen next. **Spatial**

▶ **After Reading**
Ask the red question in the student book as **ongoing assessment.**

3 Lesson Review

Answers to Stop and Think

1. The Sun lights the Moon. (pp. C12–C13)

2. A constellation is a picture made by stars. (pp. C14–C15)

 Children can learn more about the Moon by reading *Moondance* by Frank Asch. New York: Scholastic, 1994.

Retelling

Write the following scaffolding for summarizing the lesson on the board. Have children retell the lesson by filling in the circles.

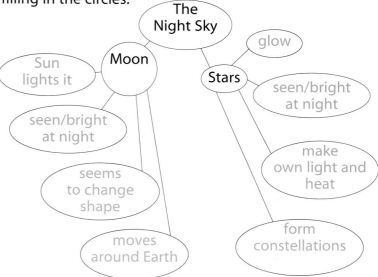

Technology

- Science Music CDs
  Twinkle, Twinkle, Little Star
  Star Light, Star Bright

The Planets

Objectives

- Explore by modeling how Earth moves around the Sun.
- Discuss likenesses and differences among the planets.

Resources

- Big Book, pp. C16–C19
- Activity Resources, pp. 66–68
- Reading in Science Resources, pp. 135–140
- Vocabulary Cards
- Reading Aid Transparency C3

Build on Prior Knowledge

Place a self-stick note on a globe to show where you live. Then shine a flashlight representing the Sun on the globe. Ask a child to turn the globe very slowly. As children observe, have them tell when it is day and when it is night where you live. Ask:

- **What does this show you about Earth?** (Earth moves.)

You may mention that this is just one way Earth moves. Ask children if they know of another way Earth moves.

1 Get Ready

Using the Illustrations

Ask:

- **Where do you think this picture of Earth was taken?** (from space)
- **What can you tell about Earth from it?** (It is round. You can see land and water.)
- **How can you show how Earth moves?** (You can make a model.)

See Science Skill Builder **Make a Model,** p. R9.

Get Ready

This is Earth. Earth moves. How can you show how Earth moves?

Science Skill

You can **make a model to show how something moves.**

C 16

 Science Background

The Planets

The nine planets in our solar system revolve around the Sun. The time it takes a planet to orbit the Sun is measured as one year. One year on Earth is 365 1/4 days. The closer a planet is to the Sun, the shorter its year. The farther away a planet is, the longer its year. Each planet also rotates on its axis. One complete rotation is measured as one day. A day on Earth is 24 hours.

 English Language Learners

How Earth Moves

Give each child a paper on which you've drawn a large oval with counterclockwise arrows. Help children to draw and label the Sun in the center, Earth on the oval, and the Moon on a path around Earth. Have children use the drawing to show how Earth turns each day, how the Moon moves around Earth, and how Earth and the Moon move around the Sun. **Spatial; Linguistic**

Explore Activity

How does Earth move around the Sun?

What to do

1. Make labels for "Earth" and "Sun." You be the "Earth." Let a partner be the "Sun."

2. Make a **model** to show how Earth moves around the Sun. Have the "Sun" stand still. Walk around the "Sun" a few times.

3. Trade labels. Let the "Earth" walk around you. How does Earth move around the Sun? Talk about it.

What you need

Earth

Earth label

Sun

Sun label

string

C 17

Alternative Explore Activity

Materials lamp without a shade, polystyrene or foam ball, knitting needle, marker

Sun and Earth in Motion Make a model of Earth by putting a knitting needle through a foam ball. Mark a dot to show where you live. Turn on the lamp and turn off the overhead lights. Slowly turn the needle to show night and day as you walk around the lamp (Sun) to show Earth's orbit. Have children take turns repeating the action.
Kinesthetic

Name _____

Sun and Earth in motion

In this activity, you will explore how Earth orbits around the Sun.

What to do

1. Hold the model of Earth. Slowly turn the needle to rotate Earth. What does this motion show?
   —————————————
   Day and night.

2. Now walk around the lamp, which stands for the Sun. What does this action show?
   —————————————
   Earth's orbit.

3. What shape does Earth make as it orbits around the Sun?
   —————————————
   An oval.

Alternative Explore Lesson 3

What you need
- lamp without a shade
- polystyrene or foam ball
- knitting needle
- marker

68 Unit C · The Sky and Weather   Use with TE textbook page C17

Activity Resources, p. 68

Explore Activity

How does Earth move around the Sun?

Science Process Skills *make a model*

Resources Activity Resources, pp. 66–67

Pacing 15–20 minutes 🕐

Grouping pairs

Plan Ahead Cut sheets of paper into thirds. Draw write-on lines as needed to help guide children as they make their labels.

What to do

Read and discuss the activity with the class before they begin.

1. Have one partner write *Earth* on a label and the other partner write *Sun*.

2. Have each child tape a label to his or her chest. Instruct the "Sun" to stand in one spot and the "Earth" to begin walking slowly around the "Sun." You may want to draw an elliptical orbit on the floor with chalk. Explain that the orbit, or path, is like a squashed circle, or oval. Draw a circle and an oval on the board to illustrate the difference between them.

3. Have partners trade labels and places and repeat. (Children should note that Earth moves around the Sun in a kind of circle.)

Going Further

Have children model how Earth spins once each day as it moves along its path (orbit) around the Sun at the same time.

Technology

- When time is short, preview the activity with the **Explore Activity Video**.

2 Read to Learn

What are the planets?

Before Reading
Have children try to answer the red question at the top of the page.

Using the Illustrations
Explain that the planets in the picture are in order from the nearest to the farthest from the Sun, but they never appear in a line as shown. Remind children that all the planets travel around the Sun in a kind of squashed circle, or oval (called an ellipse). Ask:

- **How many planets move around the Sun?** (9)
- **Which planet is nearest to the Sun?** (Mercury) **Which planet is the farthest?** (Pluto) **Which planet is third?** (Earth)
- **Which planet is the largest?** (Jupiter)
- **Which planet do you think takes the longest time to travel around the Sun?** (Pluto) **Why?** (It is farthest from the Sun.)

Developing Vocabulary

planet Display pictures of several planets as you explain that each is one of nine planets. Introduce the Vocabulary Card for the word *planet*. Place it on the word wall.

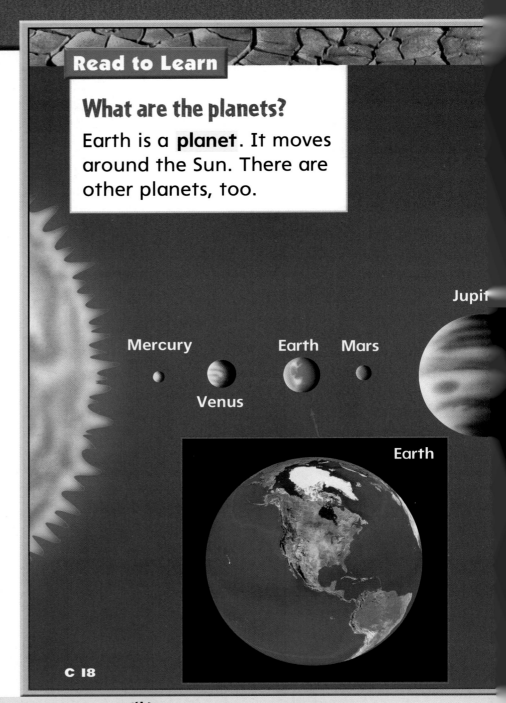

Read to Learn

What are the planets?
Earth is a **planet**. It moves around the Sun. There are other planets, too.

Mercury

Venus

Earth

Mars

Jupit

Earth

C 18

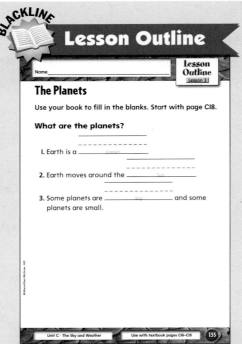

Lesson Outline

Name

Lesson Outline
Lesson 3

The Planets

Use your book to fill in the blanks. Start with page C18.

What are the planets?

1. Earth is a _____ planet _____.

2. Earth moves around the _____ Sun _____.

3. Some planets are _____ big _____ and some planets are small.

Unit C · The Sky and Weather   Use with textbook pages C16–C19   135

Reading in Science Resources, p. 135

Interpret Illustrations

Name

Reading Pictures
Lesson 3

The Planets

Place an **X** on anything that is not a planet.

An "x" should be placed over the Sun in upper right corner.

Unit C · The Sky and Weather   Use with textbook pages C16–C19   137

Reading in Science Resources, pp. 137-138

C18 UNIT C *The Sky and Weather*

Some planets are big. Some are small. Some are very close to the Sun. Others are very far away from it.

But big or small, near or far, all planets move around the Sun.

All planets move around the Sun.

 **How are the planets alike?**

Uranus

Neptune

Pluto

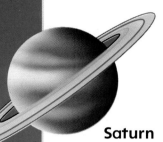

Saturn

Stop and Think

1. Does Earth stay in one place? Tell about it.

2. How are all planets alike? How are they different?

 **AT THE COMPUTER** Visit **www.mhscience02.com** to find out more about the planets.

C 19

Informal Assessment

Easy/Average Play a game with children using pages C18–C19 in the Big Book. Give clues about a planet and have children name the planet. Use the following as models.

1. I am third from the Sun. I have one moon. What planet am I? (Earth)

2. I am the sixth planet from the Sun. I have rings around me? What planet am I? (Saturn)

Invite children to make up their own clues. **Linguistic; Spatial**

Challenge Have children imagine they are on a journey through space. As they peer through the windows of their spacecrafts, have children describe what they see. Prompt with questions such as the following: **Are you passing a planet? What does it look like? How big is it? Does it have rings?** Children can use a cassette recorder to record their observations. **Linguistic**

▶ **After Reading**
Ask the red question in the student book as **ongoing assessment.**

3 Lesson Review

Answers to Stop and Think

1. No; Earth moves around the Sun. (pp. C16–C17)

2. Alike: the planets all move around the Sun. Different: some are big, some are small, some are close to the Sun, some are very far away from it. (pp. C18–C19)

Retelling

Write the following scaffolding for summarizing the lesson on the board. Have children retell the lesson by filling in the blanks.

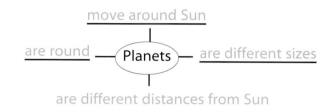

move around Sun

are round —— Planets —— are different sizes

are different distances from Sun

Moon Stories

Developing the Main Idea
Mention that Native Americans have a rich storytelling culture. Ask:

- **What might the story be about?** (the Moon)
- **Why do you think people made up stories about the Moon?** (Children may say that they did not have the tools to study the Moon or a way to travel to the Moon to see what it was really like as scientists do today.)

Thinking Further: *Drawing Conclusions*
- **What other events or things in nature do you think people of the past tried to explain in stories?** (Possible answers: why the Sun rises and sets; why there are seasons; how Earth came to be; how an animal got its spots or stripes)

Try This!
Designate a certain amount of time each day for storytelling in which children can share their stories and drawings about the Moon.

Social Studies
L·I·N·K
FOR SCHOOL OR HOME

Moon Stories
Long ago, people near and far made up stories. Some were about the Moon. Some stories told about things that lived there. Others told about what made the Moon's many shapes.

Try This!
Make up your own story about the Moon. Make drawings to go with it.

C 20

 Cultural Perspective

Storytelling
Many cultures around the world have stories to explain nature. Share with children some Native American stories about the Moon, stars, and seasons from the book *Keepers of the Earth, Native American Stories and Environmental Activities for Children* by Michael J. Caduto and Joseph Bruchac (Fulcrum Publishing, 1997). Have children illustrate or make up skits about the stories. **Linguistic; Spatial**

 Advanced Learners

What's the Real Reason?
Invite children to find and read storybooks about the Moon (Sun, stars, and seasons) in the class, school, local, and/or home library. After reading a story, challenge children to find out the real reason why, for example, the Moon seems to change shape or move across the sky. **Linguistic**

Art
L·I·N·K
FOR SCHOOL OR HOME

...ake a Star Picture

...ou can see many star ...ctures in the night sky. You ...ay see one that no one has ...efore!

...ry This!

...raw a small picture on ...me foil. Poke tiny ...oles along the picture. ...ut the foil on a paper ...owel roll. Look into it. ...hat do you see?

Science Newsroom CD-ROM
Choose **Constellations** to learn more about stars.

C 21

Science Background

...ore About Constellations
...cause Earth revolves around ... Sun, constellations in the ...ht sky change their position ...m season to season but not ...ir shape. Have interested ...dents bring in star maps ...owing the positions of ...nstellations during different ...es of the year. As a class, ...ke a plan to look for certain ...nstellations during each ...ason. **Social**

SCIENCE Reading Strategy

Sequence of Events
Developing Reading Skills
Have children use words such as *first, second, next,* and *last* to tell how to make the constellation viewer shown. Ask:

- What should you do first? (draw a picture on foil)
- What should you do next? (poke holes along the lines)
- What should you do third? (put the foil on a paper towel roll)
- What should you do last? (look into the tube)

Art
L·I·N·K

Make a Star Picture

Developing the Main Idea
Ask:

- **What do we call star pictures in the night sky?** (constellations)
- **What constellations have you seen?** (Possible answers: Big Dipper, Little Dipper, Orion)

Using the Illustrations
Ask:

- **What do the photographs show?** (how to make a star picture)
- **What materials will you need?** (paper towel roll, pencil, foil, rubber band)
- **Why might you see a star picture that no one has ever seen before?** (Everyone is making a different picture.)

Try This!
Have children take turns holding up each other's viewers and telling what star pictures they see. Alternatively, darken the room and have children shine a flashlight through the open end of the viewer toward the wall. Children can then compare the constellations they see. (Position the flashlight so that it shines at an angle slightly to the left or to the right of the open end of the viewer.)

Technology

Constellations may also be found on the Internet. Visit **www.mhscience02.com.**

Chapter Review and Test Preparation

Resources

- Big Book, pp. C22–C23
- Reading in Science Resources, pp. 141–142
- Assessment Book, pp. 25–28

Answers to Vocabulary

1. planet, p. C6
2. temperature, p. C18
3. star, p. C7
4. constellation, p. C15

Vocabulary

temperature
constellation
planet
star

Use each word once for items 1–
What does each picture show?

1

2

30°C

3
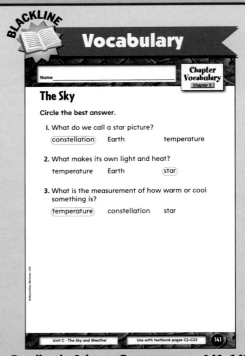

4

C 22

BLACKLINE

Vocabulary

Name _____

Chapter Vocabulary
Chapter 5

The Sky

Circle the best answer.

1. What do we call a star picture?
   (constellation)   Earth   temperature

2. What makes its own light and heat?
   temperature   Earth   (star)

3. What is the measurement of how warm or cool something is?
   (temperature)   constellation   star

Unit C · The Sky and Weather | Use with textbook pages C2–C23 | 141

Reading in Science Resources, pp. 141–142

5 What does Earth get from the Sun?

6 Why can you see the Moon at night?

7 How are the planets alike?

Science Skill: Observe

**oes each picture show morning or noon?
Tell why you think so.**

8

9

READ
Under the Night Sky by Linda Ross

C 23

Formal Assessment
CHAPTER TEST

Assessment Book, pp. 25–28

Test Taking Tip

For items 5–7, carefully read the questions and think about what you know about the Sun and Earth, the Sun and the Moon, and the Sun and the planets before you answer.

Aswers to Science Ideas

5. Earth gets light and heat from the Sun. p. C7

6. The Sun lights the Moon. p. C12

7. The planets all move around the Sun. pp. C18–C19

Answers to Science Skill: Observe

8. It is noon. The sun is high in the sky. pp. C8–C9

9. It is morning or evening. The sun is low in the sky. pp. C8–C9

Retell
Write the following scaffolding for summarizing the chapter on the board. Have children retell the chapter by filling in the blanks and telling what they learned about each object in the sky.

planets   Sun

Sky

stars   Moon

Performance Assessment
The first activity on page C56 can be used as a performance assessment. See Teacher's Edition page C56 for the scoring rubric.

Read
To find out more about the Moon and stars have children read the Grade-Level Science Book, *Under the Night Sky* by Linda Ross. For additional reading, see page C1•b.

Technology

For more review, visit
www.mhscience02.com.

Lesson Planner

Lesson	Objectives	Vocabulary	Pacing	Resources and Technology
LESSON 4 **Weather** pp. C26-C31	■ Explore wind and observe that it can move things. ■ Define *weather*. ■ Understand how rain and snow form.	**weather** **wind** **clouds**	3 days	■ Big Book, pp. C26-C31 ■ Activity Resources, pp. 69-71, 83, 85 ■ Reading in Science Resources, pp. 147-152 ■ School to Home Activities, pp. 20-21 ■ Vocabulary Cards ■ Science Center Cards 15, 17 ■ Reading Aid Transparency C4 ■ Visual Aid Transparency 17 ■ **Explore Activity Video**
LESSON 5 **Weather Changes** pp. C32-C37	■ Explore and communicate daily weather changes through the use of a chart. ■ Describe some daily weather changes, including weather changes that are harmful to living things. ■ Identify tools used to measure weather.		3 days	■ Big Book, pp. C32-C37 ■ Activity Resources, pp. 72-74, 84 ■ Reading in Science Resources, pp. 153-158 ■ Science Center Card 16 ■ Reading Aid Transparency C5 ■ **Explore Activity Video** ■ **Science Experiences Videotapes**
LESSON 6 **Spring and Summer** pp. C38-C43	■ Explore and communicate seasonal weather changes through the year. ■ Discuss weather and light conditions in spring and summer. ■ Discuss the activities and life processes of living things in spring and summer.	**season** **spring** **summer**	3 days	■ Big Book, pp. C38-C43 ■ Activity Resources, pp. 75-77 ■ Reading in Science Resources, pp. 159-164 ■ Vocabulary Cards ■ Reading Aid Transparency C6 ■ Visual Aid Transparency 18 ■ **Explore Activity Video**
LESSON 7 **Fall and Winter** pp. C44-C49	■ Explore through observation how to keep cold away from your skin. ■ Discuss weather and light conditions in fall and winter. ■ Discuss the activities and life processes of living things in fall and winter.	**fall** **winter**	3 days	■ Big Book, pp. C44-C49 ■ Activity Resources, pp. 78-80, 86 ■ Reading in Science Resources, pp. 165-170 ■ School to Home Activities, p. 22 ■ Vocabulary Cards ■ Science Center Card 18 ■ Reading Aid Transparency C7 ■ Visual Aid Transparency 19 ■ **Explore Activity Video**

Activity Planner

Activity	Process Skills	Materials	Plan Ahead
LESSON 4 Explore Activity **What can you observe about the air?** p. C27	observe	craft stick, streamer, tape, thermometer, scissors	Plan to do this activity on a breezy day. Cut the streamer paper into two-foot strips. Have children use the same thermometers as they did for the Lesson 1 Explore Activity. Refer to the Teacher Aid on p. TR6 for instructions on how to adapt the primary thermometers.
LESSON 5 Explore Activity **How does the weather change in a week?** p. C33	communicate	weather chart, thermometer, weather tool	This activity can be done by placing a thermometer outside a classroom window to be read from inside each day. Make sure it has time to register the outdoor temperature before children take their first reading. Children will need the weather tool they made for the Explore Activity in Lesson 4.
LESSON 6 Explore Activity **Is the weather the same all year?** p. C39	communicate	drawing paper, crayons	
LESSON 7 Explore Activity **How can you stay warm when it is cold outside?** p. C45	observe	small cup with ice, cloth glove	Be sure to have ice ready for the activity.

For additional activities, see Science Center Cards, pp. C56•a–C56•f.

Reading in Science Resources

McGraw-Hill Science **Reading in Science Resources** provides the following **Blackline Master** worksheets for this chapter.

Chapter Graphic Organizer

Reading in Science Resources,
p. 144

Chapter Reading Skill

Reading in Science Resources,
pp. 145-146

Chapter Vocabulary

Reading in Science Resources,
pp. 171-172

McGraw-Hill Science **Reading in Science Resources** provides the following **Blackline Master** worksheets for every lesson in this chapter.

Lesson Outline

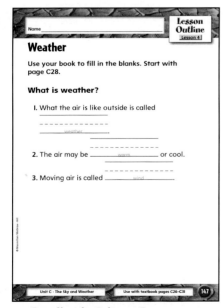

Reading in Science Resources,
pp. 147-148, 153-154, 159-160, 165-166

Interpret Illustrations

Reading in Science Resources,
pp. 149-150, 155-156, 161-162, 167-168

Lesson Vocabulary and Cloze Test

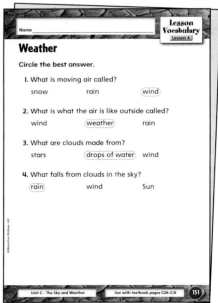

Reading in Science Resources,
pp. 151-152, 157-158, 163-164, 169-170

Activities and Assessment

McGraw-Hill Science **Activity Resources** provides the following **Blackline Master** worksheets for every lesson in this chapter.

Explore Activity and Alternative Explore Activity

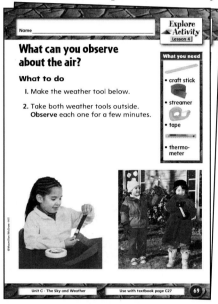

Activity Resources, pp. 69-71, 72-74, 75-77, 78-80

Science Center Card

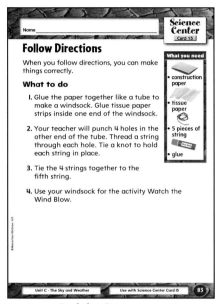

Activity Resources, pp. 83-86

Science Skill Builder

Activity Resources, pp. 185-186

All Science Skill Builders are found at the back of the Student Book.

McGraw-Hill Science **Assessment Book** provides the following **Blackline Master** worksheets for this chapter.

Chapter Test

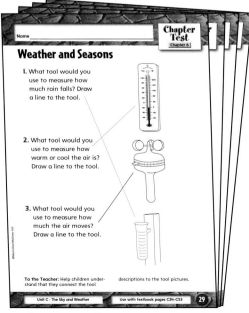

Assessment Resources, pp. 29-32

Resources

- Big Book, pp. C24–C25
- Reading in Science Resources, pp. 144–172

Did You Ever Wonder?

Invite children to look at the chapter opener photograph and describe the scene. Ask children when they have observed dark clouds like those in the photograph. Read aloud the paragraph on page C25 and have children answer the question. (The water in clouds can fall as rain, sleet, snow, or hail.)

CHAPTER

6 Weather and Seasons

C 24

Reading Skills

This chapter provides MiniLessons and other strategies for developing, practicing, and applying the following reading skills.

○ Cause and Effect
◉ Compare and Contrast: pp. C29, C32, C38, C51
○ Draw Conclusions
◉ Order of Events (act out or retell): pp. C30, C34, C41, C47,
◉ Summarize (retell): pp. C31, C37, C43, C49, C53

◉ Read pictures: pp. C30, C35, C40, C46
◉ Draw visual images based on text: pp. C31, C39, C50, C56
◉ Ask questions: pp. C26, C32, C38, C44
◉ Follow directions: pp. C27, C33, C39, C45
◉ Build on prior knowledge: pp. C26, C26, C32, C38, C44

Vocabulary

weather

wind

clouds

season

spring

summer

fall

winter

Did You Ever Wonder?

Why are rain clouds so dark? They are dark because they hold a lot of water. What will happen to the water?

C 25

Preview vocabulary by having children pronounce and spell each word. Encourage children to look up these words and their definitions in their Glossary beginning on page R35.

weather what the air is like outside, C28

wind moving air, C28

clouds made from lots of tiny drops of water that are in the air, C30

season a time of the year, C40

spring the season after winter, C40

summer the season after spring, C42

fall the season after summer, C46

winter the season after fall, C48

Technology

Visit www.mhscience02.com for an online glossary.

BLACKLINE — Vocabulary

Name _____

Chapter Vocabulary
Chapter 6

Weather and Seasons

Circle the best answer.

1. What is moving air called?
   rain   (wind)   fall

2. What do we call what the air is like outside?
   wind   season   (weather)

3. What do we call a time of year?
   (season)   wind   weather

4. What is the season after winter?
   summer   fall   (spring)

Unit C · The Sky and Weather   Use with textbook pages C24–C53   171

Reading in Science Resources, pp. 171-172

BLACKLINE — Graphic Organizer

Name _____

Chapter Organizer
Chapter 6

Weather and Seasons

To the Teacher: Guide children through the page.
1. Ask children what they see in the sky in each picture. Focus discussion on the weather and how weather changes through the seasons.
2. Ask children how the people are dressed in each picture. Focus discussion on how the weather

affects what we wear and what we do.
3. Ask children to name the season as you point to each picture. Follow the order of spring, summer, fall, and winter. Focus discussion on the fact that the sequence of the seasons is always the same.

144   Unit C · The Sky and Weather   Use with textbook pages C24–C53

Reading in Science Resources, p. 144

Weather

Objectives

- Explore wind and observe that it can move things.
- Define *weather*.
- Understand how rain and snow form.

Resources

- Big Book, pp. C26–C31
- Activity Resources, pp. 69–71, 83, 85
- Reading in Science Resources, pp. 147–152
- Vocabulary Cards
- Reading Aid Transparency C4
- Visual Aid Transparency 17
- Science Center Cards 15, 17
- School to Home Activities, pp. 20–21

Build on Prior Knowledge

Ask children to imagine they are at a picnic on a summer afternoon and to describe the weather. Begin a list of weather words and save it for use throughout the lesson.

1 Get Ready

Using the Illustrations

Ask children to imagine they are in the scene as they answer the question on the page. (Possible answer: The air probably feels warm and windy.)

See Science Skill Builder **Observe,** p. R2.

Weather

Get Ready

How do you think the air feels here? Tell about it.

Science Skill

You **observe** when you use your senses to find out about things.

C 26

 Cross Curricular Books

Additional Outside Reading

RAIN, RAIN

by Marilyn Greco
illustrated by Michael Grejniec

To order, see page C1·b.

SCIENCE FOR ALL English Language Learners

Weather Words

Have children begin a bulletin-board display with pictures that depict different weather. Make a set of weather word cards that include *foggy, windy, sunny, cloudy, rainy, snowy, icy, hot, cold,* and so on. As each picture is added to the display, have children choose the words that describe the weather and pin them to the picture. **Spatial; Linguistic**

Explore Activity

What can you observe about the air?

What you need

craft stick

streamer

tape

thermometer

What to do

1 Make the weather tool below.

2 Take both weather tools outside. **Observe** each one for a few minutes.

3 Go other places outside the school. Observe each tool for a few minutes. What did you observe about the air in different places?

C 27

Alternative Explore Activity

Materials thermometer

Air Observations Take children outdoors on a breezy day. Ask them to describe how the air feels (warm, cool, hot, cold, dry, wet) and then find things that the air (wind) is moving (leaves, branches, clouds, litter, dust). Display a thermometer and have children observe it as it registers the temperature. In the classroom, have children compare their observations to the air and temperature indoors.

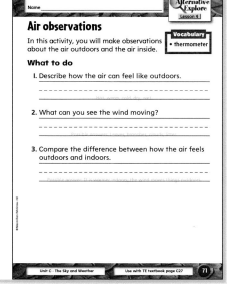

Air observations

In this activity, you will make observations about the air outdoors and the air inside.

Vocabulary
• thermometer

What to do

1. Describe how the air can feel like outdoors.

2. What can you see the wind moving?

3. Compare the difference between how the air feels outdoors and indoors.

Unit C · The Sky and Weather   Use with TE textbook page C27   71

Activity Resources, p. 71

Explore Activity

What can you observe about the air?

Science Process Skills *observe*

Resources Activity Resources, pp. 69–70

Pacing 20–25 minutes

Grouping individuals or pairs

Plan Ahead Do this activity on a day when there is a noticeable breeze. Cut the streamer paper into two-foot strips. Have children use the same modified thermometers as they did for the Explore Activity in Unit C, Lesson 1.

What to do

Read and discuss the activity with the class before they begin.

1 Help children tape the streamer paper to the craft stick. Have children hold up their completed tools and observe how the streamer hangs motionless.

2 Have children hold the thermometer in the middle or at the top rather than at the bottom so that air temperature is measured, not body temperature. Ask children to compare the position of the weather tool streamer to its position in the classroom.

3 Suggest that children stand in the shade if they were in a sunny spot in step 2. (Children's observations and answers will vary but should reflect some variation in temperature and strength or direction of wind.)

For additional activities, see Science Center Cards 15 and 17, p. C56•c and p. C56•e.

Going Further

Have children repeat the activity on a day when there is no noticeable wind. Compare the results.

Technology

■When time is short, preview the activity with the **Explore Activity Video**.

2 Read to Learn

What is weather?

Before Reading
Have children try to answer the red question at the top of the page.

Developing the Main Idea
As children read, have them identify the words that tell what it can be like outdoors and add them to the list you began at the beginning of the lesson. Ask:

- **What other words do you know that tell about weather?** (hot, windy, cold, dry, damp)

- **Is the wind blowing today, or is the air calm? If the wind is blowing, ask: How is the wind blowing?** (Possible responses: hard, gently, fast, slowly, strongly) **How can you tell?** (I can see things such as leaves and tree branches moving.)

- **What words best tell about today's weather?** (Children's responses should reflect temperature, wind, precipitation, and sky conditions.)

Developing Vocabulary

weather, wind Write the science words on the board. Ask children which one is the word for the condition of the air outside (weather) and which one is the name for moving air (wind). Have children use each word in a sentence. For example: The *weather* is warm today. The *wind* is blowing hard.
Introduce the Vocabulary Cards for the words *weather* and *wind*. Place them on the word wall.

Read to Learn

What is weather?

Weather is what the air is like outside. The air may be warm or cool. The air may be moving. The air may not be moving at all. Moving air is called **wind**.

windy and rainy

sunny

C 28

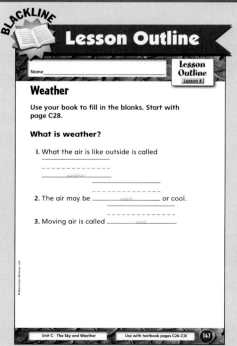

BLACKLINE **Lesson Outline**

Name_____

Lesson Outline
Lesson 4

Weather

Use your book to fill in the blanks. Start with page C28.

What is weather?

1. What the air is like outside is called
   _ _ _ _ _ _ _ _ _ _ _ _ _
   weather

2. The air may be _____ warm _____ or cool.

3. Moving air is called _____ wind _____.

Unit C · The Sky and Weather   Use with textbook pages C26–C31   **147**

Reading in Science Resources, p. 147

Cultural Perspective

Where Wind Comes From
Tell children that different cultures created stories to explain weather phenomenon such as wind. For example, the Northeast Woodland Indians said that an eagle on a mountaintop flapping its wings caused the wind. In Japan, people once thought that the god Fu Jin had a big bag of wind. If the winds were light (strong), it meant he opened the bag a little (a lot).

foggy

he sky may be sunny and lear. It may be cloudy. It hay even rain or snow.

snowy

 Tell about the weather here.
The weather is windy, rainy, sunny, snowy, and foggy.

C 29

- **How is the weather in the first picture different from weather in the picture below it? From weather in the third picture? From weather in the fourth picture?** (It is rainy and windy in the first picture, sunny and hot in the picture below it, cold and snowy in the third, and foggy in the fourth.)

- **In which picture is the wind blowing hardest?** (the first picture) **How can you tell?** (There are many waves and the flag is blowing.)

- **Why aren't the people wearing sweaters, mittens, or boots in the second picture?** (It's sunny and hot.) **If the same people were in the third picture, what might they wear?** (snowsuits, boots, hats, mittens)

▶**After Reading**
Ask about the red question in the student book as **ongoing assessment.**

SCIENCE
Reading Strategy

Compare and Contrast
Developing Reading Skills
Invite children to compare and contrast today's weather where you live with the weather in the pictures on pages C28–C29.

SCIENCE FOR ALL
Inclusion

Feeling Like the Weather
Have children look at pages C26, C28, and C29. Invite them to tell how different weather makes them feel. Ask: **Do rainy days make you sad or sleepy? How do foggy days make you feel?** Encourage children to share their feelings and discover that others may feel similarly. **Linguistic; Social**

What makes it rain or snow?

Before Reading
Have children try to answer the red question at the top of the page.

Using the Illustrations
Ask:

- **Where does the water you can't see go?** (into the air)

- **What is in the clouds?** (lots of tiny water drops) **Where did the tiny water drops come from?** (water on the Earth that went into the air) Tell children that the water in the air cools and changes into tiny droplets of water that form the clouds.

- **What is falling from the clouds?** (rain) **Where does it fall?** (to Earth) Emphasize that this movement of water between Earth and sky happens over and over. It is called the water cycle.

Developing Vocabulary

clouds Call attention to the clouds on these pages. Explain that some clouds are white and puffy, while others are dark and puffy; some clouds are high up in the sky and are thin, and others form close to the ground. If possible, show children pictures of different clouds. Introduce the Vocabulary Card for *cloud*. Put it on the word wall.

What makes it rain or snow?

Rain or snow falls from **clouds**. Clouds are made from lots of tiny water drops that are in the air.

❶ Water goes into the air. You can't see this water.

C 30

Reading | MiniLesson

Sequence of Events

Develop Explain to children that when they read, they should think about what happens first, next, then, and last.

Practice After reading about what makes it rain, write the sentences that explain the water cycle on sentence strips. Randomly arrange them along the board ledge. Have children sequence them in the same order as the student page.

Interpret Illustrations

Name _____

Reading Pictures
Lesson 4

Weather

Circle the pictures where you would feel the wind.

Unit C · The Sky and Weather   Use with textbook pages C26–C31   149

Reading in Science Resources, pp. 149–150

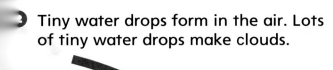

Tiny water drops form in the air. Lots of tiny water drops make clouds.

3 The water drops in clouds get bigger. When the water drops get big enough, they fall as rain or snow.

▷ **What happens when water drops in clouds get very big?**

They fall to the ground as rain or snow.

Stop and Think

1. What is weather?

2. How are rain and snow made?

HOME ACTIVITY Draw a picture of a rainy day.

C 31

Informal Assessment

Easy/Average Place a sealed bottle with some water in it in a sunny spot. After an hour, have children observe and tell what they see. (water on the sides) Ask: **What made this happen?** (the Sun's heat made the water go up, but then it cooled and collected on the sides of the bottle) **Spatial**

Challenge Have children write and illustrate a story about a drop of water that falls into a lake on Earth and then journeys back to the sky to join other tiny water drops in a cloud. Invite children to share their stories. **Linguistic**

Thinking Further: *Compare and Contrast*

■ **How are these things alike: water moving between Earth and the sky, changes in the Moon's shape, and day and night on Earth?**
(They all happen over and over.)

▶ **After Reading**
Ask the red question in the student book as **ongoing assessment.**

3 Lesson Review

Answers to Stop and Think

1. Weather is what the air is like outside. (pp. C28–C29)

2. When water goes into the air, it makes clouds. The tiny water drops get bigger. When the drops get big enough, they fall as rain. If it's cold enough, they fall as snow. (pp. C30–C31)

Retelling
Write the following scaffolding for summarizing the lesson on the board. Have children retell the lesson by filling in the blanks.

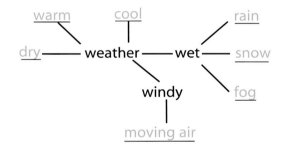

 Technology

■ Science Music CDs
What Shall We Do on a Rainy Day?
Rain, Rain Go Away

■ Visual Aid Transparency 17:
What Kinds of Weather Do You See?

Weather Changes

Objectives

- Explore and communicate daily weather changes through the use of a chart.
- Describe some daily weather changes, including weather changes that are harmful to living things.
- Identify tools used to measure weather.

Resources

- Big Book, pp. C32–C37
- Activity Resources, pp. 72–74, 84
- Reading in Science Resources, pp. 153–158
- Reading Aid Transparency C5
- Science Center Card 16

Build on Prior Knowledge

Read aloud the following: *Today will be very cold with snow beginning by noon and continuing through the evening.* Discuss with children what they would wear if they heard this weather report.

 **Get Ready**

Developing the Main Idea

Discuss the importance of knowing about weather changes. Ask:

- **Why do you think it is important to know when and how the weather is going to change?** (to know what to wear; to prepare for bad weather)

See Science Skill Builder **Communicate,** p. R6.

Get Ready

Before, it was sunny. But the weather changed. What is the weather like now?

Science Skill

You **communicate when you make a chart to tell facts.**

C 32

 Science Background

Meteorology

Meteorology is the study of the motions and interactions of Earth's atmosphere. Weather changes are often associated with the movement of cold or warm air masses, called fronts. Observing, measuring, and analyzing the wind, temperature, air pressure, precipitation, and other conditions often enables meteorologists to predict weather changes and conditions.

Reading Strategy

Compare and Contrast

Developing Reading Skills Help children to recall that when you compare and contrast, you tell how things are alike and different. Invite children to compare and contrast the weather shown on C32 with the weather outdoors.

Explore Activity

How does the weather change in a week?

What you need

weather chart

thermometer

weather tool

What to do

1. Use your chart and weather tools. Observe the weather for one week.

2. Fill in the chart each day.

3. How did the weather change? How does your chart **communicate** this?

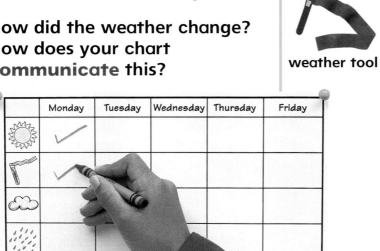

	Monday	Tuesday	Wednesday	Thursday	Friday
☀	✓				
		✓			
☁					
🌧					
❄					
🌡	Cool				

C 33

Explore Activity

How does the weather change in a week?

Science Process Skills *communicate*

Resources Activity Resources, pp. 72–73

Pacing 15–20 minutes on first day, 5 minutes each day afterward

Grouping individuals

Plan Ahead This activity may be done by placing a thermometer outside a classroom window to be read from inside each day. Children will need the same weather tools (wind tool, modified primary thermometer) that they used for the Explore Activity in Lesson 4.

What to do

Read and discuss the activity with the class before they begin.

1. All observations should be made at the same time each day.

2. Have children record the weather for one week at the same time each day.

3. Have children use their charts to discuss weather changes. (Children should tell how the weather changed from day to day. Their charts should reflect any observed changes in weather.)

Going Further

Ask:

- **Will the weather be the same next week? Why not?** (No; the weather may change because of changes in temperature, wind, sky conditions, or precipitation.)

For an additional activity, see Science Center Card 16, p. C56•d.

Technology

- When time is short, preview the activity with the **Explore Activity Video**.

Alternative Explore Activity

Materials blank calendar per child, crayons

Weather Calendars Invite children to use small pictures to record the daily weather on a calendar. Here are some possibilities: a sunny Monday could be shown by a drawing of the Sun; a cloudy morning followed by a sunny afternoon could be shown by a cloud and a Sun with a line between them; a windy day could be shown by the streamer on the wind tool out to the side.

Activity Resources, p. 74

2 Read to Learn

When does the weather change?

Before Reading
Have children try to answer the red question at the top of the page.

Using the Illustrations
Ask:

- **What do you see in the sky?** (a rainbow with the Sun coming out)
  What can you say about the weather? (It has changed; there was a storm, but the sky is clearing.)

Developing the Main Idea
Ask:

- **What was the weather like when you came to school this morning? Now look outdoors. Is the weather the same?** (Children may make observations about differences in the temperature, wind, sky, and type of precipitation.)

- **What do you think the weather will be like tomorrow? Will it be the same as today?** Record and save children's responses. Check the weather tomorrow at the same time and compare it to their predictions.

Read to Learn

When does the weather change?
The weather changes when the air outside changes. It may be rainy and cloudy. Then the rain stops. The clouds go away. Soon, it is sunny.

A tornado is a cone-shaped clou[d]; a hurricane is a large storm; when there is a drought the land is very dry; a rainbow sometimes forms after a rainfall.

a sunny day after rainfall

C 34

Reading MiniLesson

Sequence of Events

Develop Point out to children that clue words can help them recognize the sequence of events in a paragraph. Identify the two clue words *then* and *soon* on C34.

Practice Have children find other examples of sequence of events in previous lessons. Have them point out the clue words that helped them identify the examples, such as then, after, soon, first, next, last.

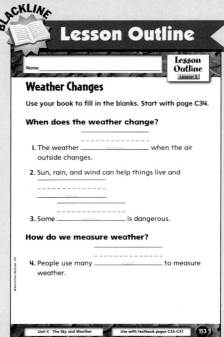

Lesson Outline

Name _____

Lesson Outline Lesson 5

Weather Changes
Use your book to fill in the blanks. Start with page C34.

When does the weather change?
_____

1. The weather ____changes____ when the air outside changes.

2. Sun, rain, and wind can help things live and _____
   ____grow____

3. Some ____weather____ is dangerous.

How do we measure weather?
_____

4. People use many ____tools____ to measure weather.

Unit C · The Sky and Weather   Use with textbook pages C32–C37   153

Reading in Science Resources, p. 153

un, rain, and wind can help things
ve and grow. But some weather is
angerous. It can harm living things.
can harm the land, too.

▶ **Tell about the weather here.**
See annotation on page C 34.

tornado

hurricane

drought

C 35

Help children read the picture labels. Ask:

- **How are a drought, a hurricane, and a tornado alike?** (All three can cause damage to people, homes, plants, animals, and the land.) **How are they different?** (A tornado is a very powerful twisting wind. A hurricane has very strong winds too, but there is so much rain that it sometimes causes flooding. In a drought there is no rain so the land dries and plants die.)

Thinking Further: *Inferring*

- **What might happen if meteorologists did not find out about the weather?** (People would have no warning about dangerous weather such as hurricanes and tornadoes.)

▶ **After Reading**
Ask the red question in the student book as **ongoing assessment.**

Technology

- Science Music CDs
  What Shall We Do on a Rainy Day?
  Rain, Rain Go Away

- **Science Experiences Videotapes**
  Sky Watch: Tracking a Winter Storm
  (Package 6)

BLACKLINE
Interpret Illustrations

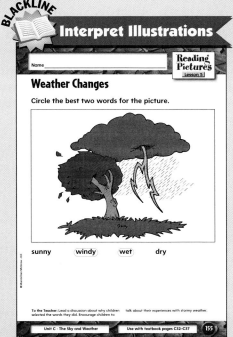

Name

Reading
Pictures
Lesson 5

Weather Changes

Circle the best two words for the picture.

sunny   windy   wet   dry

To the Teacher: Lead a discussion about why children   talk about their experiences with stormy weather.
selected the words they did. Encourage children to

Unit C · The Sky and Weather   Use with textbook pages C32–C37   155

Reading in Science Resources, pp. 155-156

Science Background

Hurricanes and Tornadoes
A hurricane is a large storm, up to 600 miles in diameter, that begins over the ocean. Winds move in a circular pattern at speeds of 75 miles and more. As a hurricane nears land, the wind and giant waves can destroy everything in their path. A tornado is a powerful twisting wind funnel. The winds may surpass 300 miles per hour and cover a diameter of up to one mile.

How do we measure weather?

Before Reading
Have children try to answer the red question at the top of the page.

Using the Illustrations
Have children recall the tools they made and used throughout the unit and what they measured. Assist children as they read the picture captions. Ask:

- **Which tools did you use in the Explore Activity?** (thermometer, wind sock) **What did those tools measure?** (temperature, wind direction and strength)

- **What most likely happens to a wind sock when the wind isn't blowing?** (It hangs down to the side of the pole.)

Direct attention to the anemometer. Point out how *thermometer* and *anemometer* both end with the word *meter*, which means "a tool for measuring." Ask:

- **What do you think happens to this tool on a windy day?** (The cups catch the wind and spin.)

- **Which tool is like a measuring cup?** (rain gauge) **How?** (It has markings on the side to show how much rain is in it.)

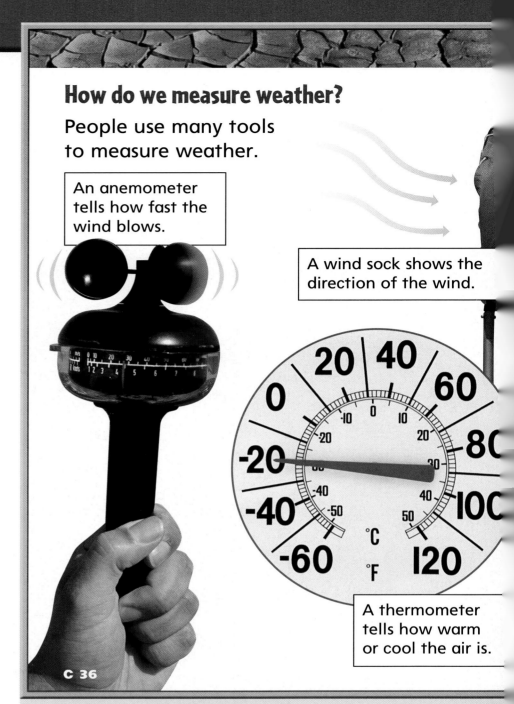

How do we measure weather?

People use many tools to measure weather.

An anemometer tells how fast the wind blows.

A wind sock shows the direction of the wind.

A thermometer tells how warm or cool the air is.

C 36

 Math MiniLesson

Comparing Rainfall Measurements

Develop Review with children that a rain gauge measures how much rain or snow falls.

Activity Give children masking tape, a jar, a marker, and a ruler. Help them to make a rain gauge (cut tape the height of the jar, mark lines 1 centimeter apart from bottom to top, place tape on the jar). Use the jar on rainy days and record measurements in a chart for a week or more. Ask:

- **Which day had the most rain? The least rain? How do you know? Spatial; Logical**

A meteorologist uses tools to measure weather.

What do these tools measure?
anemometer: wind speed;
thermometer: temperature;
wind sock: wind direction;
rain gauge: amount of rain

A rain gauge tells how much rain falls.

Stop and Think

1. When can weather change?
2. What are some things that weather tools measure?

 MORE TO READ Read **The Big Storm** by Bruce Hiscock.

C 37

Informal Assessment

Easy/Average Invite children to create a crayon-resistant and watercolor wash that depicts a storm. Begin by having children use crayons to draw a picture of a storm. Tell them to press hard. Next, have children spread a small amount of water across the picture and then spread some blue or black watercolor paint or food coloring across the damp paper. **Kinesthetic; Spatial**

Challenge Invite children to create the storm pictures as described at the left and then write a weather report to accompany the artwork. Have children present their reports as TV weather reporters reporting live from the scene. **Spatial; Linguistic**

▶**After Reading**
Ask the red question in the student book as **ongoing assessment.**

3 | Lesson Review

Answers to Stop and Think

1. Weather changes when the air outside changes. (pp. C34–C35)

2. We use weather tools to measure how hot or cool the air is, how fast the wind blows, the direction of the wind, and how much rain or snow falls. (pp. C36–C37)

MORE TO READ Children can learn more about how storms form by reading *The Big Storm* by Bruce Hiscock. New York: Aladdin Paperbacks, 2000.

Retelling
Write the following scaffolding for summarizing the lesson on the board. Have children retell the lesson by filling in the blanks.

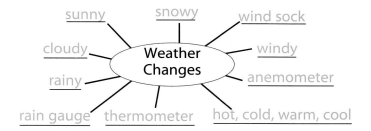

sunny   snowy   wind sock
cloudy   Weather Changes   windy
rainy   anemometer
rain gauge   thermometer   hot, cold, warm, cool

LESSON 6 Spring and Summer

Objectives

- Explore and communicate seasonal weather changes through the year.
- Discuss weather and light conditions in spring and summer.
- Discuss the activities and life processes of living things in spring and summer.

Resources

- Big Book, pp. C38–C43
- Activity Resources, pp. 75–77
- Reading in Science Resources, pp. 159–164
- Vocabulary Cards
- Reading Aid Transparency C6
- Visual Aid Transparency 18

Build on Prior Knowledge
Display pictures of your community during different seasons. The pictures should contain clues such as clothing, trees and flowers, or snow. Encourage children to identify the seasons and share experiences they have had adapting to changing weather.

1 Get Ready

Using the Illustrations
Ask:

- **Which weather words best tell about the kind of day it is here?** (sunny and warm)
- **What season of the year might it be?** (summer) **Why do you think so?** (The children are wearing warm-weather clothing.)

See Science Skill Builder **Communicate,** p. R6.

LESSON 6 Spring and Summer

Get Ready

What are these children doing? What is the weathe like here?

Science Skill

You **communicate** when you talk, draw or write to share ide

C 38

 Science Background

Seasons

Seasons are related to the tilt of Earth's axis and how much sunlight a place receives as Earth orbits the Sun. When the North Pole is tilted away from the Sun, the Northern Hemisphere has winter and the Southern Hemisphere has summer. The reverse is true when the North Pole is tilted toward the Sun. The equator gets about the same amount of sunlight throughout the year and does not have four seasons.

 Reading Strategy

Compare and Contrast
Developing Reading Skills
Remind children that when you compare and contrast you tell how things are alike and different. Invite children to compare and contrast the weather where you live with the weather depicted in the photograph on page C38.

Explore Activity

Is the weather the same all year?

What you need

drawing paper

crayons

What to do

1 Draw yourself when it is very warm outside. Draw the weather. Draw what you wear.

2 Draw yourself when it is very cold outside. Draw the weather. Draw what you wear.

3 Is the weather the same all year? Do you wear the same kinds of clothes all year? **Communicate** your ideas.

C 39

Alternative Explore Activity

Materials a variety of clothing and equipment for each season, magazine and catalog pictures to illustrate additional items

Season Sorting Invite children to sort the articles of clothing, shoes, sports apparel, and equipment used in outdoor activities by the season they would most likely use or wear them.

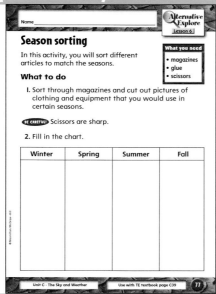

Alternative Explore
Lesson 6

Name _____

Season sorting

In this activity, you will sort different articles to match the seasons.

What you need
• magazines
• glue
• scissors

What to do

1. Sort through magazines and cut out pictures of clothing and equipment that you would use in certain seasons.

BE CAREFUL Scissors are sharp.

2. Fill in the chart.

Winter	Spring	Summer	Fall

Unit C - The Sky and Weather   Use with TE textbook page C39   77

Activity Resources, p. 77

Explore Activity

Is the weather the same all year?

Science Process Skills *communicate*

Resources Activity Resources pp. 76–77

Pacing 15–20 minutes

Grouping individuals

What to do

Read and discuss the activity with the class before they begin.

1-2 Suggest that children draw themselves in outdoor scenes. Encourage children to add details to their drawings that show what trees and other plants are like in their outdoor scenes.

3 Before discussing how the two kinds of weather are different, have children share their warm weather drawings and then their cold weather drawings, noting the characteristics of each kind of weather. (Children should conclude that the weather is not the same all year. They should also note the differences between weather conditions when it is cold and when it is warm and communicate how their choice of clothing relates to the temperature and weather outside.)

Going Further

Discuss when it is important to know what the weather will be like.

Technology

■ When time is short, preview the activity with the **Explore Activity Video**.

2 Read to Learn

What happens in spring?

Before Reading
Have children try to answer the red question at the top of the page.

Using the Illustrations
Ask:

- **What living things do you see in the pictures?** (sheep, bird, tree, people)
- **What is the weather like?** (warm) **How can you tell?** (The people are in short sleeves.)
- **What season do you think it is?** (spring) **Why?** (Birds build nests in spring, trees have blossoms in spring, people plant in spring, and some animals have their young in spring.)

Developing Vocabulary

season, spring Display pictures of the four seasons. Ask: **How many seasons does a year have?** (4) **What seasons can you name?** (winter, spring, summer, fall) As you point to each picture, ask: **What season is this?** After reviewing all four seasons, ask: **Which picture shows spring?** Introduce the Vocabulary Cards for the words *season* and *spring*. Place them on the word wall.

Read to Learn

What happens in spring?

A **season** is a time of the year. **Spring** is the season after winter. It is warmer in spring than in winter. In some places, it may rain a lot. In spring, the days get longer and the nights get shorter.

C 40

Reading in Science Resources, p. 159

Reading in Science Resources, pp. 161-162

In spring, birds build nests and lay eggs. Other animals have their young, too.

Plants grow new leaves and flowers. Many people plant seeds. Rain and warmth help the seeds grow.

 What do living things do in spring?

Plants grow new leaves and flowers; people plant seeds; birds build nests and lay eggs; other animals have their young.

C 41

Developing the Main Idea
Ask:

■ **What ideas about spring can you think of to go with each picture?**

List children's ideas on the board. Then lead them in writing a caption to accompany each picture.

Thinking Further: *Drawing Conclusions*

■ **How do you think the living things in the pictures will change as spring turns to summer?**
(The lamb, young birds, and plants will grow bigger.)

▶ **After Reading**
Ask the red question in the student book as **ongoing assessment.**

Technology

■ Visual Aid Transparency 17:
  Pond in Spring

SCIENCE
Reading MiniLesson

Sequence of Events

Develop Events that can be put in a sequence are what happens first, next, and last. Look at the bird building a nest. Ask: **What does the bird do first?** (finds a place to build its nest) **What does it do next?** (builds its nest) **Then what does it do?** (lays its eggs) **What does it do after that?** (sits on its eggs until they hatch) **What does the bird do last?** (cares for the babies until they can care for themselves)

Practice Encourage children to tell you how seeds will grow. Write or draw each part of the sequence on a strip of paper. Review the strips with children, then challenge them to arrange the strips in order.

What happens in summer?

Before Reading
Have children try to answer the red question at the top of the page.

Developing the Main Idea
Ask:

- **Which season is warmer, spring or summer?** (summer) **Why?** (The days are longer so there is more sunlight.)

- **Why do you think people spend more time outside in summer?** (The days are longer and the weather is warmer.) Have children tell about some of the things they like to do in summer.

Thinking Further: *Drawing Conclusions*

- **What season follows summer?** (fall)

- **What do you think happens as summer changes to fall?** (Days start to get shorter, the weather isn't as warm, people start wearing warmer clothing, and in some places leaves on trees begin to change color.)

Developing Vocabulary

summer Display pictures that illustrate the four seasons. As you point to each picture, ask: **What season is this? How can you tell?** Children should identify clues such as clothing, weather conditions, plant growth, or animal activity. After reviewing each season, ask: **Which picture shows summer?** Introduce the Vocabulary Card for the word *summer*. Place it on the word wall.

What happens in summer?

Summer is the season after spring. It is warmer in summer than in spring. In some places, it may be very hot. Summer days are longer than the nights.

The warmth and longer daylight hours help plants grow. Many plants grow flowers, seeds, and fruits.

C 42

Advanced Learners

Black or White

Have children place a white cloth over one thermometer in the Sun, a black cloth of the same fabric over another and read the thermometers every 5 minutes for 20 minutes. Ask: **Does the thermometer rise higher and faster under the black or white cloth?** (black) **Which color clothing will keep you cooler in summer?** (white) **Spatial; Logical**

Science Background

The First Day of Summer

In the Northern Hemisphere, summer begins with the summer solstice, the longest day of the year when the Sun is high in the sky. It occurs on either June 20 or June 21. In countries close to the Arctic Circle, the Sun does not go below the horizon for several days, and for weeks afterward, the Sun can be seen into the night.

Young animals grow bigger and look more like their parents. Many people spend more time outside in summer.

▷ **What do living things do in summer?**
Plants grow flowers, seeds, and fruits; many people spend more time outdoors; young animals grow bigger.

Stop and Think

1. What are spring and summer like?
2. What are some things living things do in spring?

 **AT THE COMPUTER** Visit **www.mhscience02.com** to learn more about the seasons.

C 43

▶**After Reading**
Ask the red question in the student book as **ongoing assessment.**

3 | Lesson Review

Answers to Stop and Think

1. In spring, the temperature gets warmer and the days get longer. In summer, the temperature is warmest and summer days are longer than summer nights. (pp. C40–C43)

2. In spring, birds and other animals have their young, plants grow new leaves and flowers, and many people plant seeds. (pp. C42–C43)

Retelling

Write the following scaffolding for summarizing the lesson on the board. Have children retell the lesson by filling in the blanks. Begin by reminding children that they have been reading about the seasons. Write Seasons on the board and ask:

- **What two seasons did you read about?**
- **What did you learn about spring? Tell at least three facts.**
- **What did you learn about summer? Tell at least three facts.**

Seasons

Spring	Summer
weather gets warm	warmest time of year
days get longer	days longer than nights
can be rainy	
birds build nests	plants grow flowers and fruits
plants grow new leaves	young animals grow
	people are outside more

 ## Technology

- Science Music CD
  The Arrival of Winter

✓ Informal Assessment

Easy/Average Invite children to create a mural of the four seasons beginning with spring and summer. Tape paper to the wall and draw a line to represent the horizon. Encourage children to discuss what to include to show spring and summer. Children can then color, paint, and cut out and paste pictures of trees and plants, animals, people, and so on to show the two seasons. Save the mural for the next lesson. **Spatial; Social**

Challenge Invite children to write weather reports for a spring or summer day. Is it warm and rainy, sunny and hot, or cool and windy? Tell children to name the season, explain what people can see and do outdoors, and suggest what people should wear. Have children draw pictures to go along with their weather reports. Then invite children to present their weather reports as TV reporters. **Linguistic**

Fall and Winter

Objectives

- Explore through observation how to keep cold away from your skin.
- Discuss weather and light conditions in fall and winter.
- Discuss the activities and life processes of living things in fall and winter.

Resources

- Big Book, pp. C44–C49
- Activity Resources, pp. 78–80, 86
- Reading in Science Resources, pp. 165–170
- Vocabulary Cards
- Reading Aid Transparency C7
- Visual Aid Transparency 19
- Science Center Card 18
- School to Home Activities, p. 22

Build on Prior Knowledge
Ask:

- **What do you know about the fall season?** (the weather gets cooler, leaves turn colors and drop from some trees, some fruits and vegetables are ready to be picked, some animals begin to store food, some animals leave the area)

1 Get Ready

Using the Illustrations
Ask:

- **What season of the year is it here?** (fall or autumn) **Why do you think so?** (The leaves turned color and dropped from the trees.)

See Science Skill Builder **Observe,** p. R2.

Fall and Winter

Get Ready

What is the season here? How do you know?

Science Skill

You **observe** when you use your senses to find out about things.

C 44

 Cross Curricular Books

Additional Outside Reading

Sheep Station

written by Shirley Frederick
illustrated by Michael A. Hobbs

To order, see page C1•b.

Cultural Perspective

Harvest Customs

Fall marks the end of the growing season and the beginning of harvest. From ancient times, different cultures have celebrated to give thanks. The Ga people of Ghana have a month-long festival called *Homowo*. They serve corn from the previous year before trying corn from the new harvest. Encourage children to tell about harvest festivals they know about such as the Jewish Sukkoth and the African-American Kwanzaa.

Explore Activity

How can you stay warm when it is cold outside?

What you need

cup with ice

glove

What to do

1 Pick up the cup. Hold it in your hand. **Observe** how it feels.

2 Wait a few minutes. Put on the glove. Hold the cup again in your hand. Observe how it feels.

3 When did your hand feel less cold? How can you stay warm when it is cold outside?

C 45

Alternative Explore Activity

Keeping Warm Tape felt around one of two jars. Fill both jars with warm water and place a thermometer in each one. Help children to check and record the temperature of the water at the start of the activity and at five-minute intervals for 15 to 20 minutes. Ask: **Which jar of water stayed warmer longer?** (the wrapped jar) **How is wrapping the cloth around the jar like wearing a coat on a cold day?** (It keeps you warm by keeping heat in.)

Keeping warm

In this activity, you will discover how water can stay warmer longer.

What to do

1. Check and record the temperature of the water in each jar at the start.

2. Record temperatures of both jars after 5 minutes, 10 minutes, 15 minutes, and 20 minutes.

3. Fill in the chart.

	Wrapped jar	Unwrapped jar
Start:		
5 minutes:		
10 minutes:		
15 minutes:		
20 minutes:		

4. Which jar of water stayed warmer longer?

_____
the wrapped jar

What you need
- tape
- felt
- 2 jars
- water
- 2 thermometers

Alternative Explore Lesson 7

80   Unit C · The Sky and Weather   Use with TE textbook page C45

Activity Resources, p. 80

Explore Activity

How can you stay warm when it is cold outside?

Science Process Skills *observe*

Resources Activity Resources pp. 78–79

Pacing 15–20 minutes

Grouping pairs

What to do

Read and discuss the activity with the class before they begin.

1 Before children pick up the cup, ask them to predict how it will feel and tell why they think so. (Ice is cold, so the cup will feel cold.) Have children hold the cup and compare their observations and predictions. (They should observe that the cup feels cold.)

2 Have children wait several minutes before putting on the glove. This will give their hands time to warm up after having touched the cold ice cup. (They should observe that when picking up the cup while wearing the glove, their hands do not feel cold or as cold.)

3 Have children compare how it feels to hold the ice cup with and without a glove on their hands. (Children should conclude that they can stay warm by wearing more clothing.)

Going Further

Ask:

- **What would you tell someone to wear when the weather turns very cold?** (long-sleeve shirt and sweater, socks, pants, boots, coat or jacket, hat, and gloves) **Why?** (Layers of clothing help keep your body warm.)

For an additional activity, see Science Center Card 18, p.C56•f.

 ## Technology

- When time is short, preview the activity with the **Explore Activity Video**.

2 | Read to Learn

What happens in fall?

Before Reading
Have children try to answer the red question at the top of the page.

Using the Illustrations
Ask:

- **Why do you think the people are picking pumpkins?** (to eat or use as decorations) Encourage children to name vegetables and fruits grown in their region that are picked in the fall.

- **What kind of clothes are the people wearing?** (clothes for cooler weather) Remind children of the Explore Activity results. Mention that clothing keeps one from feeling cold by trapping, or keeping in, body heat.

- **What letter does the flock of geese seem to form?** (the letter "V") **Where are the geese going?** (to a warmer place) **Encourage children to suggest reasons why.**

- **Which animal does not move to a warmer place?** (the squirrel) **Where might squirrels get some of the food they need in cold weather?** (They gather and store food before it gets too cold.)

Developing Vocabulary

fall Display pictures depicting the four seasons. After reviewing all four seasons, ask: **Which picture shows fall?**
Introduce the Vocabulary Card for the term *fall*. Place it on the word wall.

Read to Learn

What happens in fall?

Fall is the season after summer. It is cooler in fall than in summer. The days get shorter and the nights get longer.

Many plants stop growing in fall. In some places, leaves change color and drop to the ground. In many places, fruits are ripe. People pick the fruits.

C 46

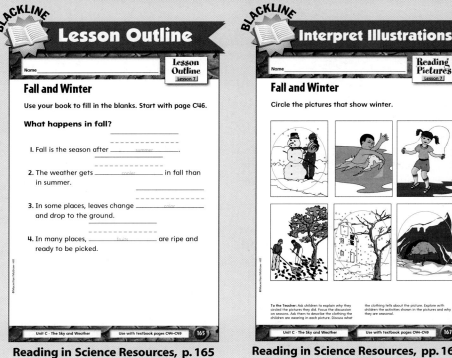

BLACKLINE **Lesson Outline**

Lesson Outline
Lesson 7

Name _____

Fall and Winter

Use your book to fill in the blanks. Start with page C46.

What happens in fall?

1. Fall is the season after _____ summer.

2. The weather gets _____ cooler _____ in fall than in summer.

3. In some places, leaves change _____ color and drop to the ground.

4. In many places, _____ fruits _____ are ripe and ready to be picked.

Unit C · The Sky and Weather   Use with textbook pages C44–C49   165

Reading in Science Resources, p. 165

BLACKLINE **Interpret Illustrations**

Reading Pictures
Lesson 7

Name _____

Fall and Winter

Circle the pictures that show winter.

To the Teacher: Ask children to explain why they circled the pictures they did. Focus the discussion on seasons. Ask them to describe the clothing the children are wearing in each picture. Discuss what the clothing tells about the picture. Explore with children the activities shown in the pictures and why they are seasonal.

Unit C · The Sky and Weather   Use with textbook pages C44–C49   167

Reading in Science Resources, pp. 167–1

Some animals move to warmer places in fall. Others store food to eat in winter.

 What do living things do in fall?

People pick ripe fruits; leaves of some trees change color and fall to the ground; some animals move to warmer places; some animals store food.

C 47

Developing the Main Idea

Begin a chart. Label columns *Spring, Summer, Fall, Winter.* At the left, write *weather.* As children answer the questions, fill in the chart: Ask:

- **What is spring weather like?** (warm) **Which season is the warmest?** (summer) **Is it warmer or cooler in fall than in summer?** (cooler)

Write *plants* just below weather. Ask:

- **What grows on many plants in spring?** (New leaves grow.) **In summer?** (Flowers, fruits, and seeds grow.) **What happens to many plants in fall?** (Some plants stop growing, leaves change color and drop, and fruits are ripe.)

Write *animals* next. Ask:

- **What happens among many animals in spring?** (They have young.) **How do the babies change by summer?** (They grow bigger.) **What do some animals do in fall?** (move to warmer places or store food for winter)

Write *days/nights* last. Ask:

- **How do days and nights change in spring?** (days grow longer, nights grow shorter) **In summer?** (Days are longer than nights.) **In fall?** (Days grow shorter and nights grow longer.)

Thinking Further: *Making Predictions*

- **What changes will there be in winter?** (The weather becomes colder, some plants die, some animals sleep, and nights are longer than days.)

▶ **After Reading**

Ask the red question in the student book as **ongoing assessment.**

 English Language Learners

Seasons Game

Write one of these words in each box of a tic-tac-toe grid: *seasons, summer, winter, spring, fall, hot, cold, warm, cool.* Other words may include s*nowy, rainy, nest, harvest.* Call out a word. Before pairs of children can mark an *X* or *O* on their grids, they must tell something about the word using gestures, drawings, or words. **Linguistic**

Science Background

Seasonal Migrations

Some species of birds, fish, insects, and mammals migrate twice a year. Some animals migrate between northern and southern latitudes. Others migrate between higher and lower elevations. Scientists do not know exactly what triggers a migration, but among some groups of animals it may be the dwindling food supply as a result of seasonal changes.

What happens in winter?

Before Reading
Have children try to answer the red question at the top of the page.

Developing the Main Idea
Complete the chart you started earlier.
Ask:

- **Which season is the coldest?** (winter)

- **Are winter days longer or shorter than spring, summer, or fall days?** (shorter) **Are winter nights longer or shorter than spring, summer, or fall nights?** (longer)

- **Which trees do not make food in winter?** (trees that lose their leaves) **Why?** (Leaves make the food a tree needs.) **Explain that many seed plants die in winter, and although trees that lose their leaves (deciduous) may look dead, they are not. They will grow the leaves they need to make food again in spring.**

Thinking Further: *Making Generalizations*

- **What other cycles do you know?** (cycle of day and night, the Moon's cycle, the water cycle)

Developing Vocabulary

winter Display pictures depicting the four seasons. After reviewing all four seasons, ask:
Which picture shows winter?
Introduce the Vocabulary Card for the term *winter*. Place it on the word wall.

What happens in winter?

Winter is the season after fall. It is colder in winter than in fall. In some places, it may be very cold. People wear warm clothes. Winter days are shorter than the nights.

In many places, some plants die. Some stay alive but have no leaves. Evergreens make food all year.

C 48

Reading MiniLesson

Sequence of Events

Develop Review with children that sequence is the order in which events happen. Write *spring* on the board. Ask which season comes next and record the response. Repeat for each of the seasons. Review the sequence with children.

Practice Have children use the completed seasons chart to tell how the weather, plants, or days and nights change from spring through winter.

Science Background

Hibernation

The body functions of a hibernating animal nearly shut down. The animal does not eat, its body temperature falls, and its respiration rate slows down. Hibernating animals include door mice, woodchucks, and bats. Bears and other animals go into a kind of hibernation. They sleep deeply for long periods, but may wake up and leave their dens for food. This is not true hibernation.

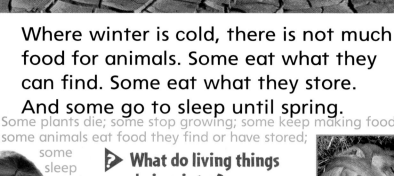

Where winter is cold, there is not much food for animals. Some eat what they can find. Some eat what they store. And some go to sleep until spring.

Some plants die; some stop growing; some keep making food; some animals eat food they find or have stored; some sleep until spring.

▶ **What do living things do in winter?**

Stop and Think

1. What do some living things do in fall?
2. What is winter like?

AT THE COMPUTER

Visit **www.mhscience02.com** to learn more about the seasons.

C 49

Informal Assessment

Easy/Average Invite children to continue the seasons mural they started in Lesson 6. Encourage children to discuss what to include on the mural to show fall and winter. Children can then color, paint, and cut out and paste pictures of trees and plants, animals, people, and so on to show the two seasons. **Spatial; Social**

Challenge Invite children to plan an imaginary trip to a place with specific fall or winter weather. Ask children to pretend to pack what they will need for this particular kind of seasonal weather. Have children then describe the contents of their suitcase to classmates to see if classmates can guess what seasonal weather the traveler will be experiencing. **Linguistic**

▶ **After Reading**
Ask the red question in the student book as **ongoing assessment.**

3 Lesson Review

Answers to Stop and Think

1. Some plants stop growing; others lose their leaves. Animals may store food for the winter or move to where the weather is warm. People pick fruits. (pp. C46–C47)

2. In winter, the weather is cold. Winter days are shorter than nights. (pp. C48–C49)

Retelling

Write the following scaffolding for summarizing the lesson on the board. Have children retell the lesson by filling in the blanks. Begin by reminding children that they have been reading about the seasons. Write *Seasons* on the board and ask:

■ **What two seasons did you read about?**

■ **What did you learn about fall? Tell at least three facts.**

■ **What did you learn about winter? Tell at least three facts.**

Seasons

Fall
weather gets cooler
days get shorter
some animals store food
some plants stop growing

Winter
weather gets cold
days shorter than nights
some animals sleep until spring
some plants die

Technology

■ Science Music CD
*The Arrival of Winter
Is That the Sweet Sound?*

■ Visual Aid Transparency 19:
Pond in Winter

Reading

L·I·N·K

Busy Seasons

Developing the Main Idea
Encourage children to describe fall where they live.
Ask:

- **Do the leaves on the trees change? How?**
  (Depending on where children live, they may
  say that the leaves turn color and drop.)

- **Does the weather change? How?** (Depending
  on where children live, they may say that
  weather gets cooler.)

- **Do the days get longer or shorter?** (shorter)

- **Do you need to wear a jacket or sweater at
  times? Why?** (Depending on where children
  live, they may answer yes because the weather
  is cooler.)

- **What do some animals do in fall?** (Depending
  on where children live, they may say that some
  animals move to warmer places and other
  animals begin to store food for winter.)

Direct attention to the book *Fall is Fun*. Have
children suggest reasons why fall is fun and list
their ideas on the board. Then have them read the
book and compare their ideas about fall with those
of the author.

Have children read the Grade-Level Science Book,
Fall is Fun. For additional reading, see p. C1·b.

Try This!
Invite children to brainstorm a list of things
that people do in winter. Record their ideas on the
board and let them choose their favorites to
illustrate in their books. Have children write or dictate
a caption for each drawing and make a cover with the
title and their names. Invite children to read each
other's books.

Reading

L·I·N·K
FOR SCHOOL OR HOME

Busy Seasons

Find out about some
things people do in
fall. Read *Fall is Fun*
by Joe Smith.

Fall is Fun!

by Joe Smith
illustrated by Selina Alko

Try This!

Make your own book. Call it
Winter Is Fun. Show things
that people do in winter.

C 50

SCIENCE

Reading | MiniLesson

Sequence of Events

Develop Remind children that
sequence is the order in which
events happen. To help children
understand the cyclic pattern of
the seasons, draw a graphic
organizer in the shape of a circle
and connect the four seasons
with arrows.

Practice Have volunteers come
to the board and point to any
season. Then ask the class
which season comes next,
which season comes after that,
and so on. Have children
describe what happens in each
season and add this to the
graphic organizer.

Measure Temperature

hat is the temperature like
a season? Does it change
lot from day to day? Find out.

Try This!

Work with an adult. Find out the
emperature each day. Use a radio,
a TV, or a thermometer. Do it at the
ame time each day. Do it for a few
weeks. Record the temperatures.
What are they like?

C 51

Math
L·I·N·K

Measure Temperature

Using the Illustrations
Focus attention on the photograph and ask:

- **What season do you think it is?** (winter) **How can you tell?** (Possible answer: It snows in winter in some places; people are dressed in clothing that will keep them warm on a snowy winter day.)

- **What is the temperature like in winter?** (cold)

- **What tool can you use to measure the temperature?** (thermometer)

Try This!
Review with children how to use and read a thermometer. Provide them with a blank calendar page to record the temperature each day. Children can also draw a symbol to indicate whether it is sunny, cloudy, rainy, snowy, or windy on any particular day. Invite children to share and compare the readings. Discuss whether the temperature changed a lot from day to day.

Reading Strategy

Compare and Contrast
Developing Reading Skills
Remind children that when you compare and contrast you tell how things are alike and different. Invite children to compare and contrast the temperature readings they recorded over the course of a few weeks. Ask:

- **When were the temperatures most alike? Different?** (probably from day to day; probably from day to evening or from week to week)

Science Background

How a Thermometer Works
The most common type of thermometer is a hollow glass tube that holds mercury or colored alcohol. When the temperature goes up, the liquid expands, takes up more space inside the tube; as a result, the liquid rises. When the temperature falls, the liquid contracts, takes up less space, and moves down. Have children compare temperature readings on a thermometer with Fahrenheit and Celsius scales.

Chapter Review and Test Preparation

Resources
- Big Book, pp. C52–C53
- Reading in Science Resources, pp. 171–172
- Assessment Book, pp. 29–32

Answers to Vocabulary

1. fall, p. C40
2. clouds, p. C48
3. summer, p. C42
4. spring, p. C46
5. winter, p. C30

Test Taking Tip

For items 6–8, look for key words in each sentence that may suggest the meaning of the missing word.

6. season, p. C40
7. wind, p. C28
8. weather, p. C28

Chapter 6 Review

Vocabulary

weather
wind
season
spring
summer
fall
winter
clouds

Use each word once for items 1–8. What does each picture show?

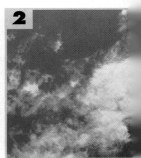

Complete each sentence.

6. A time of year is called a ____.

7. Moving air is called ____.

8. What the air is like outside is called ____.

C 52

Reading in Science Resources, pp. 171–172

Science Ideas

Tell what each weather tool measures.

9

10

Science Skill: Communicate

11 What makes it rain or snow?
Use the picture to tell what happens.

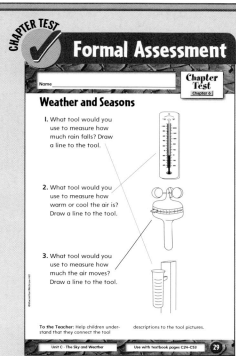

READ
Fall Is Fun! by Joe Smith

C 53

CHAPTER TEST

Formal Assessment

Name _____

Chapter Test
Chapter 6

Weather and Seasons

1. What tool would you use to measure how much rain falls? Draw a line to the tool.

2. What tool would you use to measure how warm or cool the air is? Draw a line to the tool.

3. What tool would you use to measure how much the air moves? Draw a line to the tool.

To the Teacher: Help children understand that they connect the tool descriptions to the tool pictures.

Unit C · The Sky and Weather   Use with textbook pages C24–C53   29

Assessment Book, pp. 29–32

Answers to Science Ideas

9. wind direction, p. C36
10. how warm or cool the air is, or temperature, p. C36

Answers to Science Skill: Communicate

11. When water goes into the air, clouds form. The tiny drops get bigger. When the water drops in the clouds get very big, they fall to the ground as rain or snow. pp. C30–C31

Retell
Write the following scaffolding for summarizing the chapter on the board. Have children retell the chapter by filling in the blanks to tell about different kinds of weather and to identify the four seasons.

Weather and Seasons

snowy	summer
windy	fall
sunny	winter
rainy	spring
snowy	
cold	
hot	
warm	
cool	

Performance Assessment
The second activity on page C56 can be used as a performance assessment. See Teacher's Edition page C56 for the scoring rubric.

Read
To find out more about the fall season, have children read the Grade-Level Science Book, *Fall Is Fun* by Ron Archer. For additional reading, see page C1•b.

Technology

For more review, visit
www.mhscience02.com.

People in Science

People in Science

Objective

- Discuss that storm chasers are people that look for tornadoes.

Build on Prior Knowledge

Ask children to share their experiences either viewing or being caught in a thunderstorm. Discuss where they were and what they observed about the storm.

- **Have you ever seen a thunderstorm? What was it like?** (Possible answers: Heavy rain, dark clouds, thunder, lightning, heavy winds)

- **Have you ever seen a tornado? What was it like?** (Possible answers: Dangerous winds, dark clouds, heavy rain, clouds shaped like a funnel, large hail)

Warren Faidley
Storm Chaser

Developing the Main Idea
Ask:

- **What is a tornado?** (a large and very dangerous thunderstorm.)

- **What do storm chasers do?** (They drive to where the thunderstorms are forming and watch the clouds.)

- **What do the storm chasers do if they see a tornado forming?** (They tell other people the location of the tornado, and the possible direction of the tornado.)

Warren Faidley
Storm Chaser

Warren Faidley is a storm chaser. He looks for tornadoes.

C 54

Science Background

Storm Chasers

Storm chasers, or spotters, gather information from local National Weather Service stations on such conditions as wind fields, wind shear, and dew point, some of the ingredients necessary to the possible formation of a supercell thunderstorm that can produce damaging winds, large hail, and weak-to-moderate tornadoes.

Storm chasers drive to areas where supercells may possibly form or have already been reported. They listen to the reports of other storm chasers in the area and police reports on ham radios. And they relay their own information about storm features to the National Weather Service station, local police, and other chasers as well. Given enough warning, people are able to seek shelter from the destruction of tornadoes.

...ornadoes happen in some ...understorms. Warren drives ...o where these thunderstorms ...re forming. He watches the ...louds. If Warren sees a ...ornado, he tells others where ...t is. He also tells where the ...torm may be going. This ...nformation can save lives.

 How does Warren Faidley help save lives?

 Visit **www.mhscience02.com** to find out more about storm chasers.

C 55

Developing the Main Idea

■ **Why do you think it is important to know about tornadoes?** (Possible answers: to get to safe shelter, or not travel to where a tornado is heading.)

■ **How do storm chasers help save lives?** (If they see a tornado, they tell others where it is and where it might be going.)

Answer to Journal Question

Children's writing should include that Warren Faidley can tell where a tornado might occur and tell people to avoid that area.

Retelling

Check children's understanding by asking them to tell about storm chasers and their work.

 Advanced Learners

The Weather Forecast

Have children take turns using the Internet, newspapers, or television to research the location of tornadoes locally, or in other regions of the United States throughout the week. Have children present the features of a tornado, drawing pictures of a tornado. Children can make a poster warning people about the dangers of tornadoes. **Linguistic**

SCIENCE
Workshop

Unit C Performance Assessment

1. Tell About Things in the Sky (Chapter 5)

Materials: drawing paper, crayons

Teaching Tips: Have children complete each drawing as directed. Ask which drawing they would label *Day* and which drawing they would label *Night*. Encourage children to explain why and have them add the correct label to each drawing. Continue by having children use the reverse side of their drawings to answer the three questions.

2. Compare Winter and Summer (Chapter 6)

Materials: drawing paper, crayons

Teaching Tips: Have children label their drawings *Winter* and *Summer*. Invite them to share their drawings with a partner, describing what they are doing and what they are wearing. Ask why they would not wear summer clothing in winter or winter clothing in summer. Then have children write sentences about summer weather, winter weather, plants and animals in summer, and plants and animals in winter on the reverse side of their drawings.

---

1. **Tell about things** in the sky. Draw your school. Show the Sun. Draw your house. Show the Moon and stars. Then write an answer for each question below.

- What happens each time the Earth turns?
- What lights the Moon?
- What is a constellation?

2. **Compare winter and summer** where you live. Draw pictures of what you do and wear in summer and winter. Then write a sentence about:

- the weather in summer
- the weather in winter

C 56

Rubrics for Science Workshop

1. Tell About Things in the Sky (5-point rubric)

1 point = for drawing the Sun in the day sky

1 point = for drawing the Moon in the night sky

1 point = for writing that each time Earth turns, there is one day

1 point = for writing that the Sun lights the Moon

1 point = for writing that a constellation is a star picture

2. Compare Winter and Summer (5-point rubric)

2 points = for both drawings of what is worn and done in summer and winter

1 point = for writing that it is warm or hot in summer

1 point = for writing that it is cool or cold in winter

1 point = for writing what some plants and animals do in your area

---

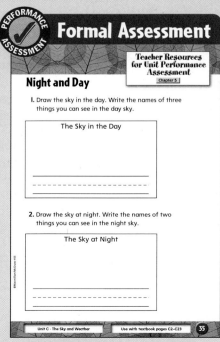

Formal Assessment

Teacher Resources for Unit Performance Assessment
Chapter 5

Night and Day

I. Draw the sky in the day. Write the names of three things you can see in the day sky.

> The Sky in the Day

2. Draw the sky at night. Write the names of two things you can see in the night sky.

> The Sky at Night

Unit C · The Sky and Weather   Use with textbook pages C2–C23   35

Assessment Book, pp. 33–36

Science Center Card 13

The Sky and Weather
Why do we have day and night?

Objectives

- Children shine a flashlight on their partners and have their partners rotate to learn why we have day and night.

What you need

- **Science Center Card 13**
- Activity Resources, Science Center Card 13, p. 81
- flashlight; Sun label; Earth label; string; hole punch

What to do

- Make the two labels, then punch holes in the top corners of each label. Thread and knot the two ends of the string in each hole to make a necklace.
- Make sure the flashlight works.
- Make the room as dark as possible before starting the activity.
- Read the Science Center Card aloud to assure that children understand the activity.
- Model for the children how to turn around but stay in the same place, if necessary.
- Tell children to shine the flashlight in the "Earth's" chest area and not into the eyes.
- Remind children to return the labels and flashlight to the activity center for the next group of children to use.

Informal Assessment

- Show children a globe and a flashlight. Point out where North America is. Ask children to position the globe to show day and night in North America.
- Check children's filled-in worksheets.

Follow-Up

- Help children understand that when it is day for our part of the world, it is night for another part of the world. Challenge children to identify a country or continent that has night when we have day.

Science Center Card

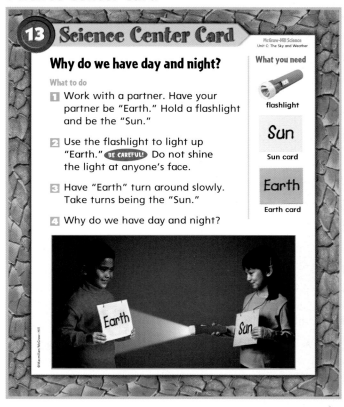

Activity Resources, Page 81

Science Center Card 14

The Sky and Weather
Ask a Question

Objectives

- Children ask questions about a picture of the Moon.

What you need

- **Science Center Card 14**
- Activity Resources, Science Center Card 14, p. 82

What to do

- Be sure children understand the activity before they begin. Go through each step and make sure children know what they will be doing.
- Review with children question words they can use, such as *who, what, when, where, why* and *how,* and that questions always end with a question mark.
- Remind children that we ask questions to find out more about something.

Informal Assessment

- Show children an unusual photo of the Moon. Tell them to ask a question about the photo. Tell them to identify the question word they used.
- Check children's filled-in worksheets.

Follow-Up

- Challenge children to find answers to their questions. Have each child choose one of the questions he or she asked. Provide reference books where children can locate the answers. Allow time for children to share any information they found.

Science Center Card

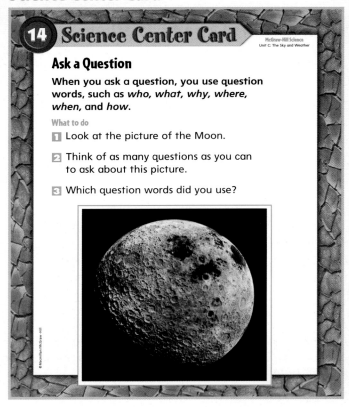

Activity Resources, Page 82

Science Center Card 15

The Sky and Weather
Follow Directions

Objectives

- Children follow directions to make a windsock.

What you need

- **Science Center Card 15**
- Activity Resources, Science Center Card 15, p. 83
- construction paper; tissue paper; 5 pieces of string; glue; hole punch

What to do

- Cut enough 1-inch tissue paper strips so that each windsock will have six to eight pieces.
- Cut string into 4-inch and 6-inch pieces. Each windsock needs 4 smaller pieces and one larger piece.
- Place all materials in the Science Center.
- Provide damp paper towels for any glue spills.
- Assure that children understand the activity before they begin by reading each step aloud.
- Punch four holes, evenly spaced, around one edge of each windsock.
- Model for children how to tie double knots with the string. Allow time for children to practice, if needed.
- Remind children to clean the Science Center for the next students.

Informal Assessment

- Show children a windsock that has been assembled incorrectly. (The string is glued in place of the tissue paper and the tissue paper strips are tied together.) Ask children to describe which part of the directions wasn't followed correctly.

Follow-Up

- Have children search for areas around the school where they can hang their windsocks. The best spots would be outside a classroom window. If that isn't possible, choose an area children can see easily.

Science Center Card

Activity Resources, Page 83

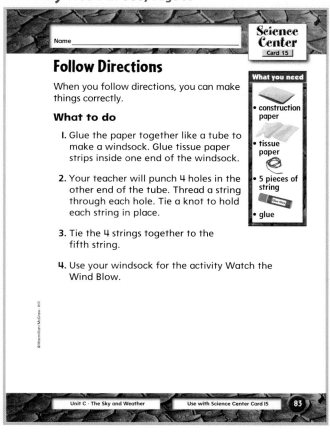

Science Center Card 16

The Sky and Weather
Watch the Wind Blow

Objectives

- Children observe a windsock for 5 days and observe how the wind changes from day to day.

What you need:

- **Science Center Card 16**
- Activity Resources, Science Center Card 16, p. 84
- windsock; wind chart

What to do:

- Before the activity, choose a place outside where you will hang the windsocks. Children should be able to observe them easily.

- Read the activity aloud to assure that children understand each step.

- Choose a specific time during the day when children will observe and record wind on their charts.

- Show children the chart on the worksheet. Be sure they understand the difference between the illustrated windsocks.

Informal Assessment:

- Observe children as they observe the windsocks to see if they accurately match the windsock's position with the windsock illustrations on the chart.

- Ask children to explain how the wind chart helped them answer the questions on the worksheet. (It provided a way to review what the wind was like at another time.)

- Check children's filled in worksheets.

Follow-Up

- Bring in the weather section of the local newspaper and read the wind directions for each day. Have children compare the newspaper's information with the information they collected. How is it similar? How is it different?

Science Center Card

Activity Resources, Page 84

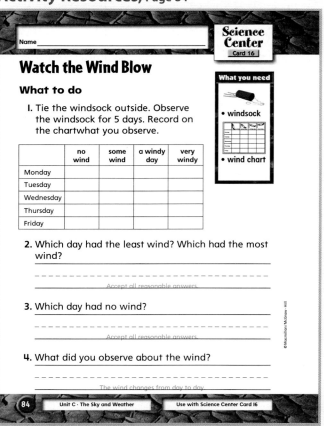

Science Center Card 17

The Sky and Weather
Use a Pattern

Objectives

- Children observe a pattern of rainfall from clouds and predict what comes next.

What you need

- **Science Center Card 17**
- Activity Resources, Science Center Card 17, p. 85

What to do

- Read the Science Center Card and worksheet aloud so that children understand the activity.
- Ask children to define the word *predict,* to use what you know to tell what might happen in the future.
- Review the water cycle with children and discuss how the photos are similar to the water cycle.

Informal Assessment

- Ask children to draw or describe a pattern based on the Sun. (Children might illustrate or describe day, night, day, night for their patterns.)
- Check children's filled in worksheets.

Follow-Up

- Challenge children to make a pattern using three different pictures. Allow time for them to swap patterns with a friend who must figure out what comes next in their patterns.

Science Center Card

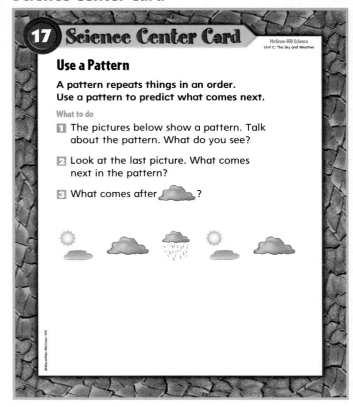

Activity Resources, Page 85

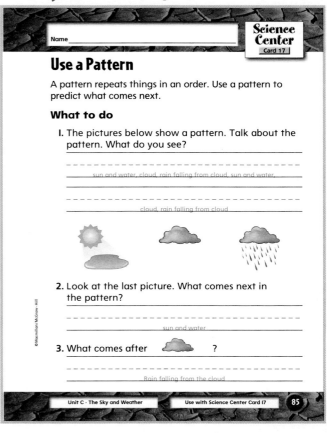

Science Center Card 18

The Sky and Weather
Be a Weather Tracker

Objectives

■ Children track how the weather changes from fall to spring.

What you need

■ **Science Center Card 18**
■ Activity Resources, Science Center Card 18, p. 86, weather charts, p. 73
■ crayons; thermometer; weather tool

What to do

■ Staple together 3 copies of the weather chart with a cover sheet to make a science journal for each child.
■ Label each weather chart in the science journal with a season — fall, winter, and spring.
■ Read the activity aloud so that children understand what to do.
■ Review with children how to read a thermometer.
■ Review with children how to use the weather tool from Unit C in the pupil edition.
■ Collect and store the science journals once children have completed one season so they won't be misplaced before the next season arrives.

Informal Assessment

■ After each season, have children describe the weather they observed. Was it the usual weather for that time of year in your region? Allow children to explain why they think it was or wasn't.
■ Check children's filled in worksheets.

Follow-Up

■ Have children choose a part of the United States where the weather is different from where they live. Discuss the weather differences and how signs of seasonal change are different in different places.

Science Center Card

Activity Resources, Page 86

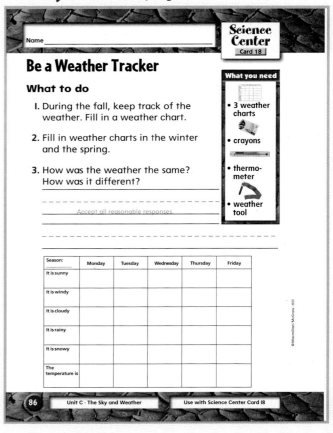

Earth Science

UNIT D

Caring for Earth

NATIONAL GEOGRAPHIC

Caring for Earth

Main Idea: Natural resources, such as soil, water, air, and plants, are important for life, but limited. They must be conserved.

UNIT D

Unit Organizer

Grade-Level Science Books

EASY

A family is in the country for a picnic. Two of the children go nature hunting and find interesting things. The third child goes for a swim and is surprised when nature – a frog – finds him.

EASY

A lake is a habitat for animals and a resource for people. Many animals live in a lake, and people use a lake for recreation.

CHALLENGE

Billy goes to a party on a boat. During the festivities, the people dump their garbage and food into the ocean.

To order from Macmillan/McGraw-Hill, call 800-442-9685

Cross Curricular Books from McGraw-Hill

A Bath for Mick by Jeannette Mara

Dig for Clams by Paula Oliver

The Land by Wendy Pearl

Learning from Our Mothers by Leya Roberts

To order, call 800-442-9685

Student Bibliography

Asch, Frank. **Water.** San Diego: Gulliver Green/Harcourt Brace and Company, 1995.

Cherry, Lynne. **The Great Kapok Tree.** San Diego: Harcourt Brace, 1990.

Gibbons, Gail. **Recycle!** Boston: Little, Brown, and Company, 1996.

Thornhill, Jan. **Before & After: A Book of Nature Timescapes.** Washington, D.C.: National Geographic Society, 1997.

Reading in Science

McGraw-Hill Science

Teacher Editions provide point-of-use strategies and resource support for students to practice reading skills as they read their science texts.

- **Reading MiniLessons**
- **reduced Blackline Masters** *from Reading in Science Resources*
- **additional Reading Strategies**

Reading in Science Resources

Boxes beneath the reduced Pupil Edition pages identify specific places in a lesson where students can complete worksheets from the ***Reading in Science Resources*** blackline masters. Reduced worksheets for this unit are found on the following pages of this Teacher Edition.

Lesson Outlines: pp. D6, D12, D18, D24, D28, D40, D46

Interpret Illustrations (Reading Pictures): pp. D7, D12, D18, D24, D29, D40, D46

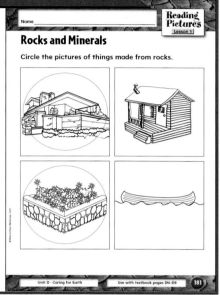

Reading in Science Resources, p. 181

Reading MiniLesson

Reading MiniLessons provide a brief tutorial and an activity for children to practice a specific reading skill for each chapter. In this unit, the chapter reading skills are:

Compare and Contrast: pp. D7, D28

Summarize (retell): pp. D41, D47

Reading Skills

Additional opportunities for students to develop and apply reading skills are provided in this unit as follows:

- ◉ **Cause and effect:** p. D42
- ○ **Compare and contrast**
- ◉ **Draw conclusions:** p. D19
- ◉ **Find the main idea:** pp. D13, D30
- ○ **Order of events (act out or retell)**
- ◉ **Summarize (retell):** pp. D9, D15, D21, D25, D31, D43, D49

- ◉ **Read pictures:** pp. D7, D12, D18, D24, D29, D40, D46
- ◉ **Draw visual images based on text:** pp. D21, D33
- ◉ **Ask questions:** pp. D4, D10, D16, D22, D26, D38, D44
- ◉ **Follow directions:** pp. D5, D11, D17, D23, D27, D39, D45
- ◉ **Build on prior knowledge:** pp. D4, D10, D16, D22, D26, D38, D44

CROSS CURRICULUM IDEAS for integrating science

L·I·N·K·S

Meeting Individual Needs

McGraw-Hill Science **includes all children in the learning process by providing a variety of strategies in this unit.**

 English Language Learners

Moving Air

Pair children learning English with native speakers. Have the non-native speaker act out or mime one thing that air (wind) can move. Have the native speaker help him or her form a descriptive sentence in English and practice writing and saying it. **Intrapersonal; Linguistic**

 Advanced Learners

Salty or Fresh

Place one carnation flower in fresh water, and another in saltwater overnight. Then ask children to draw conclusions about which cup held salty water and which held fresh water. (The cup with the wilted flower contains salt water.) Ask them to explain their conclusion. (Since people cannot drink salt water, it probably also is not good for plants.) **Logical; Visual**

 Inclusion

Plant Collage

Have children collect samples of plant materials used to make things people use, such as wood and cotton, and cut out pictures of plants that are used in some way as food. Help them make a collage titled *Why Plants Are Important.* As students continue the lesson, have them add to the collage and label each item to explain why it is important. **Visual; Spatial**

For additional support, see pp. D6, D14, D19, D22, D26, D38, D42, D49.

Learning Styles

Children acquire knowledge in a variety of ways that reflect different, often distinct, learning styles. The seven learning styles are:

- ⦿ **Kinesthetic** pp. D15, D25
- ⦿ **Social** pp. D14, D21, D49
- ⦿ **Intrapersonal** pp. D22, D31, D42
- ⦿ **Linguistic** pp. D6, D7, D9, D15, D22, D26, D31, D43, D49
- ⦿ **Logical/Mathematical** pp. D14, D19, D28, D42
- ○ **Auditory/Musical**
- ⦿ **Visual/Spatial** pp. D6, D7, D21, D26, D43

Technology for McGRAW-HILL SCIENCE

CD-ROMs

Science Newsroom CD-ROM

Science Newsroom CD-ROM, Primary Edition, is available on the Web site.

Chapter 8: Parts Puzzle

Children learn how things are made of parts, and how parts can be put together.

Join me in the Science Newsroom

Videotapes

Explore Activity Videos

All Explore Activities are available on video. Introduce lessons with these Explore Activities on Video.

Lesson 1: How can you classify rocks?

Lesson 2: How do some soils compare?

Lesson 3: What happens to rain?

Lesson 4: What can make the balloon move?

Lesson 5: What comes from plants and animals?

Lesson 6: What is in the air?

Lesson 7: How can you make something new from something old?

Science Experiences Videos

Chapter 7:

Lesson 1 Rocks and Minerals

Volcanoes: Churning and Burning (Package 5)

Lesson 3 Water

Researching the Ocean Depths (Package 7)

Science Music CDs

Lesson 3: What Shall We Do on a Rainy Day?; Rain, Rain, Go Away

Lesson 5: My Oak Tree; Mill Song

Transparencies

Visual Aid Transparencies

- **20** What is soil?
- **21** Oceans
- **22** How do parts help things move? (sail boat)
- **23** What comes from trees?

Reading Aid Transparencies

- D1-D7

Science Skills and Handbook Transparencies

- Who's a Scientist? ■ Science Handbook

Internet Resources

McGRAW-HILL SCIENCE is online at *www.mhscience02.com* with projects and activities for students, teachers, and parents.

At the Computer PE pp. D15, D25, D43, D55

Chapter Review TE pp. D34-D35, D52-D53

National Geographic pp. D54-D55

Glossary Preview Vocabulary TE pp. D3, D37
Glossary PE pp. R35-R48 also online.

NATIONAL GEOGRAPHIC

* To order National Geographic Society Products, visit us online at *www.nationalgeographic.com/education* or call 1-800-368-2728. To order NGS PictureShow and NGS PicturePack, call McGraw-Hill at 1-800-442-9685.

NGS PictureShow CD-ROM
Dynamic Earth

NGS PicturePack Transparencies
Rocks and Minerals

Process Skills

Science Process Skills	Explore Activities (Pupil Edition)	Science Skill Builders
Observe	p. D39	Pupil Edition, p. R2 Teacher Edition, p. R2 Activity Resources, pp. 175-176
Compare	p. D11	Pupil Edition, p. R3 Teacher Edition, p. R3 Activity Resources, pp. 177-178
Measure		Pupil Edition, p. R4 Teacher Edition, p. R4 Activity Resources, pp. 179-180
Classify	pp. D5, D27	Pupil Edition, p. R5 Teacher Edition, p. R5 Activity Resources, pp. 181-182
Communicate	p. D17	Pupil Edition, p. R6 Teacher Edition, p. R6 Activity Resources, pp. 183-184
Put Things in Order		Pupil Edition, p. R7 Teacher Edition, p. R7 Activity Resources, pp. 185-186
Infer	p. D23	Pupil Edition, p. R8 Teacher Edition, p. R8 Activity Resources, pp. 187-188
Make a Model		Pupil Edition, p. R9 Teacher Edition, p. R9 Activity Resources, pp. 189-190
Predict		Pupil Edition, p. R10 Teacher Edition, p. R10 Activity Resources, pp. 191-192
Investigate	p. D45	Pupil Edition, p. R11 Teacher Edition, p. R11 Activity Resources, pp. 193-194
Draw a Conclusion		Pupil Edition, p. R12 Teacher Edition, p. R12 Activity Resources, pp. 195-196

Science Center Cards

The six *Science Center Cards* for this unit on caring for Earth reinforce objectives and skills presented in the unit lessons. Each card is a hands-on activity that children can do independently in your classroom Science Center. Companion worksheets are available as blackline masters in *Activity Resources*. See pages D56•a–D56•f for instructions on using these cards.

Science Center Card 19

Good for Growing

What to do

1. Put the light soil in cup A. Put the dark soil in cup B.
2. Plant a bean in each cup. Wet the soil.
3. Observe the cups for one week. Draw what you observe.
4. Measure each plant with the ruler. Which soil is best for growing beans?

What you need
- 2 kinds of soil
- 2 beans
- 2 cups
- ruler

Good for Growing

Children observe the growth of bean seeds in two different soils for one week. *(Use after Lesson 2.)*

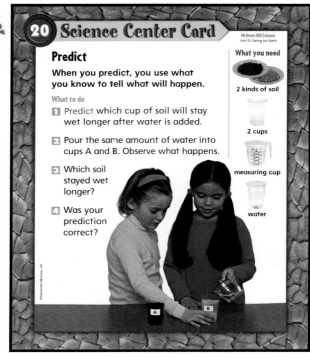

Science Center Card 20
McGraw-Hill Science
Unit D: Caring for Earth

Predict

When you predict, you use what you know to tell what will happen.

What to do

1. Predict which cup of soil will stay wet longer after water is added.
2. Pour the same amount of water into cups A and B. Observe what happens.
3. Which soil stayed wet longer?
4. Was your prediction correct?

What you need
- 2 kinds of soil
- 2 cups
- measuring cup
- water

Predict

Children pour water onto two different kinds of soil to observe which soil holds water better. *(Use after Lesson 2.)*

21 Science Center Card
McGraw-Hill Science
Unit D: Caring for Earth

Make a Model

You can make a model to find out how much of Earth's water is fresh water.

What to do

1. Color 2 squares white. Color I square light blue. Color the rest dark blue.

2. White is frozen water. Light blue is fresh water. Dark blue is salt water.

3. What kind of water does Earth have the most of? The least of?

4. How does your model help you learn about the water on Earth?

What you need

crayons

chart

Make a Model
Children make a model to show how much salt water, frozen water, and fresh water is on Earth. *(Use after Lesson 3.)*

22 Science Center Card
McGraw-Hill Science
Unit D: Caring for Earth

Make a Pinwheel

What to do

1. Bring the 4 ends of the pinwheel to the center dot.

2. Push the pin through the center of the pinwheel. **BE CAREFUL!** Push the pin into the pencil eraser. Hold the pin by the top only.

3. Make the pinwheel move. What did you do to move the pinwheel?

What you need

pin

pinwheel pattern

pencil with eraser

Make a Pinwheel
Children follow directions to make a pinwheel. *(Use after Lesson 4.)*

23 Science Center Card
McGraw-Hill Science
Unit D: Caring for Earth

Thanks for Everything!

What to do

1. Put sand in the can. Put the branch in the sand.

2. Use tape or string to hang things made from trees on the branch.

3. Which things on the tree can you eat? Which things do you use every day?

4. Why is it important for people to take care of trees?

What you need

tree branch

can

sand

things from trees

string

tape

Thanks for Everything!
Children attach items to a tree branch to show which things come from trees. *(Use after Lesson 5.)*

24 Science Center Card
McGraw-Hill Science
Unit D: Caring for Earth

Make a Graph

When you make a graph, information is easy to read.

What to do

1. How many things can be recycled? How many can not? Sort the things.

2. Look closely at the things we recycle. Sort them into smaller groups.

3. Show the information in a graph.

4. Which group has the most items? Which group has the least?

What you need

12 things

crayons

Make a Graph
Children make a graph to show which items can be recycled and which cannot. *(Use after Lesson 7.)*

Materials

Consumable materials (based on six groups)

Materials	Quantity	Kit Quantity	Lessons
Balloon, 9"	1	35	4
Can, coffee	1		Science Center Card 23
Crayons			Science Center Card 21, 24
Cups, plastic, 300 mL	4	50	Science Center Card 19, 20
Index cards		100	Science Center Card 23
Jelly, petroleum		4 oz	6
Newspaper			7
Notes, self-stick			5
Paint			7
Pencil, w/eraser	1		Science Center Card 22
Plant, branch, large tree	1		Science Center Card 23
Plates, paper	3	100	2
Sand, fine		2.5 kg	3, Science Center Card 23
Seeds, Oriental Mung Bean	2	60 g	Science Center Card 19
Soil, clay		5 kg	2, Science Center Card 19, 20
Soil, loam		2.5 kg	2
Soil, potting		16 lbs	Science Center Card 19, 20
Soil, sandy		2.5 kg	2
Sticks, craft		50	Science Center Card 23
Straws, plastic, wrapped	1	100	4
String		200 ft	Science Center Card 23
Tape			4, Science Center Card 23

Materials	Quantity	Kit Quantity	Lessons
"old, clean things" yogurt container (8 ounce plastic), milk container, paper towel and toilet paper tubes, shoebox, empty egg carton, plastic water bottle, coffee can			7
"12 objects – can and cannot be recycled"			Science Center Card 24

Non-consumable materials (based on six groups)

Materials	Quantity	Kit Quantity	Lessons
Brush, paint	1	6	7
Cup, plastic measuring, 500 ml	2	6	3, Science Center Card 20
Hand lens	3	6	1, 2, 6
Pan, aluminum foil, 13" x 10" x 2"	1	6	3
Pin, straight	1	150	Science Center Card 22
Rock, basalt specimen pack		1	1
Rock, limestone specimen pack		1	1
Rock, obsidian specimen pack		1	1
Rock, sandstone specimen pack		1	1
Rock, schist specimen pack		1	1
Ruler	1		Science Center Card 19

Caring for Earth

LOOK!

People planted these trees. Why do people plant trees? What can people get from them?

D1

Resources

- Reading in Science Resources, Unit Vocabulary, pp. 229–231
- School to Home Activities, pp. 23-27
- Cross Curricular Projects, pp. 21-27

LOOK!

People might plant trees to replace trees that were cut down. We get oxygen, wood, and food from trees.

Assessment Strand

McGraw-Hill Science provides a variety of strategies for assessing students' learning and progress, including ongoing assessment, informal assessment, formal assessment, and performance assessment.

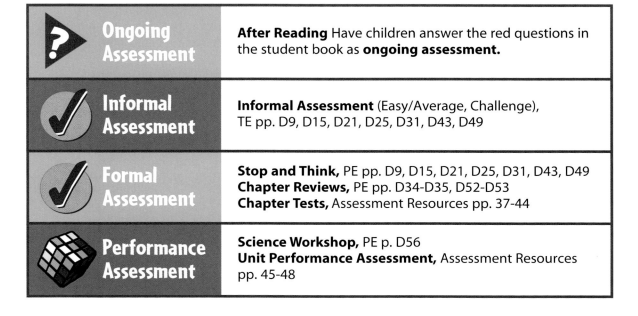

?	**Ongoing Assessment**	**After Reading** Have children answer the red questions in the student book as **ongoing assessment.**
✓	**Informal Assessment**	**Informal Assessment** (Easy/Average, Challenge), TE pp. D9, D15, D21, D25, D31, D43, D49
✓	**Formal Assessment**	**Stop and Think,** PE pp. D9, D15, D21, D25, D31, D43, D49 **Chapter Reviews,** PE pp. D34-D35, D52-D53 **Chapter Tests,** Assessment Resources pp. 37-44
▦	**Performance Assessment**	**Science Workshop,** PE p. D56 **Unit Performance Assessment,** Assessment Resources pp. 45-48

Lesson Planner

Lesson	Objectives	Vocabulary	Pacing	Resources and Technology
LESSON 1 **Rocks and Minerals** pp. D4-D9	■ Explore ways to classify rocks. ■ Define a natural resource. ■ Identify ways that people use rocks and minerals.	**rocks** **minerals** **natural resource**	3 days	■ Activity Resources, pp. 87-89 ■ Reading in Science Resources, pp. 179-184 ■ School to Home Activities, p. 24 ■ Vocabulary Cards ■ Reading Aid Transparency D1 ■ **Explore Activity Video** ■ **Science Experiences Video**
LESSON 2 **Soil** pp. D10-D15	■ Explore and compare different soils. ■ Identify the components of soil and understand that soils are different. ■ Recognize the importance of soil as a natural resource.	**soil**	3 days	■ Activity Resources, pp. 90-92, 108-109 ■ Reading in Science, pp. 185-190 ■ School to Home Activities, p. 25 ■ Vocabulary Cards ■ Science Center Cards 19, 20 ■ Reading Aid Transparency D2 ■ Visual Aid Transparency 20 ■ **Explore Activity Video**
LESSON 3 **Water** pp. D16-D21	■ Explore and communicate how rain water travels. ■ Identify places where water is found on Earth. ■ Recognize the importance of water as a natural resource.		3 days	■ Activity Resources, pp. 93-95, 110-111 ■ Reading in Science, pp. 191-196 ■ Science Center Card 21 ■ Reading Aid Transparency D3 ■ Visual Aid Transparency 21 ■ **Explore Activity Video** ■ **Science Experiences Video**
LESSON 4 **Air** pp. D22-D25	■ Explore through inferring that air can move things. ■ Recognize the importance of air as a natural resource.	**oxygen**	2 days	■ Activity Resources, pp. 96-98, 112 ■ Reading in Science Resources, pp. 197-202 ■ Vocabulary Cards ■ Science Center Card 22 ■ Reading Aid Transparency D4 ■ Visual Aid Transparency 22 ■ **Explore Activity Video**
LESSON 5 **Plants and Animals Are Resources** pp. D26-D31	■ Explore and classify things we use that come from plants and animals. ■ Name ways plants and animals are important natural resources.		3 days	■ Activity Resources, pp. 99-101, 113 ■ Reading in Science Resources, pp. 203-208 ■ School to Home Activities, p. 26 ■ Science Center Card 23 ■ Reading Aid Transparency D5 ■ Visual Aid Transparency 23 ■ **Explore Activity Video**

Activity Planner

Activity	Process Skills	Materials	Plan Ahead
1 Explore Activity **How can you classify rocks?** p. D5	classify	assorted rocks such as black obsidian, brown sandstone, black basalt, brown mica, schist, and brown limestone; hand lens	
2 Explore Activity **How do some soils compare?** p. D11	compare	three plates of different soil samples, hand lens, newspaper, water soap, paper towels	Make sure you have water, soap, and paper towels available for hand washing. Cover work areas with newspaper for easy clean up.
3 Explore Activity **What happens to rain?** p. D17	communicate	sand, water in a plastic container, deep tray, newspaper, paper towels for hand clean up	Cover work areas with newspaper for easy clean up. For each team, put several cups of moist sand in a large, deep pan. Each team also needs approximately one pint of water.
4 Explore Activity **What can make the balloon move?** p. D23	infer	one balloon, one straw per child, tape	Balloons pose a choking hazard. Do not allow children to inflate their own balloons, but do so yourself in advance. A balloon pump can save both time and effort.
5 Explore Activity **What comes from plants and animals?** p. D27	classify	sticky notes	Use a paper cutter to cut large sticky notes into smaller strips or use the small sticky notes.

Reading in Science Resources

McGraw-Hill Science ***Reading in Science*** provides the following **Blackline Master** worksheets for this chapter.

Chapter Graphic Organizer

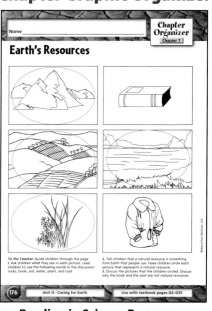

Reading in Science Resources,
p. 176

Chapter Reading Skill

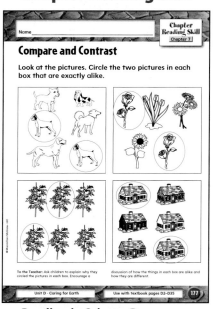

Reading in Science Resources,
pp. 177-178

Chapter Vocabulary

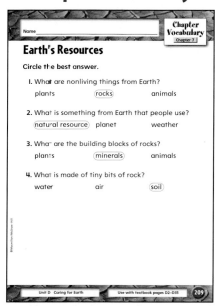

Reading in Science Resources,
pp. 209-210

McGraw-Hill Science ***Reading in Science*** provides the following **Blackline Master** worksheets for every lesson in this chapter.

Lesson Outline

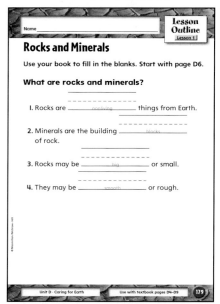

Reading in Science Resources, pp. 179-180, 185-186, 191-192, 197-198, 203-204

Interpret Illustrations

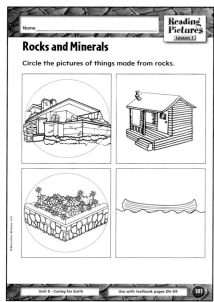

Reading in Science Resources, pp. 181-182, 187-188, 193-194, 199-200, 205-206

Lesson Vocabulary and Cloze Test

Reading in Science Resources, pp. 183-184, 189-190, 195-196, 201-202, 207-208

Activities and Assessment

McGraw-Hill Science **Activity Resources** provides the following **Blackline Master** worksheets for every lesson in this chapter.

Explore Activity and Alternative Explore Activity

Activity Resources, pp. 87-89, 90-92, 93-95, 96-98, 99-101

Science Center Card

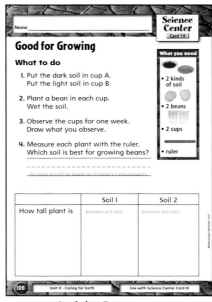

Activity Resources, pp. 108-113

Science Skill Builder

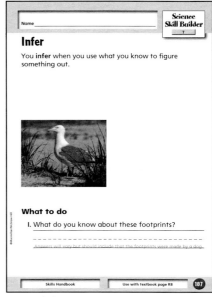

Activity Resources, pp. 187-188

All Science Skill Builders are found at the back of the Student Book.

McGraw-Hill Science **Assessment Book** provides the following **Blackline Master** worksheets for this chapter.

Chapter Test

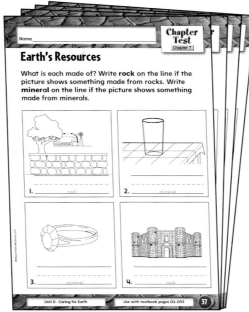

Assessment Resources, pp. 37-40

CHAPTER 7
Earth's Resources

Resources

- Big Book, pp. D2–D3
- Reading in Science Resources, pp. 176–210

Did You Ever Wonder?

Have children look at the photograph on pages D2–D3 and describe what they see. (This picture from Glacier National Park on Montana's border with Canada shows rocks, soil, snow, water, and other features of Earth.)

Ask children where water comes from. (They may say clouds in the form of rain; streams; melting snow.) If children say water comes from taps, spigots, or hoses, ask them to try to identify where it was before that (for example, lake, river, stream, reservoir).

Have children brainstorm a list of reasons we need water and write them on the board. (Examples include washing, cooking, drinking, watering gardens, growing food.)

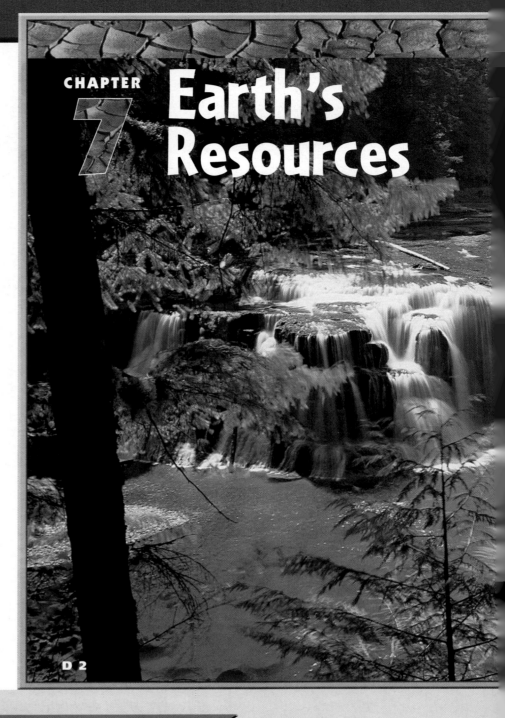

CHAPTER
7 Earth's
Resources

D 2

Reading Skills

This chapter provides MiniLessons and other strategies for developing, practicing, and applying the following reading skills.

- ○ Cause and effect
- ◉ Compare and Contrast: pp. D7, D28
- ◉ Find the Main Idea: pp. D13, D30
- ○ Order of Events (act out or retell)
- ◉ Summarize: pp. D9, D15, D21, D25, D31

- ◉ Read pictures: pp. D7, D12, D18, D24, D29
- ◉ Draw visual images based on text: pp. D21
- ◉ Ask questions: pp. D4, D10, D16, D22, D26
- ◉ Follow directions: pp. D5, D11, D17, D23, D27
- ◉ Build on prior knowledge: pp. D4, D10, D16, D22, D26

Vocabulary

rocks

minerals

natural resource

soil

oxygen

Did You Ever Wonder?

Where does water come from? Water falls to Earth as snow or rain. It flows into streams and rivers. Then it collects in ponds, lakes, and oceans. Why is water important?

D 3

Vocabulary Preview

Preview vocabulary by having children pronounce and spell each word. Encourage children to look up these words and their definitions in their Glossary beginning on page R35.

rocks nonliving things from Earth, D6

minerals the building blocks of rocks, D6

natural resource something from Earth that people use, D8

soil tiny bits of rock with dead plants and animals in it, D12

oxygen the part of air that people need to live, D25

Technology

Visit **www.mhscience02.com** for an online glossary.

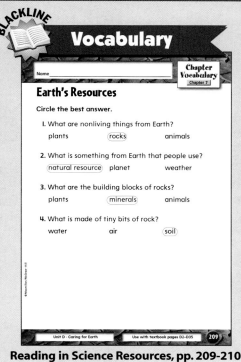

Reading in Science Resources, pp. 209-210

Reading in Science Resources, p. 176

Rocks and Minerals

Objectives

- Explore ways to classify rocks.
- Define a *natural resource*.
- Identify ways that people use rocks and minerals.

Resources

- Big Book, pp. D4–D9
- Activity Resources, pp. 87–89
- Reading in Science Resources, pp. 179–184
- Vocabulary Cards
- Reading Aid Transparency D1
- School to Home Activities, p. 24

Build on Prior Knowledge
Ask:

- **Are all rocks you have seen or touched alike?** (no) **How are they different?** (They are different shapes, sizes, colors, and textures.)

1 Get Ready

Using the Illustrations
Ask:

- **Have you ever collected rocks? Where did you find them?** (Possible answers: schoolyard, road, gravel pit, garden, on the sidewalk, at the beach, and so on)

- **How can you put rocks into groups?** (Rocks can be grouped by size, color, smoothness or texture, and shape.)

See Science Skill Builder **Classify**, p. R5.

Get Ready

Did you ever collect rocks? How can the rocks be put into groups?

Science Skill

You **classify** when you group things by how they are alike.

D 4

 Cross Curricular Books

Additional Outside Reading

The Land

written by Wendy Pearl
illustrated by Alexandra Wallner

To order, see page D1·b.

Science Background

Classifying Rocks
Geologists classify rocks as sedimentary (layers deposited by water or wind), igneous (formed from cooled molten material), or metamorphic (changed from either sedimentary or igneous by heat or pressure). Shale, sandstone, and limestone are sedimentary rocks. Igneous rocks include obsidian, basalt, granite, and pumice. Slate, schist, marble, and gneiss are metamorphic rocks.

Explore Activity

How can you classify rocks?

What you need

rocks

hand lens

paper

1. Look at each rock with the hand lens. Feel each rock.

2. Draw two sorting rings. **Classify** the rocks. Label the groups you make.

3. How did you classify the rocks?

D 5

Explore Activity

How can you classify rocks?

Science Process Skills classify

Resources Activity Resources, pp. 87–88

Pacing 15–20 minutes

Grouping pairs

What to do

Read and discuss the activity with the class before they begin.

1. Show children how to use a hand lens to see greater detail in the rocks. Ask children to handle the rocks carefully and to observe them with and without the hand lens. Have pairs discuss their observations. (Descriptions will include color words as well as *rough, smooth, gritty, hard*, and other texture words.)

2. Encourage children to discuss the properties of the rocks they can use to sort them. If necessary, help children to label their sorting rings.

3. Ask each pair to explain how they classified their rocks. (The rocks may be classified by color, size, shape, and texture.)

Going Further

Draw two overlapping circles side by side on the chalkboard. Label one circle *rough rocks*. Label the other circle *black rocks*. Label the overlapping area *black, rough rocks*. Ask children to show which rocks they would place in each area.

Technology

- When time is short, preview the activity with the **Explore Activity Video.**

Alternative Explore Activity

Materials mixture of three types of uncooked pastas and rices.

Classify Ask children to observe the mixture and discuss different ways the pastas and rices can be classified. Then have children use the sorting rings to show the different ways the parts of the mixture can be classified, such as by color, size, shape, or other properties.

Name _____

Alternative Explore
Lesson 1

Classify

In this activity, you will classify different types of food.

What you need
- mixture of three types of pastas and rices

What to do

1. Your teacher will show you a mixture of three types of pastas and rices.

2. Draw your own sorting rings. Inside each ring, write a different way that the pastas and rices can be classified.

_____
_____
Possible answers: They roll; different shapes; different colors.

3. Name other foods that can be classified each of these ways.

_____
Possible answers: Color: fruit; size: nuts; shape: beans.

Unit D · Caring for Earth   Use with TE textbook page D5   89

Activity Resources, p. 89

2 Read to Learn

What are rocks and minerals?

Before Reading
Have children try to answer the red question at the top of the page.

Using the Illustrations
Ask:

- **Where are the rocks in this picture?** (They are everywhere. The land is made of rock.)

- **Are the rocks here all the same?** (No, they are different colors, shapes, and textures.)

Developing Vocabulary

rocks, minerals Give children several colors of plastic interlocking or snap-together blocks. Tell children that the blocks represent minerals, the building blocks of rocks. Have children snap together blocks to form "rocks" of all one mineral (all the same color blocks) or several different minerals (different color blocks).

Introduce the Vocabulary Cards for the terms *rocks* and *minerals*. Place them on the word wall.

Read to Learn

What are rocks and minerals?

Rocks are nonliving things from Earth. The land we live on is mostly rock.

Minerals are the building blocks of rock. They give rocks their color. Some rocks are made of many minerals. Other rocks are made of only one mineral.

mineral

D 6

English Language Learners

Language Rock
Pair children learning English with native English speakers. Have partners work together to list as many different words as they can to describe rocks, such as *hard, shiny, rough, smooth, black*, and so on. Then ask partners to share their lists as you record the words on the chalkboard. **Spatial; Linguistic**

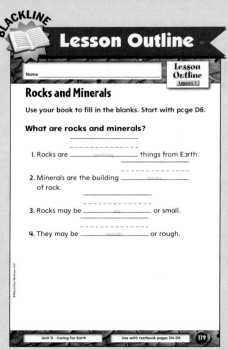

BLACKLINE
Lesson Outline

Reading in Science Resources, p. 179

.ocks may be big or small. They
nay be smooth or rough. They
nay be different colors, too.

▶ **Tell how these rocks are
alike and different.**
Children should discuss observed
similarities and differences in color,
size, shape, or texture.

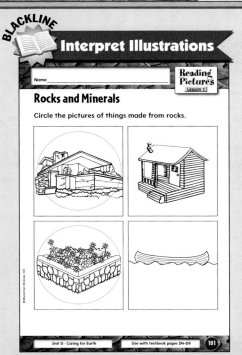

D 7

■ **How can you describe the rocks on page D7?**
(Children use their own words to tell about the
shape, color, size, and texture of the rocks.)

Developing the Main Idea
Ask:

■ **How do you know rocks are nonliving things?**
(They do not grow, use energy, move, or have
young.)

Discuss the fact that some rocks, like limestone, are
made up of mostly one mineral (calcite). Others, like
granite, are made up of many different minerals
(quartz, feldspar, and mica). There are more than
3,000 different minerals. The type of minerals found in
rocks is what gives them their shape, color, hardness,
and texture.

Thinking Further: *Inferring*

■ **Do you think these rocks all formed in the
same way? Why?** (They look so different, so
they probably did not form the same way.)

▶**After Reading**
Ask the red question in the student book as
ongoing assessment.

BLACKLINE
Interpret Illustrations

Reading Pictures
Lesson 1

Rocks and Minerals

Circle the pictures of things made from rocks.

Unit D · Caring for Earth | Use with textbook pages D4–D9 | **181**

Reading in Science Resources, pp. 181-182

SCIENCE
Reading | **MiniLesson**

Compare and Contrast

Develop Remind children that
comparing and contrasting
involves telling how things are
alike and different. When
comparing and contrasting
things, you need to carefully
observe characteristics, or
properties, such as size, shape,
color, and texture.

Activity Have children look at
the rocks pictured in the lesson.
Help children to make a list on
the board of words and phrases
that describe the different
properties of the rocks. Ask:
**Which rocks are similar?
How? Which rocks are
different? How? Spatial;
Linguistic**

Why are rocks and minerals important?

Before Reading
Have children try to answer the red question at the top of the page.

Using the Illustrations
Ask:

- **How are rocks and minerals being used here?**
  (to build things, to build on, and to make glass, jewelry, and metals)

Exploring the Main Idea
Explain that a natural resource is anything that occurs in nature that people use in some way. Some natural resources include trees, wind, plants, animals, soil, water, rocks, minerals, oil, coal, and natural gas. Have children draw pictures or cut photographs from old magazines of examples of natural resources. Display these on one side of a bulletin board. Label this side of the bulletin board *Natural Resources*.

Developing Vocabulary

natural resource Have children draw pictures or clip pictures from magazines that show ways we use natural resources. Add them to the other side of the bulletin board display. Label it *Things Made from Natural Resources.*

Introduce the Vocabulary Card for the word *natural resource*. Place it on the word wall.

Why are rocks and minerals important?

A rock is a natural resource. So is a mineral. So is land. A **natural resource** is something from Earth that people use.

D 8

Reading Strategy

Summarize (Retell)
Developing Reading Skills
Have children look at the pictures and reread the text on pages D8–D9. Ask:

- **Can you tell in your own words why rocks and minerals are important?**
Record children's statements on the board. Help children to compare the statements with the information in their books to be sure the statements are accurate.

Math   MiniLesson

Measurement and Volume

Develop Measurement involves quantifying the properties of objects, processes, and events. One property of objects is that they take up space. This property is called volume.

Activity Use rocks to introduce the concept of volume. Partially fill a plastic container with water. Mark the water level with a piece of tape or self-stick note. Let children gently drop rocks into the water. Ask: **What happens to the water level?** (It rises.) Explain that the rocks take up space and push the water out of the way.

We use rocks to build things.
We use minerals to make glass, jewelry, and metals.

How are rocks and minerals used here?

...are used to build homes; minerals are used to make metals, glass, and jewelry.

Stop and Think

1. What is a natural resource?
2. How do people use rocks and minerals?

HOME ACTIVITY Which rocks and minerals do you use at home?

D 9

✔ **Informal Assessment**

Easy/Average Ask children to tell what a natural resource is and to give some examples. **Linguistic**

Challenge Have children tell what a natural resource is, give some examples, and describe how the natural resource is used. **Linguistic**

Thinking Further: *Classifying*

■ **How are the things shown on page D9 alike?**
(They are all made from natural resources—things that come from the Earth.)

Mention that glass is made from sand (a mineral), the metal ring is made from gold (a mineral), and the metal slide is made from iron ore (a mineral).

▶**After Reading**
Ask the red question in the student book as **ongoing assessment.**

3 | Lesson Review

Answers to Stop and Think

1. A natural resource is something from Earth that people use. (p. D8)

2. People make buildings from rocks and minerals. They also make glass, jewelry, and metal from minerals. (pp. D8–D9)

Retelling

Write the following scaffolding for summarizing the lesson on the chalkboard. Have children retell the lesson by filling in the blanks.

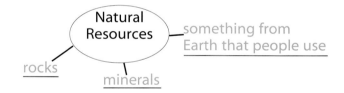

Natural Resources — something from Earth that people use

rocks

minerals

Technology

■ **Science Experiences Videotapes**
Volcanoes: Churning and Burning (Package 5)

LESSON 2 Soil

LESSON 2 Soil

Get Ready

The machine digs into the ground. It pulls up soil. Does all this soil look the same?

Science Skill

You **compare**, when you learn how things are alike and different.

D 10

Objectives

- Explore and compare different soils.
- Identify the components of soil and understand that soils are different.
- Recognize the importance of soil as a natural resource.

Resources

- Big Book, pp. D10–D15
- Activity Resources, pp. 90–92, 108-109
- Reading in Science Resources, pp. 185–190
- Vocabulary Card
- Reading Aid Transparency D2
- Visual Aid Transparency 20
- Science Center Cards 19, 20
- School to Home Activities, p. 25

Build on Prior Knowledge
Ask:

- **Have you ever planted seeds? What did you put the seeds in?** (dirt, soil)
- **What did you notice about the soil you planted in?** (Children may describe the color or texture of garden soil or potting soil.)

1 Get Ready

Using the Illustrations
Ask:

- **What does the machine dig up?** (dirt, soil)
- **What observations can you make about soil?** (Not all soil is the same.)

See Science Skill Builder **Compare,** p. R3.

 Science Background

Soils
Although the layers in a soil profile may look different, they are the same soil type. What makes the layers look different is the amount of organic matter (decayed plants and animals) in each layer and the size and number of rocks. Potting soil is made up of sand, vermiculite, perlite, pumice, peat, sphagnum moss, and manure. Minerals needed for plant growth are also added.

Explore Activity

How do some soils compare?

What you need

3 plates of different soils

hand lens

1 Use a hand lens. **Compare** each soil. How does each soil look and smell?

2 Squeeze each soil with your hand. What happens to each soil? Wash your hands.

3 What is different about each soil?

topsoil

sandy soil

clay soil

D 11

Alternative Explore Activity

Materials 3 clear plastic jars nearly full of water with lids, 3 different soil samples

Soil Shaker Place each soil sample into each of the jars. Shake them. Ask: **What does the water in each jar look like?** (Colors and cloudiness vary with soil type.) Let the jars sit for a while. Ask: **How does the water compare now?** (Sandy soil settles out more than clay or topsoil. The water looks clearer.)

Alternative Explore Lesson 2

Soil Shaker

In this activity, you will see what happens when soil is shaken.

What to do

1. Shake soil samples into the jar.

2. Describe what happens to the water.

_____ The water becomes cloudy and turns color._____

3. Look at the jars after they have sat overnight. Describe how the soil samples compare.

_____ Possible answers: The sandy soil settled best._____

_____ The water looks clear. The clay sample is still cloudy._____

What you need
• three clear plastic jars, nearly full with water, with lids
• three different soil samples

92 | Unit D · Caring for Earth | Use with TE textbook page D11

Activity Resources, p. 92

Explore Activity

How do some soils compare?

Science Process Skills *compare*

Resources Activity Resources pp. 90–91

Pacing 15–20 minutes

Grouping small groups

Plan Ahead Make sure you have water, soap, and paper towels available for washing hands. Cover work areas with newspaper for easy cleanup.

What to do

Read and discuss the activity with the class before they begin.

1 Let children explore the samples freely, but *no tasting!* Circulate among the teams and encourage children to verbalize their observations. List descriptive words and phrases on the board. (Children should observe that each soil smells and looks different.)

2 Encourage each child to squeeze the different soils. (Children should observe that when squeezed, the topsoil and clay soil stick together, but the sandy soil does not.) Have children wash and dry their hands.

3 Children should observe that each soil has a different color, and smells and feels different.

Going Further

Ask children to bring in a sample of soil from their garden, lawn, or a houseplant. Compare the color, texture, and "squeezability" of children's samples with the soil types used in this activity.

For additional activities, see Science Center Cards 19 and 20, p. D56•a and p. D56•b.

Technology

■ When time is short, preview the activity with the **Explore Activity Video**.

2 Read to Learn

What is soil?

Before Reading
Have children try to answer the red question at the top of the page. Label a column on the board *I Think Soil Is Made Of…*. Record children's responses.

Using the Illustrations
Ask:

- **What do you see in this soil?** Record children's observations in a second column on the board. Label the column *I Observe that Soil Is Made Of…*. Compare children's observations with their initial thoughts.

Thinking Further: *Inferring*

- **How do you think rocks become part of soil?** (They get broken and crushed into little pieces.)

- **What do you think happens to animals and plants that die in soil?** (They rot and become part of it.)

- **Can you see the air and water in soil? How do you know they are there?** (Water seeps into soil when it rains or when snow melts. Air fills up the spaces between the tiny bits of soil.)

Developing Vocabulary

soil Write *soil* on an index card and tack it to a bulletin board. Ask children to work with a partner to state a question that can be answered by the word *soil*. Write children's questions on strips of paper and tack them around the term *soil* in the shape of spokes of a wheel.
Introduce the Vocabulary Card for the word *soil*. Place it on the word wall.

Read to Learn

What is soil?

Soil is made of tiny bits of rock. It may also have bits of dead animals and plants in it. There is also air and water in soil.

In most places, soil covers the land. Soils can be very different.

D 12

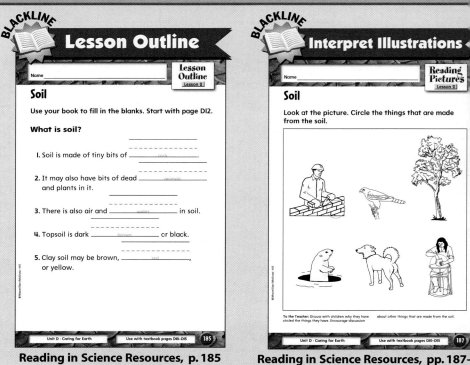

Reading in Science Resources, p. 185

Reading in Science Resources, pp. 187-

Topsoil is dark brown or black. It sticks together when you squeeze it. It holds some water. Plants grow best in topsoil.

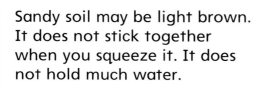

Clay soil may be brown, red, or yellow. It sticks together when you squeeze it. It holds a lot of water.

Topsoil is dark and rough–looking; clay soil is reddish, moist, and clumpy; sandy soil is light colored, dry, and rough.

Sandy soil may be light brown. It does not stick together when you squeeze it. It does not hold much water.

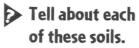

▶ **Tell about each of these soils.**
See above.

D 13

Developing the Main Idea
Ask:

- **What is topsoil (humus) like?** (dark brown or black, sticks together when you squeeze it, holds some water)
- **What is clay soil like?** (brown, red, yellow or gray in color, sticks together when you squeeze it, holds water)
- **What is sandy soil like?** (light-colored, dry, rough, doesn't hold much water)

Point out to children that each kind of soil has a different amount of decayed plants and animals (organic matter) in it, as well as a different amount of clay and sand. These things determine how a soil feels and how much water it will hold. Topsoil (humus) has the most amount of decayed plants and animals in it. This means that topsoil is rich in minerals and other things plants need to grow. Sandy soil has the least amount of decayed plants and animals in it. Not as many plants can grow in sandy soil.

Thinking Further: *Inferring*

Ask:

- **Why do you think plants grow best in top-soil?** (It holds some water but not too much. It has a lot of dead plants and animals in it.)

▶ **After Reading**
Ask the red question in the student book as **ongoing assessment.**

Technology
- Visual Aid Transparency 20: *What Is Soil?*

Reading Strategy

Find the Main Idea

Developing Reading Skills
Have children reread pages D12 and D13. Ask them to identify the topic (soil). Then ask:

- **What is the main idea on page D12?** (what soil is made of)

- **What is the main idea on page D13?** (Soils can be different.)

Why is soil important?

Before Reading
Have children try to answer the red question at the top of the page.

Developing the Main Idea
As children read this page, ask them to recall what a natural resource is. (something from the Earth that people use)

Using the Illustrations
Ask:

- **What things are pictured here?** (clay pottery, bricks, a plowed field, an animal in soil)
- **What are bricks and clay pots made from?** (clay soil)
- **Is soil a natural resource?** (Yes.) **Why?** (It comes from the Earth and is used by people.)

Why is soil important?
Soil is a natural resource. People use it to make things like bricks and clay pots.

D 14

 Cultural Perspective

Bricks Around the World
Brickmaking predates 4000 B.C. when the first true arch of sun-baked brick was erected in Mesopotamia. Descendants of the ancient Egyptians called mud brickmaking *tobe*. The Arabs gave the word to the Spanish who brought it to the New World as *adobe*. The Great Wall of China is made of both burned and sun-dried bricks. Children may enjoy learning how these techniques differ.

 Advanced Learners

Plants in Soil
Plant dried beans in cups filled with different kinds of soil. Water well and place in a sunny spot. Have children watch how they grow, comparing and discussing color, height, and size and number of leaves. Ask children to share ideas about why the beans grow differently in the different soils.
Logical; Social

People grow plants in soil. People and animals eat these plants. Soil is also the home for many animals.

▷ How is soil used here?

Soil is used to make clay pots, to make bricks, and to grow plants in. Some animals live in soil.

Stop and Think

1. What is soil made of?
2. Why is soil important?

Visit **www.mhscience02.com** to learn more about soil.

D 15

✓ Informal Assessment

Easy/Average Ask children to tell what soil is and to tell some reasons why it is important. **Linguistic**

Challenge Give children a soil sample inside a brown paper bag. Tell them to feel and smell the sample, but not to look inside the bag. **Can you tell whether the soil is topsoil, clay, or sandy soil? How?** Once children have identified their samples, ask them to tell why they identified the soil sample as they did. **Kinesthetic; Linguistic**

Thinking Further: *Compare and Contrast*

Ask:

■ **Can you think of ways that soil is important to animals?** (Worms, ants, termites, moles, rabbits, mice, and many other animals live in soil. Many animals eat the plants that grow in soil.)

▶ **After Reading**
Ask the red question in the student book as **ongoing assessment.**

3 | Lesson Review

Answers to Stop and Think

1. Soil is made of tiny bits of rock, dead plants and animals, air, and water. (p. D12)

2. Soil is important because the plants we and other animals use for food grow in it, and people use it to make things. (pp. D14—D15)

Retelling
Write the following scaffolding for summarizing the lesson on the chalkboard. Have children retell the lesson by filling in the blanks.

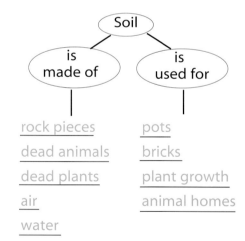

```
                    Soil
              /             \
          is                  is
        made of            used for
           |                   |
      rock pieces           pots
      dead animals          bricks
      dead plants           plant growth
      air                   animal homes
      water
```

LESSON 3 Water

Objectives

- Explore and communicate how rain water travels.
- Identify places where water is found on Earth.
- Recognize the importance of water as a natural resource.

Resources

- Big Book, pp. D16–D21
- Activity Resources, pp. 93–95, 110-111
- Reading in Science Resources, pp. 191–196
- Reading Aid Transparency D3
- Visual Aid Transparency 21
- Science Center Card 21

Build on Prior Knowledge

Sing "The Itsy, Bitsy Spider" together and teach children the hand motions that accompany it. Talk about rain—where children think it comes from, where it goes, and how it affects living things.

1 Get Ready

Using the Illustrations
Ask:

- **What does rain do when it falls on a mountain?**
  (Some soaks into the soil. Some runs down the mountain and gathers in streams that run into rivers and lakes.)

See Science Skill Builder **Communicate,** p. R6.

LESSON 3 Water

Get Ready

It rains in the mountains. The water forms a stream. Where does it go?

Science Skill

You **communicate** when you talk, write, or draw.

D 16

 ## Science Background

The Water Cycle
The total amount of water on Earth never changes. Water recycles itself, continually being purified and reused through the processes of evaporation, condensation, and precipitation. Along with air, water is the most fundamental of the life-sustaining natural resources.

Explore Activity

What happens to rain?

1 Use the sand to make a mountain.

2 Pour water on the model mountain. Pour it at the top of the mountain. Wash your hands.

3 What happens to the water? **Communicate your ideas.**

What you need

sand

water

deep tray

D 17

Alternative Explore Activity

Material pan, sand, water, bowl, cheesecloth, rubber band

Groundwater Cover a bowl with cheesecloth and secure it with a rubber band. Form a sand "mountain" over the bowl. Pour water slowly onto the sand. Look in the bowl. Ask: **How did water get here?** (It soaked through the sand.) Water that soaks through the ground and collects is called groundwater.

Activity Resources, p. 95

Explore Activity

What happens to rain?

Science Process Skills *communicate*

Resources Activity Resources, pp. 93–94

Pacing 15–20 minutes

Grouping small groups

Plan Ahead Cover work areas with newspaper for easy cleanup. For each group, put several cups of moist sand into a large, deep tray or pan.

What to do

Read and discuss the activity with the class before they begin.

1 Help groups mold the sand into a packed mound to form their "mountain."

2 Tell children to pour the water directly onto the top of the "mountain" from a height of about three inches (eight centimeters). Instruct children not to trickle the water but to pour it slowly and steadily without moving the cup around.

3 Have children discuss their observations. (Children should observe that the water runs down the sides of the mountain in little streams and forms puddles at the bottom.)

Going Further

Repeat the experiment, this time pouring from a watering can with a sprinkler attachment. Ask children to tell how the results differ. (The sprinkler spreads the water out, so less runs down in streams.)

For an additional activity, see Science Center Card 21, p. D56·c.

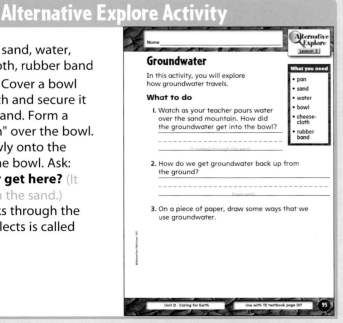

Technology

■ When time is short, preview the activity with the **Explore Activity Video.**

Where is Earth's water?

Before Reading
Have children try to answer the red question at the top of the page.

Developing the Main Idea
Ask:

- **How are rivers and lakes alike?** (They have fresh water in them.) **How are they different from oceans?** (They are much smaller than oceans and are not usually salty.)

- **Where does rain come from?** (clouds)

- **Where does rain fall?** (onto the land where it flows into streams, rivers, and lakes)

- **How do we use fresh water?** (We use it to drink, cook, and wash.)

Thinking Further: *Compare and Contrast*

Have children recall the Explore Activity. Ask:

- **What happened to the water in the Explore Activity?** (It flowed down the "mountain" and collected in a puddle at the bottom.)

- **What happens to rain water that runs down a mountain?** (It flows down the land and ends up in streams, rivers, and lakes.) Discuss with children that small streams run into rivers and lakes. Rivers eventually run into the ocean.

- **How is the movement of rain water similar to what happened in the Explore Activity?** (Water flows down an incline and collects in some fashion at the bottom.)

Read to Learn

Where is Earth's water found?

Most of Earth has water on it. Rain falls from clouds. It flows from the land into streams, rivers, and lakes. There is fresh water in clouds, streams, rivers, and lakes. Fresh water is the kind of water you drink.

river

D 18

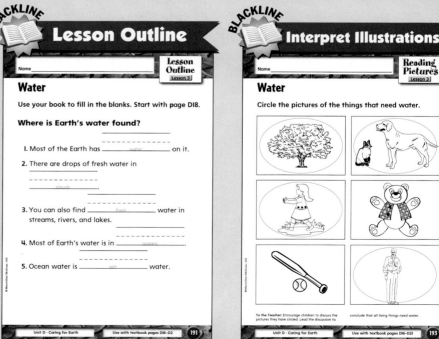

Reading in Science Resources, p. 191

Reading in Science Resources, pp. 193-194

Most of Earth's water is in oceans. Ocean water is salt water. People can not drink salt water. But many plants and animals live in salt water.

Most of Earth is covered with water.

➤ Where is Earth's fresh water found?
clouds, streams, rivers, lakes

lake

ocean

D 19

- **Has anyone ever visited the ocean? What was it like?** (It is big with salt water and has sandy or rocky beaches.)
- **How is ocean water different from fresh water?** (It is salty. People cannot drink it.)

Exploring the Main Idea
Explain to children that water covers about three fourths of Earth's surface. To help children understand this concept, give each a paper plate. Explain that it is a model of Earth. Demonstrate on the board how to draw four quarters. Discuss that if all Earth's water was collected in one place, it would cover three of the four equal parts of the circle, and that land would occupy the fourth part. Have children color three fourths of their plates to help them visualize the concept.

▶**After Reading**
Ask the red question in the student book as **ongoing assessment.**

Technology

- Visual Aid Transparency 21:
  Oceans

- Science Music CDs
  What Shall We Do on a Rainy Day?
  Rain, Rain Go Away

- **Science Experiences Videotapes**
  Researching the Ocean Depths
  (Package 7)

SCIENCE FOR ALL   Advanced Learners

What Will Happen?
Place one carnation or other flower in fresh water and another in salt water. Ask children to predict what will happen. (The flower in salt water will wilt.) After several hours, have children verify their predictions and draw conclusions about plants and salt water. (Most plants cannot live in salt water.) **Logical**

SCIENCE   Reading Strategy

Draw Conclusions
Developing Reading Skills
Make a fresh cut at the ends of two carnation stems. Place one flower in fresh water, the other in saltwater, but don't tell children that there is any difference. Leave the flowers overnight. The next day, ask children to explain what they observe. Some may guess that some difference in the water caused one to droop and shrivel, while the other stayed fresh and healthy.

Why is water important?

Before Reading
Have children try to answer the red question at the top of the page.

Exploring the Main Idea
Have children think about everything they do before going to bed. List their responses on the board. Ask:

■ **How many of these things involve water?**
(bath, brushing teeth, drinking water)

Developing the Main Idea
As children read these pages, ask them to tell ways their families use water every day. Ask:

■ **What would happen if we did not have fresh water?** As you discuss children's answers, guide them toward understanding the important role water plays in our lives.

■ **Can water move things?** (Yes.) **How do you know?** (Water from a garden hose can move leaves on a sidewalk. Ocean waves can bring shells to the shore, and so on.) Explain that moving water from a dam can move turbines to make electricity that we use in our homes.

Why is water important?

Water is a natural resource. All living things need water.

People use water to drink, to cook, and to clean. People travel across water. People use water to have fun, too.

D 20

 Science Background

Hydroelectric Power
The power of moving water can be harnessed to generate electrical power. Moving water, either passing through dams, falling at waterfalls, or the natural tides, can be used to generate electrical power. The moving water turns turbines, which in turn power an electrical generator. Nearly seven percent of the world's power is provided by hydroelectric power.

 Cultural Perspective

Rain Dance
Successful crops depend on rain, and cultures from ancient times through today have invoked the rains in ceremony, ritual, and dance. The Pueblo people of the American Southwest perform a rain dance accompanied by rattle-and-song. The rain dance of the Hopi tribe asks snakes to carry prayers to the Rainmakers.

People use moving water to make power. The power lights and heats their homes.

for brushing teeth; for travel; for fun rides; for making power

▷ **How is water used here?**

Stop and Think

1. Where is most of Earth's water?

2. How do people use water?

HOME ACTIVITY How do you use water to have fun? Make a drawing.

D 21

3 | Lesson Review

Answers to Stop and Think

1. Earth's water is in oceans, rivers, lakes, streams, and clouds. (pp. D18–D19)

2. People use water for drinking, cooking, cleaning, having fun, growing plants, travel, and making power (electricity). (pp. D20–D21)

Retelling
Write the following scaffolding for summarizing the lesson on the chalkboard. Have children retell the lesson by filling in the blanks.

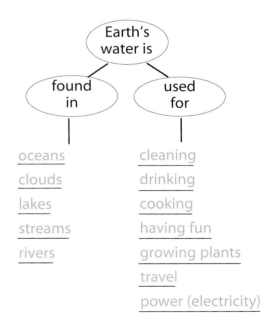

Earth's water is

found in

used for

oceans
clouds
lakes
streams
rivers

cleaning
drinking
cooking
having fun
growing plants
travel
power (electricity)

✓ Informal Assessment

Easy/Average Ask children to draw a picture showing some places where water is found on Earth and some ways in which people use it. **Spatial**

Challenge Create a class collage called "Water Resources." Have children make drawings of every use of water they see or know about. Have children include the obvious, such as dishwashing and making soup, along with the less obvious, such as fish dinners (food caught in a lake or ocean) and breakfast toast (rain makes wheat grow). **Spatial; Social**

LESSON 4 Air

Objectives

- Explore through inferring that air can move things.
- Recognize the importance of air as a natural resource.

Resources

- Big Book, pp. D22–D25
- Activity Resources, pp. 96–98, 112
- Reading in Science Resources, pp. 197–202
- Vocabulary Cards
- Reading Aid Transparency D4
- Visual Aid Transparency 22
- Science Center Card 22

Build on Prior Knowledge
Ask:

- **Can you see air?** (no)
- **How do you know air exists?** (You blow up a party balloon with air. Moving air can move things like leaves and litter. You can feel air on your face.)

1 Get Ready

Using the Illustrations
Ask:

- **What is inside this balloon?** (hot air)
- **How does the hot air balloon move?** (Air pushes it.)

See Science Skill Builder **Infer**, p. R8.

LESSON 4 Air

Get Ready

What makes the balloon move across the sky?

Science Skill
You **infer** when you use what you know to figure something out.

D 22

 Science Background

Air

Air is a mixture of invisible gases—essentially odorless, tasteless, and colorless. We cannot see air, but we can see its effects. It takes up space (fills balloons and lungs), has mass (pushes down on Earth), and has power (the force of moving air or wind).

 English Language Learners

Moving Air

Pair children learning English with native speakers. Have the nonnative speaker act out or mime one thing that air (wind) can move. Have the native speaker help him or her form a descriptive sentence in English and practice saying it.
Intrapersonal; Linguistic

Explore Activity

What can make the balloon move?

What you need

balloon

drinking straw

tape

1 Tape a finish line to the floor.

2 Use the straw. Move the balloon to the finish line. Do not touch the balloon with the straw.

3 **Infer** what makes the balloon move. How could you move it faster with the straw? Try it.

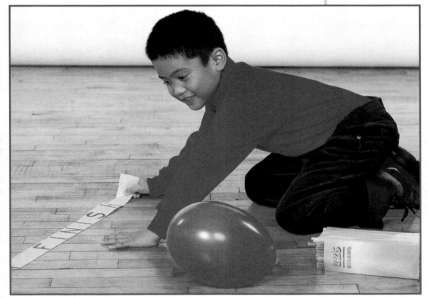

D 23

Alternative Explore Activity

Materials 6" x 6" squares of construction paper, scissors, tape, pencils with erasers, spool or coin, straight pins

Make a Pinwheel Have children follow the directions in the Activity Resources to build their pinwheels. Then children can test different ways to make their pinwheels move.

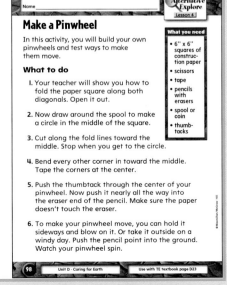

Make a Pinwheel

In this activity, you will build your own pinwheels and test ways to make them move.

What to do

1. Your teacher will show you how to fold the paper square along both diagonals. Open it out.

2. Now draw around the spool to make a circle in the middle of the square.

3. Cut along the fold lines toward the middle. Stop when you get to the circle.

4. Bend every other corner in toward the middle. Tape the corners at the center.

5. Push the thumbtack through the center of your pinwheel. Now push it nearly all the way into the eraser end of the pencil. Make sure the paper doesn't touch the eraser.

6. To make your pinwheel move, you can hold it sideways and blow on it. Or take it outside on a windy day. Push the pencil point into the ground. Watch your pinwheel spin.

Alternative Explore
Lesson 4

What you need
- 6" x 6" squares of construc-tion paper
- scissors
- tape
- pencils with erasers
- spool or coin
- thumb-tacks

98 | Unit D · Caring for Earth | Use with TE textbook page D23

Activity Resources, p. 98

Explore Activity

What can make the balloon move?

Science Process Skills *infer*

Resources Activity Resources, pp. 96–97

Pacing 15–20 minutes

Grouping individual or pairs

Plan Ahead Do not allow children to inflate their own balloons. A balloon pump can save you both time and effort.

What to do

Read and discuss the activity with the class before they begin.

1 If you have enough space to make a long finish line, all teams may share the same one.

2 Caution children not to share straws. Don't make suggestions about blowing through the straw to move the balloon. Let children discover this method for themselves.

3 This is not a race. Sidestep competition and focus instead on the value of this experience for each child. (Children should conclude that moving air makes the balloon move. Blowing harder through the straw will make the balloon move faster.)

Going Further

Challenge children to use only their straws to keep their balloons suspended in the air.

For an additional activity, see Science Center Card 22, p. D56·d.

Technology

- When time is short, preview the activity with the **Explore Activity Video.**

Why is air important?

Before Reading
Have children try to answer the red question at the top of the page.

Using the Illustrations
Ask:

- **How do you know air is being used in each picture if you can't see it?** (You can hear air make sound or see it move things. I know that planes fly through air and that people breathe it.)

- **Why is air a natural resource?** (It is something from Earth that people use.)

Developing the Main Idea
Have children recall the Explore Activity in which they used air to move a balloon. Ask:

- **What happened when you blew harder through the straw?** (The balloon traveled faster.)

Explain that moving air is a powerful force. It powers sail boats and carries hot air balloons across the sky. It turns wind turbines that produce electricity—in much the same way that moving water does. Ask:

- **Is oxygen the same as air?** (No; oxygen is one part of air that people need to live.)

Developing Vocabulary

oxygen Place a small candle inside a glass jar with a tight lid. Light the candle, then seal the jar. Let children watch the candle until the flame is extinguished. Discuss possible reasons why it might have gone out. Explain that candles can't burn and animals can't survive without oxygen. Introduce the Vocabulary Card for the word *oxygen*. Place the card on the word wall.

Read to Learn

Why is air important?

Air is a natural resource. Air fills basketballs. People fly planes in the air. They use air to move sailboats and make music. Moving air can even make power for homes.

D 24

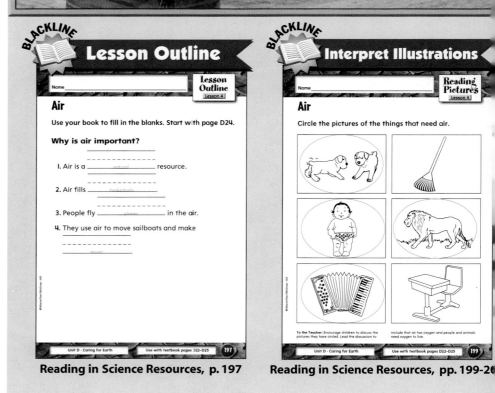

BLACKLINE Lesson Outline

Name_____

Lesson Outline
Lesson 4

Air

Use your book to fill in the blanks. Start with page D24.

Why is air important?
_____

1. Air is a _____ natural _____ resource.

2. Air fills _____ basketballs _____.

3. People fly _____ planes _____ in the air.

4. They use air to move sailboats and make
_____
_____ music _____.

Unit D · Caring for Earth | Use with textbook pages D22–D25 | 197

Reading in Science Resources, p. 197

BLACKLINE Interpret Illustrations

Name_____

Reading Pictures
Lesson 4

Air

Circle the pictures of the things that need air.

To the Teacher: Encourage children to discuss the pictures they have circled. Lead the discussion to | include that air has oxygen and people and animals need oxygen to live.

Unit D · Caring for Earth | Use with textbook pages D22–D25 | 199

Reading in Science Resources, pp. 199–2

People take in air. Air has **oxygen** in it. Oxygen is a part of air that people need to live.

▶ **How is air used here?** to breathe, fill things, fly a plane, make music, sail boats, make power

Stop and Think

1. What are some ways people use air?
2. What is in air that people need?

AT THE COMPUTER — Visit **www.mhscience02.com** to learn more about air.

D 25

Informal Assessment

Easy/Average Play "Sssh!-Air-ades." Ask children to act out, without words, one or two things that air does. **Kinesthetic**

Challenge As a class, invent ways to use moving air to make sound. Build air-powered instruments and form an air band. Ask children to draw pictures to show how their air instruments work. **Kinesthetic**

3 Lesson Review

Answers to Stop and Think

1. People use air to breathe, fill things, make music, sail boats, and make power. (pp. D24–D25)

2. People need the oxygen in air. (p. D25)

Retelling

Write the following scaffolding for summarizing the lesson on the chalkboard. Have children retell the lesson by filling in the blanks.

lets people and animals live

moves boats and balloons

makes music — **Things Air Does** — fills things

supports airplanes   makes power

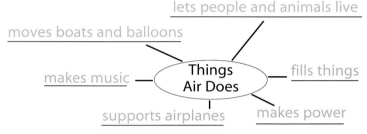

Technology

■ Visual Aid Transparency 22: *How Do Parts Help Things Move?*

LESSON 5

Living Things Are Resources

Objectives

- Explore and classify things we use that come from plants and animals.
- Name ways plants and animals are important natural resources.

Resources

- Big Book, pp. D26–D31
- Activity Resources, pp. 99–101, 113
- Reading in Science Resources, pp. 203–208
- Reading Aid Transparency D5
- Visual Aid Transparency 23
- Science Center Card 23
- School to Home Activities, p. 26

Build on Prior Knowledge

Discuss with children what they ate for breakfast. Make a list on the board. Then ask children if they know what their breakfast foods were made from. As children respond, write plant or animal next to each entry on the list.

1 Get Ready

Using the Illustrations
Ask:

- **What foods do you see here?** (Children should point to and name foods pictured.)

Add any foods not mentioned by children at the beginning of the lesson to the list on the board. As children identify which foods come from plants and animals, add the classifications to the list.

See Science Skill Builder **Classify,** p. R5.

LESSON 5

Living Things Are Resources

Get Ready

Do you eat any of these foods? Which come from plants? Which come from animals?

Science Skill

You **classify** when you group things by where they come from.

D 26

 Cross Curricular Books

Additional Outside Reading

DIG FOR CLAMS

written by Paula Oliver
illustrated by Diane Blasius

To order, see page D1•b.

SCIENCE FOR ALL Inclusion

Plant Collage

Have children collect samples of plant materials that are made into things people use, such as wood and cotton, and cut out pictures of plants that are used in some way as food. Help children make a collage titled *Why Plants Are Important*. As children continue the lesson, have them add to the collage and label each item to explain why it is important.
Spatial; Linguistic

Explore Activity

What comes from plants and animals?

What you need

sticky notes

crayons

1. Write the word *plant* on some sticky notes. Write the word *animal* on other sticky notes.

2. Go around the classroom. **Classify** where some things come from. Put sticky notes on them.

3. Talk about the things you classified.

D 27

Alternative Explore Activity

Materials old magazines, scissors

Food Classification Have children cut out pictures of foods, then sort them into two groups—plant or animal foods. If a food has many ingredients, children should classify it by the major ingredient. For example, crackers belong in the plant group because their major ingredient is flour, which is made from grains. Collect pictures into posters or a class bulletin board.

Name _____

Alternative Explore Lesson 5

Food Classification

In this activity, you will sort pictures of food into two groups.

What you need
• old magazines
• scissors

What to do

1. Find pictures of foods in the magazines. Cut out the pictures. **BE CAREFUL!** Scissors are sharp!

2. Now sort the pictures into two groups: plant foods or animal foods.

3. List all the foods in the chart.

Plant foods	Animal foods
Answers will vary.	Answers will vary.

Unit D · Caring for Earth Use with TE textbook page D27 101

Activity Resources, p. 101

Explore Activity
What comes from plants and animals?

Science Process Skills *classify*

Resources Activity Resources, pp. 99–100

Pacing 15–20 minutes

Grouping small goups

What to do

Read and discuss the activity with the class before they begin.

1. Have group members write the word *plant* on some sticky notes and the word *animal* on others.

2. Ask groups to identify objects around the room and discuss whether they come from plants or animals before applying the sticky notes. Circulate and talk with each group. Ask questions to help children identify the origins of objects that puzzle them.

3. Ask children to explain how they classified. (They may identify cotton or linen clothes, rubber boots, rubber erasers, and wooden objects such as pencils, table, desk, floor, and meterstick as coming from plants. They may classify leather belts, shoes, gloves, woolen clothes, milk, yogurt, and meat products as coming from animals.)

Going Further

Let children put *Don't Know* labels on objects that puzzle them, such as plastics. Explain that plastics (polyester, vinyl, etc.) come from petroleum—the decayed remains of both plants and animals.

For an additional activity, see Science Center Card 23, p. D56•e.

Technology

■ When time is short, preview the activity with the **Explore Activity Video**.

Why are plants important?

Before Reading
Have children try to answer the red question at the top of the page.

Using the Illustrations
Ask:

■ **What things do you see that you can eat?**
(wheat bread, syrup) Discuss with children that wheat is ground into flour, which is used to make bread and cereals. Also mention that people collect the sap from maple trees by tapping a hollow tube (spigot) into the tree. The clear liquid is boiled in sugar houses for many hours until it becomes a thick, brown syrup called maple syrup.

■ **What things here come from plants?**
(Everything pictured comes from plants.)
Besides the things shown here, what other things come from trees? (furniture, building materials for homes)

Read to Learn

Why are plants important?
Plants are a natural resource. People eat plants. They use plants for food. People also use wood from trees to make many things.

wheat bread

wood blocks

D 28

Reading MiniLesson

Compare and Contrast

Develop Remind children that when you compare and contrast, you tell how things are alike and different.

Activity Have children compare and contrast the items on pages D28–D29. Ask:

■ **How are all the items on these pages the same?** (All come from plants.)

■ **How are all the items on these pages different?** (They have different uses. Some are used as food, and some are used to make things that people use). **Logical**

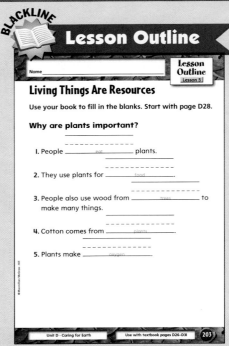

BLACKLINE

Lesson Outline

Name _____

Lesson Outline
Lesson 5

Living Things Are Resources

Use your book to fill in the blanks. Start with page D28.

Why are plants important?

1. People _____ eat _____ plants.

2. They use plants for _____ food _____

3. People also use wood from _____ trees _____ to make many things.

4. Cotton comes from _____ plants _____

5. Plants make _____ oxygen _____

Unit D · Caring for Earth | Use with textbook pages D26–D31 | 203

Reading in Science Resources, p. 203

otton comes from plants. People
se cotton to make many things.

lants make oxygen. People need
xygen to live.

**cotton
towels**

**How are plants
used here?**

to make bread, toys,
cotton towels,
maple syrup

maple syrup

D 29

- **What do both cotton plants and maple trees
  make that you cannot see, but that people
  need to live?** (oxygen) Review page D25 and
  explain that the oxygen that is in the air comes
  mostly from plants.

Thinking Further: *Making Generalizations*

Go on a nature walk and have children point out as
many plants as they can. Ask:

- **What do all the plants make that we cannot
  see but need to live?** (oxygen)

▶**After Reading**
Ask the red question in the student book as
ongoing assessment.

Technology

- Science Music CDs
  Mill Song
  My Oak Tree

- Visual Aid Transparency 23:
  What Comes from Trees?

Reading in Science Resources, pp. 205-206

Why are animals important?

Before Reading
Have children try to answer the question at the top of the page.

Using the Illustrations
Ask:

■ **Where does honey come from?** If children do not know, explain that honey is made by bees and then collected from beehives by people.

■ **What is the person doing to the sheep?** (Removing its wool. The wool is then spun into wool threads that are used to make clothing.)

■ **What is the person doing to the cow?** (milking it)

■ **Can you describe in your own words what is happening in the other pictures?** (The police officers are using horses in their work. The dog is trained to guide a person who is unable to see.)

Developing the Main Idea
As children read this page, ask them to talk about any animals they may own or care for and how they help people. Discuss why animals are important to people. (They are used for food and clothing. They provide companionship for people and help people to do work.) Ask:

■ **Why are living things natural resources?** (They come from Earth and are used by people.)

Why are animals important?

Animals are a natural resource. Many people eat meat from animals. Milk and eggs come from them, too. Some wool comes from sheep. Things made from wool keep people warm.

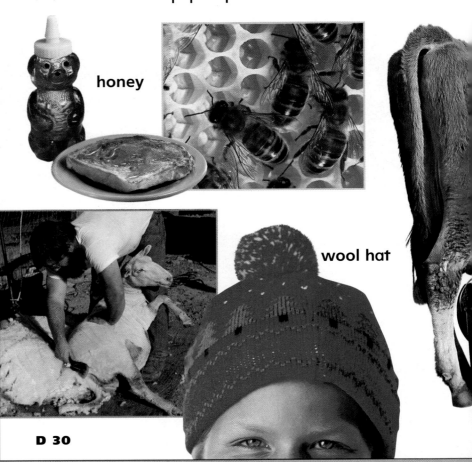

honey

wool hat

D 30

 Cultural Perspective

Animal Clothing

Inuit peoples used many animals to make clothes. They made needles from bone or ivory and thread from animal sinew. They wore animal pelts fur-side in. They used the skins of birds for clothing and feathers for decoration. They made boots from sealskin and waterproof capes from the intestines of seals and walrus. Have children discuss ways we use animals for clothing.

 SCIENCE **Reading Strategy**

Find the Main Idea

Developing Reading Skills
Have children identify the main idea of pages D30–D31. Ask:

■ **Which sentence tells the most important idea?** (Animals are a natural resource.)

■ **What do the other sentences tell about the main idea?** (We use animals for food, wool, pets, and help getting from place to place.)

Many people have animals as ets. Some animals help eople get from place to place.

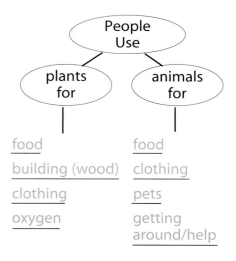

How are animals used here?

ple eat bees' honey; ep's wool is used for hes; people drink vs' milk; horses and de dogs help people around.

milk

Stop and Think

1. What are two ways people use plants?

2. What are two ways people use animals?

MORE TO READ Read **The Great Kapok Tree** by Lynne Cherry.

D 3I

✓ **Informal Assessment**

Easy/Average Point to objects in the room and ask children to identify whether they come from plant or animal sources. Ask children to explain their answers.
Linguistic

Challenge Ask children to make collections of discarded items that come from plant or animal sources. They can display their collections in shoeboxes and label them "Plant Products" and "Animal Products."
Intrapersonal

▶ **After Reading**
Ask the red question in the student book as **ongoing assessment.**

3 | Lesson Review

Answers to Stop and Think

1. People use plants for food, wood, cotton, and oxygen. (pp. D28–D29)

2. People use animals for food and clothing. They use them as pets and for getting around. (pp. D30–D31)

MORE TO READ Children can learn more about plants by reading *The Great Kapok Tree* by Lynne Cherry. San Diego: Harcourt Brace, 1990.

Retelling

Write the following scaffolding for summarizing the lesson on the chalkboard. Have children retell the lesson by filling in the blanks.

```
              People
              Use
        /              \
   plants            animals
   for                for
     |                  |
   food              food
   building (wood)   clothing
   clothing          pets
   oxygen            getting
                     around/help
```

Social Studies

Getting Water

Using the Illustrations
Ask:

- **What is the person in the picture doing?** (pumping water)

- **What does a pump do?** (moves water from one place to another)

- **How do people get water if they don't have water taps or pumps?** (They carry it from a stream in a bucket or jar, collect rainwater in a barrel, or melt snow or ice over a fire.)

Try This!
Let children create a picture essay titled "Water—Then and Now." After talking with adults, have children draw or look for pictures in magazines that show how people used to get water and how they washed things. Invest in a disposable camera. Give each child a chance to take a picture of a way people get or use water today. Tack the pictures to a bulletin board and caption them with sentences that children write or dictate.

Social Studies
L·I·N·K
FOR SCHOOL or HOME

Getting Water

You get water from a sink. But long ago, people did n[o]t have water in their homes.

Try This!

Talk with an adult. What would life be like without water in your home? Where would you get water to drink? How would you wash things?

Math | MiniLesson

Measuring Volume

Develop The volume of water and other liquids can be measured.

Practice Let children pour water between containers of different sizes and shapes. Ask:

Does the amount of water change? (Some children will think a taller container must have more water in it. Others will realize that the amount of water stays the same.)

Provide children with measuring spoons and cups in several sizes. Show them how to use the devices to measure amounts of water. Hang liquid measuring devices on a bulletin board and caption them according to the amount they hold, such as one teaspoon, one cup, or one liter.

A Poem About Earth

ead this poem with an adult.
's about Earth's air and land.

I'm glad the sky is painted blue,
And the earth is painted green,
With such a lot of nice fresh air
all sandwiched in between.
—Anonymous

Vrite your own poem about Earth's
ir, land, or water. Make drawings to
o with your poem.

SCIENCE Reading Strategy

Use Context Clues

Developing Reading Skills
The impact of a poem lies in the freshness of its ideas and the originality of its language.

Activity Let children exchange poems and read them aloud; or ask children to follow along as you read them. Discuss the ideas, words, and images used to express the meaning of each poem to make it unique and valuable.

A Poem About Earth

Developing the Main Idea
Discuss what makes something a poem. (Children may focus on rhyme and rhythm; try to elicit the use of sound and imagery to suggest thoughts, impressions, and feelings.)

Ask:

- **What images does this poem use?** (color, air "sandwiched" between earth and sky)
- **What do you think this poem means?** (It shows appreciation for earth, sky, and air.)

Exploring the Main Idea
Get some books of children's poetry from the library and read some poems about nature together. Talk about the images used and what each poem means. Discuss how the poems make children feel as they read them.

Try This!
Some children may want to try writing a poem in haiku format—three lines of five, seven, and five syllables respectively. Children might enjoy hearing this example of a haiku written by one first grader:

> Clean Earth sings with joy.
> Polluted Earth weeps and dies.
> I will help Earth sing.

Ask volunteers to read their poems to the class. Then bind children's poems and pictures together to make a class book of poems about Earth.

Chapter Review and Test Preparation

Resources

- Big Book, pp. D34–D35
- Reading in Science Resources, pp. 209–210
- Assessment Book, pp. 37–40

Test Taking Tip

When using each word only once, if one answer seems to fit more than one picture, tell children to first match the ones they are sure of, then see what is left. For example, *natural resource* could be used for any of the pictures, but after the other words are matched with the pictures, the choice becomes evident.

Answers to Vocabulary

1. rocks, p. D8
2. mineral, p. D12
3. oxygen, p. D6
4. natural resources, p. D25
5. soil, p. D6

Answers to Science Ideas

6. Things live and grow in each of the three types of soil and they are made up of bits of rock and dead animals and plants. The soils are different colors and hold different amounts of water. **pp. D12–D13**

Chapter 7 Review

Vocabulary

rocks

mineral

soil

natural resource

oxygen

Use each word once for items I–5. What does each picture show?

1

2

3 **4** **5**

Science Ideas

6 Tell how these soils are alike and different.

clay soil   topsoil   sandy soil

D 34

BLACKLINE

Vocabulary

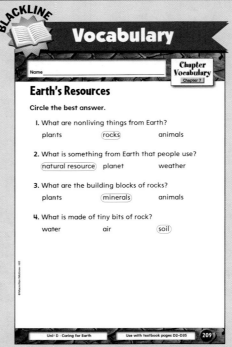

Name_____

Chapter Vocabulary
Chapter 7

Earth's Resources

Circle the best answer.

I. What are nonliving things from Earth?

plants   (rocks)   animals

2. What is something from Earth that people use?

(natural resource)   planet   weather

3. What are the building blocks of rocks?

plants   (minerals)   animals

4. What is made of tiny bits of rock?

water   air   (soil)

Unit D · Caring for Earth   Use with textbook pages D2–D35   209

Reading in Science Resources, pp. 209–210

7 Tell where you can find Earth's water.

8 What are some ways people use air?

Science Skill: Classify

Tell if each thing comes from plants, animals, or rocks.

9

10

11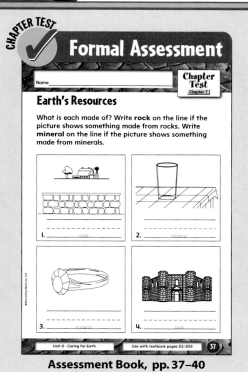

12

7. Earth's water is in clouds, streams, rivers, lakes, and oceans. **pp. D18–D19**

8. People breathe air. They use it to move things such as kites and sailboats, to fill things such as rafts and tires, to make music, and to make power. **pp. D24–D25**

Answers to Science Skills: Classify

9. plants, p. D8
10. rocks, p. D31
11. plants, p. D28
12. plants, p. D29

Retell
Write the following scaffolding for summarizing the chapter on the board. Have children retell the chapter by filling in the blanks.

Natural Resources

soil   rocks   water   air (oxygen)

minerals   animals   plants

Performance Assessment
The first activity on page D56 can be used as a performance assessment. See Teacher's Edition page D56 for the scoring rubric.

Technology

For more review, visit
www.mhscience02.com.

CHAPTER TEST
Formal Assessment

Name _____

Chapter Test
Chapter 7

Earth's Resources

What is each made of? Write **rock** on the line if the picture shows something made from rocks. Write **mineral** on the line if the picture shows something made from minerals.

1. _____ rock
2. _____ mineral
3. _____ mineral
4. _____ rock

Unit D · Caring for Earth   Use with textbook pages D2–D53   37

Assessment Book, pp. 37–40

Lesson Planner

Lesson	Objectives	Vocabulary	Pacing	Resources and Technology
LESSON 6 **Pollution** pp. D38-D43	■ Explore what may be found in air by observing. ■ Identify different types of pollution (air, water, land). ■ Discuss the effects of pollution.	**pollution**	3 days	■ Big Book D38-D43 ■ Activity Resources, pp. 102-104 ■ Reading in Science Resources, pp. 215-220 ■ School to Home Activities, p. 27 ■ Vocabulary Cards ■ Reading Aid Transparency D6 ■ **Explore Activity Video**
LESSON 7 **Caring for Earth's Resources** pp. D44-D49	■ Explore ways to reuse things through investigation. ■ Discuss reusing, recycling, and reducing as ways to stop pollution and take care of Earth's natural resources.	**reuse** **recycle** **reduce**	3 days	■ Big Book D44-D49 ■ Activity Resources, pp. 105-107, 114 ■ Reading in Science Resources, pp. 221-226 ■ Vocabulary Cards ■ Science Center Card 24 ■ Reading Aid Transparency D7 ■ **Explore Activity Video**

Activity Planner

Activity	Process Skills	Materials	Plan Ahead
6 Explore Activity **What is in the air?** p. D39	observe	white paper, petroleum jelly, hand lens, paper towels for hand clean up	
7 Explore Activity **How can you make something new from something old?** p. D45	investigate	clean, used things; acrylic paints; paint brush, crayons, and other art supplies; newspaper; paper towels	Cover the work surfaces with newspaper. Have paper towels available for clean up.

Reading in Science Resources

McGraw-Hill Science ***Reading in Science*** provides the following **Blackline Master** worksheets for this chapter.

Chapter Graphic Organizer

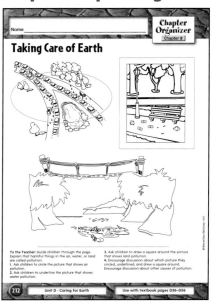

Reading in Science Resources, p. 212

Chapter Reading Skill

Reading in Science Resources, pp. 213-214

Chapter Vocabulary

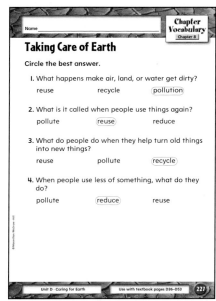

Reading in Science Resources, pp. 227-228

McGraw-Hill Science ***Reading in Science*** provides the following **Blackline Master** worksheets for every lesson in this chapter.

Lesson Outline

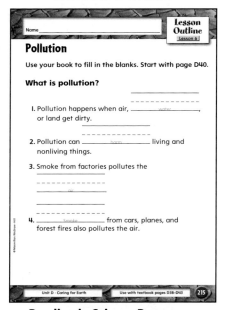

Reading in Science Resources, pp. 215-216, 221-222

Interpret Illustrations

Reading in Science Resources, pp. 217-218, 223-224

Lesson Vocabulary and Cloze Test

Reading in Science Resources, pp. 219-220, 225-226

Activities and Assessment

McGraw-Hill Science **Activity Resources** provides the following **Blackline Master** worksheets for every lesson in this chapter.

Explore Activity and Alternative Explore Activity

Activity Resources,
pp. 102-104, 105-107

Science Center Card

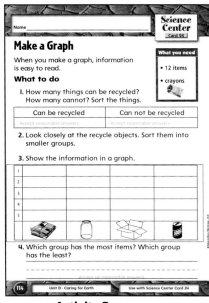

Activity Resources,
pp. 114

Science Skill Builder

Activity Resources, pp. 189-190

All Science Skill Builders are found at the back of the Student Book.

McGraw-Hill Science **Assessment Book** provides the following **Blackline Master** worksheets for this chapter.

Chapter Test

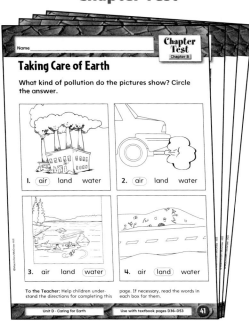

Assessment Resources, pp. 41-44

8 Taking Care of Earth

Resources

- Big Book, pp. D36–D37
- Reading in Science Resources, pp. 212–228

Did You Ever Wonder?

Invite children to look at the chapter opener photograph and describe the natural resources shown. (plants, bears, and water) Ask children if they have ever visited a local, state, or national park. Have them describe what they saw there.

Read aloud the paragraph on page D37 as children follow along. Discuss why people set aside parks. (Possible answers: recycling, saving resources, not littering, not polluting water or air)

CHAPTER

8 Taking Care of Earth

D 36

Reading Skills

This chapter provides MiniLessons and other strategies for developing, practicing, and applying the following reading skills.

- ◉ **Cause and Effect:** p. D42
- ○ **Compare and Contrast**
- ○ **Draw Conclusions**
- ○ **Find the Main Idea**
- ○ **Order of Events (act out or retell)**
- ◉ **Summarize (retell):** pp. D41, D43, D47, D49

- ◉ **Read pictures:** pp. D40, D46
- ◉ **Ask questions:** pp. D38, D44
- ◉ **Follow directions:** pp. D39, D45
- ◉ **Build on prior knowledge:** pp. D38, D44

Vocabulary

pollution

reuse

recycle

reduce

Did You Ever Wonder?

How can we take care of land, water, air, and living things? One way is to make parks. These bears stay safe in their park home. How else can we take care of land, water, air, and living things?

D 37

Vocabulary Preview

Preview vocabulary by having children pronounce and spell each word. Encourage children to look up these words and their definitions in their Glossary beginning on page R35.

pollution harmful things in the air, water, or land, D40

reuse to use something again in a new way, D46

recycle turn old things into new things, D47

reduce to use less of something, D48

Technology

Visit **www.mhscience02.com** for an online glossary.

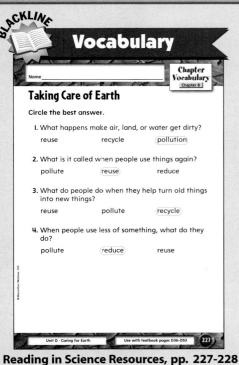

Reading in Science Resources, pp. 227-228

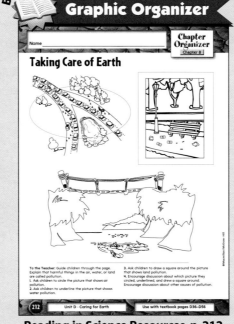

Reading in Science Resources, p. 212

LESSON 6 Pollution

Objectives

- Explore what may be found in air by observing.
- Identify different types of pollution (air, water, land).
- Discuss the effects of pollution.

Resources

- Big Book, pp. D38–D43
- Activity Resources, pp. 102–104
- Reading in Science Resources, pp. 215–220
- Vocabulary Card
- Reading Aid Transparency D6
- School to Home Activities, p. 27

Build on Prior Knowledge
Use the following questions to begin a discussion about pollution. Ask:

- **Have you ever seen pollution such as smog or smoke, or garbage in water or on land? How do you think it got there? What do you think people can do to clean it up?**

1 Get Ready

Using the Illustrations
Ask:

- **Where does the smoke go?** (The smoke goes into the air.)

- **Do you think the smoke is harmful to living things? Why or why not?** Allow discussion. Record responses on the chalkboard to be referred to later in the lesson.

See Science Skill Builder **Observe,** p. R2.

LESSON 6 Pollution

Get Ready

Do you see the smoke? Where does it go?

Science Skill

You **observe** when you use your senses to find out about things.

D 38

 Cross Curricular Books

Additional Outside Reading

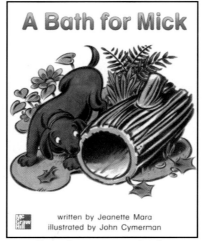

A Bath for Mick

written by Jeanette Mara
illustrated by John Cymerman

To order, see page D1•b.

Science Background

Air Pollution
The most dangerous air pollutants are invisible. Carbon dioxide from burning fuels is colorless and odorless, but its increasing concentration in the atmosphere is causing Earth to become warmer. CFCs (chlorofluorocarbons) from refrigerators and air conditioners deplete Earth's protective ozone layer and rob living things of their natural protection against the Sun's harmful ultraviolet rays.

Explore Activity

What is in the air?

1. Wipe some petroleum jelly on the paper. **Observe** it with the hand lens. Wash your hands.

2. Place the paper outside for a few hours. Put something on the paper to hold it in place.

3. Observe the paper again with the hand lens. What is on the paper? How do you think it got there?

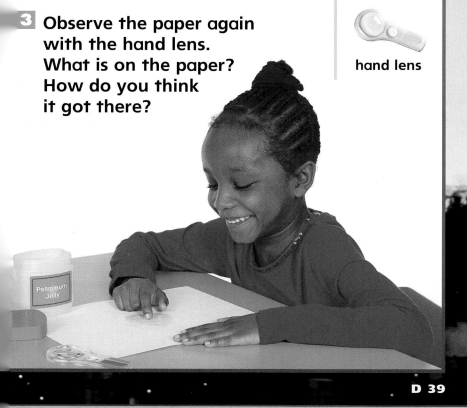

white paper

petroleum jelly

hand lens

D 39

Alternative Explore Activity

Materials coarse, dry spices; water; two clear plastic jars with lids; sieve; coffee filter

Water Watching Add water to one jar. Ask: **How does the water look?** (clear) Add spices and shake. **How does the water look now?** (It has little bits in it.) Pour the water into the other jar through the filter in the sieve. **What happens?** (The water in the jar is nearly clear again.) **Why?** (The little pieces stayed in the filter.) Talk about how filters are used to clean water.

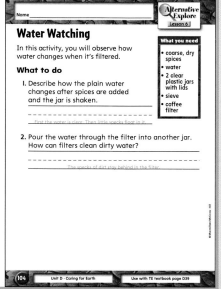

Alternative Explore Lesson 6

Water Watching
In this activity, you will observe how water changes when it's filtered.

What to do

1. Describe how the plain water changes after spices are added and the jar is shaken.

   First the water is clear. Then little specks float in it.

2. Pour the water through the filter into another jar. How can filters clean dirty water?

   The specks of dirt stay behind in the filter.

What you need
- coarse, dry spices
- water
- 2 clear plastic jars with lids
- sieve
- coffee filter

104   Unit D · Caring for Earth   Use with TE textbook page D39

Activity Resources, p. 104

Explore Activity

What is in the air?

Science Process Skills *observe*

Resources Activity Resources, pp. 102–103

Pacing 15 minutes to set up; wait period of several hours; 15 minutes to observe results

Grouping individuals or pairs

What to do

Read and discuss the activity with the class before they begin.

1. Show children that only a very thin coat of petroleum jelly is needed over a small patch of the paper.

2. This activity works best on a breezy day. On a still day, leave papers outdoors for a longer period of time.

3. Children may share hand lenses. (Children should observe dirt, soot, dust, seeds, and so on. They should conclude that the items were carried by the air and trapped by the petroleum jelly on the paper.)

Going Further

Cover several pieces of white cardboard with double-stick tape. Nail or tack the cardboard pieces in different locations where they can stay for several days. Then have children observe the tape and note any differences. Discuss the condition of the pieces of tape from different locations. Ask: **What conclusions can you draw about the different locations?** (Some are dirtier than others. Some get different types of pollutants.)

Technology

- When time is short, preview the activity with the **Explore Activity Video.**

2 Read to Learn

What is pollution?

Before Reading
Have children try to answer the red question at the top of the page.

Using the Illustrations
Ask:

- **What signs of pollution do you see in these pictures?** (smoke, smog)

- **What causes this pollution?** (factories, cars, planes, forest fires) Explain that airplanes and cars use gasoline in their engines that give off wastes (carbon monoxide) that are dangerous for people to breathe. States have laws that control the amount of wastes that cars can give off to help control air pollution.

- **Did people make all this pollution?** (Yes for cars, but lightning could have started the forest fire.) Discuss that people do not cause all pollution. Many forest fires start by lightning strikes. Volcanoes send ash and harmful gases into the air. Hard rains wash ashes from fires and volcanoes into streams and rivers, polluting the water.

Developing Vocabulary

pollution Ask children to think about examples of pollution. Make a list on the chalkboard of harmful things that they have seen in the air, water, or on land. Introduce the Vocabulary Card for the word *pollution*. Place it on the word wall.

Read to Learn

What is pollution?

Harmful things in the air, water, or land are called **pollution**. Pollution happens when air, water, or land gets dirty. It can harm living and nonliving things.

D 40

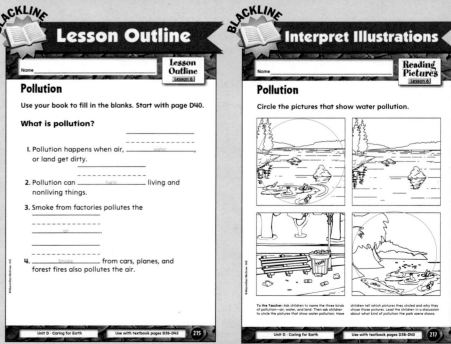

Reading in Science Resources, p. 215   **Reading in Science Resources, pp. 217-218**

Smoke from factories pollutes the air. So does smoke from cars, planes, and forest fires.

Air pollution may make people sick. They can't breathe the way they should. smoke from factories, cars, planes, and forest fires

▷ **What pollutes the air?**

D 41

Developing the Main Idea

As children read this page, have them recall the Explore Activity and how moving air carried soot, dirt, pollen, and other things in it. Discuss that we breathe things carried by air and that some of those things can make living things sick. That is why it is important to stop air pollution.

Thinking Further: *Making Predictions*

■ **What would happen to the air if people walked or rode bicycles instead of driving cars? Why?** (The air would be less polluted because people wouldn't be putting harmful substances from their car engines into the air.)

▶ **After Reading**
Ask the red question in the student book as **ongoing assessment.**

Reading MiniLesson

Summarize (Retell)

Develop Discuss with children that being able to summarize what you have learned by retelling it using your own words shows that you understand the topic.

Activity Ask children to summarize, or retell in their own words, what they have learned by reading page D41. (Children should show an understanding that smoke from factories, cars, planes, and forest fires pollutes the air and can make people sick.)

What pollutes the water?

Before Reading
Have children try to answer the red question at the top of the page.

Exploring the Main Idea
Display two glasses of water. Add some coarsely ground pepper to one and stir. Ask:

- **Is the water still pure and clean?** (No.) **How do you know?** (The pepper makes it dirty. You can see the pepper in it.)

Then add some sugar to the other and stir. Ask:

- **Is this water still pure and clean?** (No.) **How do you know?** (Children should respond that they saw you put something into it.) **How is this water different from the water in the first glass?** (It still appears clear, unlike the first glass.) Discuss the fact that not all pollution is visible.

Developing the Main Idea
As children read this page, ask them if they have seen or smelled any signs of water pollution in their community.

▶After Reading
Ask the red question in the student book as **ongoing assessment.**

What pollutes the water?

Wastes pollute the water. Wastes are things left over from factories. Dirty water is not safe to drink.

Sometimes people throw trash into water. When animals eat this trash, they may get sick and die.

Water pollution made the fish d

 What happened to the fish?

D 42

 Reading Strategy

Cause and Effect
Developing Reading Skills
An *effect* is something that happens and a *cause* is why it happens.

- **What is the cause of pollution shown on this page?** (Wastes going into the water.)
- **What is the effect of this?** (Fish died.)
- **What is another possible effect of this pollution?** (People and animals that drink the water may get sick.)

Advanced Learners

Pollution Solutions
Have children make a class list of as many sources of pollution they can think of, both big and small. Have them brainstorm ways to help stop or reduce the types of pollution listed. Invite children to present their ideas to the class for discussion.
Logical; Intrapersonal

hat pollutes the land?

rash pollutes the land. So do
ctory wastes. Land pollution may
arm animals, plants, and soil. Plants
nd crops can't grow in polluted soil.

➡ **What pollutes the land here?** trash

Stop and Think

1. What are three kinds of pollution?

2. How may pollution harm living things?

AT THE COMPUTER Visit **www.mhscience02.com** to learn more about pollution.

D 43

Informal Assessment

Easy/Average Ask children to name three kinds of pollution and give an example of each. (air, water, land) **Linguistic**

Challenge Ask children to draw two pictures: one showing three kinds of pollution and the other showing no pollution. (First picture: Children may draw dirt in water and air and trash on land. They may draw dead animals and dying plants. Second picture: Children may draw clean air and water and healthy plants and animals.) **Visual; Spatial**

What pollutes the land?

Before Reading
Have children try to answer the red question at the top of the page.

Developing the Main Idea
As children read this page, ask them to suggest specific ways that land pollution can harm animals, plants, and soil. For example, poisoning plants kills animals that eat them. Polluted soil cannot grow food.

Exploring the Main Idea
Let children choose a pollutant to experiment with. (Oil, detergent, or salt is a good choice.) Have them add a little pollutant to some soil in cups, then plant bean seeds. Also have them plant some beans in unpolluted soil. Over the next few weeks, have children describe and measure differences in the plants' health and growth.

▶ **After Reading**
Ask the red question in the student book as **ongoing assessment.**

3 Lesson Review

Answers to Stop and Think

1. Air, water, and land pollution are three kinds of pollution. (pp. D40–D43)

2. Pollution may harm people and other animals by making them sick. Plants cannot grow in polluted soil. (pp. D40–D43)

Retelling
Write the following scaffolding for summarizing the lesson on the chalkboard. Have children retell the lesson by filling in the blanks.

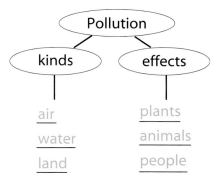

LESSON 7 Caring for Earth's Resources

Objectives

- Explore ways to reuse things through investigation.
- Discuss reusing, recycling, and reducing as ways to help stop pollution and take care of Earth's natural resources.

Resources

- Big Book, pp. D44–D49
- Activity Resources, pp.105–107, 114
- Reading in Science Resources, pp. 221–226
- Vocabulary Cards
- Reading Aid Transparency D7
- Science Center Card 24

Build on Prior Knowledge

Ask children to recall what they learned about pollution in Lesson 6. Ask them to suggest ways to stop or reduce pollution. Children may have ideas of their own or may know about recycling programs or other pollution-reduction efforts in their community.

1 Get Ready

Using the Illustrations
Ask:

- **What material was used to make this house?** (glass bottles)

- **How could making a house from this material help to stop pollution?** (By reusing materials to make something new instead of throwing them away, you help to stop pollution.)

See Science Skill Builder **Investigate,** p. R11.

LESSON 7 Caring for Earth's Resources

Get Ready

Look closely. What is this house made of? How else can people use things to make something new?

Science Skill

You **investigate** when you make a plan and try it out.

D 44

 Cross Curricular Books

Additional Outside Reading

Learning from Our **Mothers**

by Leya Roberts
illustrated by Ellen Dreibelbis

To order, see page D1·b.

Science Background

Recycling

The Environmental Defense Fund estimated that curbside recycling saves at least $187 (in 1995) per ton in energy costs alone. Other benefits include reducing pollution, conserving natural resources, cutting landfill and incinerator costs, creating jobs, and making manufacturing industries more competitive.

Explore Activity

ow can you make something new from something old?

1 **Investigate** how you can use clean, old things to make something new. Think about what you want to make.

2 Make a plan. Think about what you will use to make it. Try it out.

3 Tell how you used something old in a new way.

What you need

clean, old things

art supplies

D 45

Alternative Explore Activity

Materials blender, water, fine screen stretched onto a wooden frame, old paper

Papermaking Place small pieces of paper into the blender with plenty of water and chop into a slurry. Have children press a thin layer of the slurry onto the screen. Press out the water. When dry, lift off the sheet of recycled paper from the screen. Paper can be made with flowers, seeds, colors, scents, and other additives.

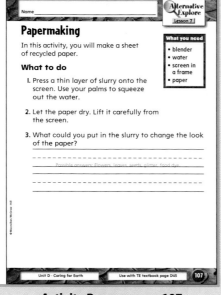

Name _____

Alternative Explore Lesson 7

Papermaking

In this activity, you will make a sheet of recycled paper.

What you need
- blender
- water
- screen in a frame
- paper

What to do

I. Press a thin layer of slurry onto the screen. Use your palms to squeeze out the water.

2. Let the paper dry. Lift it carefully from the screen.

3. What could you put in the slurry to change the look of the paper?

_____
Possible answers: Flowers, leaves, seeds, glitter, food dye.
_____
_____

Unit D · Caring for Earth   Use with TE textbook page D45   107

Activity Resources, p. 107

Explore Activity

How can you make something new from something old?

Science Process Skills *investigate*

Resources Activity Resources, pp. 105–106

Pacing 20–30 minutes

Grouping pairs

Plan Ahead Cover the work surfaces with newspaper. Have paper towels available for cleanup. Several days before the activity, have children bring in clean used things such as yogurt and milk containers, paper towel and toilet paper tubes, shoeboxes, plastic water bottles, egg cartons, and the like.

What to do

Read and discuss the activity with the class before they begin.

1 Have children begin by discussing possible projects. Suggest some or encourage children to come up with ideas of their own. Give partners time to discuss their ideas.

2 Have children make plans for what they want to create and compile a list of materials they will need. Let children dictate or draw plans for their construction. Plans may require modification or expansion. Give children time to make their objects. More than one trial may be needed as problems surface. This is a natural part of the process and should be encouraged.

3 Have pairs take turns describing how they used old, unwanted things in new ways.

Going Further

Plan a project that the whole class can make using old items in a new way. A large sculpture made from discarded items is one idea.

For an additional activity, see Science Card 24, p. D56•f.

Technology

- When time is short, preview the activity with the **Explore Activity Video**.

2 Read to Learn

Why should people reuse things?

Before Reading
Have children try to answer the red question at the top of the page.

Exploring the Main Idea
Have children talk about the meaning of the words in this old adage: Use it up or wear it out. Make it do or do without.

Using the Illustrations
Ask:

- **What do you see?** (jar used for holding jewelry, margarine tub used to hold buttons, plastic milk jug used as bird feeder, rummage sale)

- **How are the things you see in these pictures fighting pollution?** (Things are being used again and not thrown away to create trash and pollution.)

Discuss with children that when old things are reused, new ones don't have to be made. This helps save Earth's natural resources such as aluminum for making new cans, petroleum for making new plastics, trees for making new paper, minerals for making glass, and so on. Reusing things also means that fewer things end up as trash in landfills. This means that there is less land pollution.

Recall the Explore Activity. The child reused a container as a pencil holder, which means he did not have to buy one. It also means that the plastic container did not end up in the trash causing land pollution.

▶ **After Reading**
Ask the red question in the student book as **ongoing assessment.**

Developing Vocabulary

reuse Ask children to look at the picture on page D45. Ask: **What is the child doing?** (making a pencil holder) **How does this fight pollution?** (It won't go in the trash and pollute the land.) **What is the word for using something again?** (reuse)
Introduce the Vocabulary Card for the term *reuse*. Place it on the word wall.

Read to Learn

Why should people reuse things?

When people **reuse** things, they use them again in a new way. They don't throw these things away. They don't have to buy new things.

> **How do people reuse things here?**
> See above.

D 46

Lesson Outline

Caring for Earth's Resources

Reading in Science Resources, p. 221

Interpret Illustrations

Caring for Earth's Resources

Reading in Science Resources, pp. 223-2

Why should people recycle?

When people **recycle,** they help turn old things into new things. Old paper is used to make new paper. This means trees are not cut to make new paper. This saves trees.

▶ **What do these children recycle?**
cans, paper

D 47

Reading | MiniLesson

Summarize (Retell)

Develop Discuss with children that being able to summarize what you have learned by retelling it using your own words shows that you understand the topic.

Activity Ask children to summarize what they have learned by reading pages D46–D47. (Children should show an understanding that reusing and recycling both help save natural resources and reduce pollution.)

Why should people recycle?

Before Reading
Have children try to answer the red question at the top of the page.

Exploring the Main Idea
Ask children if they save cans, glass, plastic, cardboard, or newspaper at home. Ask if they know why this is done. If you do not participate in recyling programs at your school, you may wish to learn about such programs in your area and get the class involved in recycling.

Using the Illustrations
Ask:

■ **What are these people doing?** (putting cans and paper into recycling containers) Remind children that bauxite and trees—from which aluminum and paper are made respectively— are natural resources. When old cans are used to make new ones, bauxite need not be taken from the land. When old paper is used to make new paper, trees don't have to be cut down.

▶ **After Reading**
Ask the red question in the student book as **ongoing assessment**.

Developing Vocabulary

recycle If you have not yet done the Alternative Explore Activity, you may wish to do it now. Use the word *recycle* to describe making new paper from old. Introduce the Vocabulary Card for the word *recycle*. Place it on the word wall.

Why should people reduce what they use?

Before Reading
Have children try to answer the red question at the top of the page.

Developing the Main Idea
As children read page D48, have them brainstorm other ways they can reduce the use of things to help save natural resources. List their ideas on the chalkboard.

Thinking Further: *Compare and Contrast*

- **How are reusing, recycling, and reducing similar?** (All do something with objects that typically are thrown away. They all help save natural resources and reduce pollution.)

- **How are they different?** (Reusing means to use an object again for a different or similar purpose. Recycling means to turn old things into new things, such as recyling old paper to make new paper. Reducing means to use less of something.)

▶ **After Reading**
Ask the red question in the student book as **ongoing assessment**.

Developing Vocabulary

reduce Ask children to explain how the girl in the picture is reducing paper use. (By using a cloth towel instead of a paper towel, the girl reduces the use of paper.) Introduce the Vocabulary Card for the word *reduce*. Place it on the word wall.

Why should people reduce what they use?

When people **reduce** what they use, they use less of it. Then there is more left over for later. You can reduce how much paper you use when you write on both sides. This saves paper.

 Who uses less paper here? Tell how.

The girl; by using a cloth towel instead of a paper towel, she saves paper.

D 48

Math MiniLesson

Comparing Weight on a Bar Graph

Develop Weight is a property of objects and materials. It can be determined using a scale. Different weights may be compared on a bar graph.

Activity Collect the waste paper the class generates in a day. Weigh it on a scale. Make a bar graph on chart paper and record the weight. Continue collecting and weighing every day for a predetermined period of time, trying hard to reduce waste. Ask: **Do the numbers get smaller? What does that mean?**

hat else can people do?

ople can take care of resources in her ways. They take care of air when ey drive cars less. They take care of ater when they keep it clean. They take re of land when they put trash in cans.

How do these people take care of resources?
They pick up trash to protect the land and water.

Stop and Think

1. Why is it important to reuse, recycle, and reduce?

2. How can you help stop pollution and take care of natural resources? Tell one way.

Read **Recycle!** by Gail Gibbons.

D 49

✓ Informal Assessment

Easy/Average Ask children to define reuse, reduce, and recycle and to give an example of ways they can do each. **Linguistic**

Challenge Compile a class anthology of "Use It Up, Wear It Out" tales. Have children make up stories about someone who reuses, reduces, or recycles. They can dictate their stories to you, then illustrate them with pictures. Display the stories for all to see. **Linguistic**

SCIENCE FOR ALL   Inclusion

Class Recycling Project
As a class, decide on a recycling activity you can undertake. Perhaps you can gather paper around the school or collect aluminum cans from the lunch area. If possible, tour a recycling plant to learn how new objects and materials are made from old. **Social**

What else can people do?

Before Reading
Have children try to answer the red question at the top of the page.

Developing the Main Idea
Review the adage discussed with page D46: Use it up or wear it out. Make it do or do without. Talk about how following the advice helps people care for natural resources.

Exploring the Main Idea
Hold up an object from the classroom trash. As children read page D49, ask them to suggest a way to reuse it, recycle it, or reduce its use. Choose other items from the classroom trash. Continue with discussing possible ways to reuse, recycle, or reduce the use of the items.

▶**After Reading**
Ask the red question in the student book as **ongoing assessment**.

Children can learn more about ways to recycle by reading *Recycle!* by Gail Gibbons. Boston: Little, Brown, and Company, 1996.

3 Lesson Review

Answers to Stop and Think

1. They help to stop pollution and take care of natural resources. (pp. D46–D49)

2. Possible answers: Reduce, reuse, recycle; put trash in cans; use less water, and so on. (pp. D46–D49)

Retelling
Write the following scaffolding for summarizing the lesson on the chalkboard. Have children retell the lesson by filling in the blanks.

Three Ways to Care for Earth's Resources

reuse   recycle   reduce

Reading L·I·N·K

A Trip to the Park

Exploring the Main Idea

Discuss with children what dangers threaten plants and animals in parks. Make a list on the board. (Possible answers include traffic killing animals and people trampling plants. People may disturb nesting or breeding areas or destroy animal habitats—perhaps without realizing they are doing so.)

If possible, take the class for a walk in a local park. Have children make notes about the different things people are doing (for example, picnicking, playing ball, running) as well as the plants and animals they see. Have children try to spot what has been done to protect plants and animals there, such as traffic barriers, paved walkways, and "Keep Off the Grass" signs.

Try This!

When the class returns from the park, discuss what people can do to protect plants and animals in parks. List ideas on the board and add to the list as children work on their books. (Some ideas may include banning cars from parks, restricting where people can walk, prohibiting fire building or overnight camping, picking up trash.)

Have children read the Grade-Level Science Book, *Going for a Walk*. For additional reading, see p. D1·b.

Reading L·I·N·K
FOR SCHOOL OR HOME

Going for a Walk

written by Kana Riley   *illustrated by Margaux Lucas*

A Trip to the Park

Find out some things you can see and do in a park. Read *Going for a Walk* by Kana Riley.

Try This!

How can people keep a park's living things safe? How can people keep a park's land, air, and water clean? Make a picture book to show how. Call the book *Save Our Parks.*

D 50

Inclusion

Mimic and Mime

Let children pantomime a scene about a park. Challenge children to invent roles for every class member. Each will mimic a person, plant, or animal in a park. Let children decide what the theme or message of their scene will be. The class might enjoy experimenting with costumes or facepainting to ensure that the characters in their silent drama appear realistic. **Social**

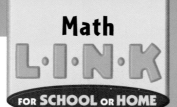

Make Less Trash

ach person in your family
akes 4 pounds of trash each
ay. But only I pound of that
ash is reused or recycled!

Try This!

ow much trash does
our family make each
ay? Add to find out.
ow much of that
ash is reused or
ecycled? Add to
ind out.

Science Newsroom CD-ROM
Choose **Parts Puzzle** to find out
how parts of things work together.

D 51

Math
L·I·N·K

Make Less Trash

Exploring the Main Idea
Ask:

- **What kinds of trash do you make?** (Possible answers: food wrappers and peels, school papers, lunch bags, cans, bottles, juice boxes)

- **Does any of your trash get reused or recycled?** (Children may report on recycling activities in the family, school, or community.)

Give children a feel for how much trash one person makes in a day by having them lift a bag containing four pounds of potatoes or apples. Or let children stand on a bathroom scale holding a basket and watching the numbers as you add potatoes or apples to the basket.

Ask a volunteer to remove one pound of "trash." Have children compare the amount recycled to the amount that gets thrown into landfills.

Try This!
Have children write a tally mark on a piece of paper for each of their family members including themselves. Then, ask children to write the number *4* next to each tally mark and add the numbers to find out how much trash their families make in one day. Discuss how children might be able to tell if their ideas for making less trash are working. (Children should say they could weigh the trash each day to see if they are producing less, or notice that smaller bags, or less of a bag is used for trash.)

Technology

Parts Puzzle may also be found on the Internet. Visit **www.mhscience02.com.**

Using a Circle Graph

Develop A circle graph shows the parts of a whole.

Activity Show children how to draw or trace a circle. Help them to draw two lines to divide the circle into four equal parts. Have them color in one of the parts. Ask:

- **How many parts does the circle have?** (four)
- **How many are colored?** (one)

Reread the text, drawing children's attention to the amount of trash that is recycled. Ask:

- **What does the colored part of your circle stand for?** (the one pound of trash that is recycled)
- **What do the uncolored parts stand for?** (the three pounds of trash that are not recycled)

Chapter Review and Test Preparation

Resources

- Big Book, pp. D52–D53
- Reading in Science Resources, pp. 227–228
- Assessment Book, pp. 41–44

Answers to Vocabulary

1. pollution, p. D40
2. reuse, p. D47
3. reduce, p. D48
4. recycle, p. D46

Test Taking Tip

When telling about the pictures in items 1–4, remind children that they need not use the vocabulary word in exactly the same form as it is shown. For example, the form of the word can tell about the present (recycle), the past (recycled), or the future (will recycle); it can give advice (should recycle) or describe a habit (always recycles). Names of things, such as pollution, can be changed into action words, such as pollute.

Vocabulary

pollution
reduce
reuse
recycle

Use each word once for items 1–4. What does each picture show?

D 52

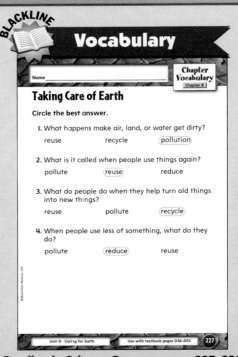

Vocabulary

Name _____

Chapter Vocabulary
Chapter 8

Taking Care of Earth

Circle the best answer.

1. What happens make air, land, or water get dirty?

   reuse   recycle   (pollution)

2. What is it called when people use things again?

   pollute   (reuse)   reduce

3. What do people do when they help turn old things into new things?

   reuse   pollute   (recycle)

4. When people use less of something, what do they do?

   pollute   (reduce)   reuse

Unit D · Caring for Earth   Use with textbook pages D36–D53   227

Reading in Science Resources, pp. 227–228

ience Ideas

What happens if people don't take care of the air?

Name some things that make pollution.

Tell one way that people can reuse things.

ience Skill: Observe

What natural resources are not taken care of here? How do you know?

READ

In the Lake by Gary Apple
Billy Fish by Edward S. Popper

D 53

Formal Assessment

Name_____

Chapter Test
Chapter 8

Taking Care of Earth

What kind of pollution do the pictures show? Circle the answer.

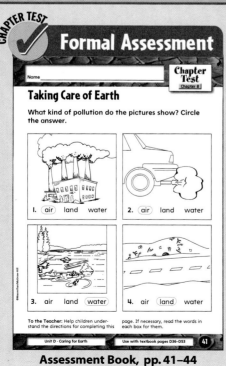

1. (air) land water   2. (air) land water

3. air land (water)   4. air (land) water

To the Teacher: Help children understand the directions for completing this page. If necessary, read the words in each box for them.

Unit D · Caring for Earth   Use with textbook pages D36–D53   41

Assessment Book, pp. 41–44

Answers to Science Ideas

5. If people don't take care of the air, it gets polluted. p. D40

6. Factory wastes, smoke, forest fires, and trash make pollution. pp. D40–D41

7. Possible answers: People can reuse things by using them in new ways. A jar can be used to store things. A gallon jug can be reused as a bird feeder. p. D46

Answers to Science Skill: Observe

8. The water is in danger because wastes are pouring into it. Animals such as fish are in danger because the wastes make them sick and kill them. p. D42

Retell

Write the following scaffolding for summarizing the chapter on the board. Have children retell the chapter by filling in the blanks.

Fight
Pollution

reduce   reuse   recycle

Performance Assessment

The second activity on page D56 can be used as a performance assessment. See Teacher's Edition page D56 for the scoring rubric.

Read

To find out more about places where water is found and pollution of the ocean, have children read the Grade-Level Science Books *In the Lake* by Gary Apple and *Billy Fish* by Edward S. Popper. For additional reading see page D1·b.

Technology

For more review, visit
www.mhscience02.com.

Objective

■ Recognize that the American bison is no longer on the verge of being extinct.

Build on Prior Knowledge
Ask:

■ **Have you ever seen a buffalo? Where?**
(Children might have seen a buffalo at the zoo, or in a national park.)

Discuss with children that once bison roamed freely across the country, and were large in number.

The Return of the American Bison

Developing the Main Idea
Ask:

■ **What happened to the bison?** (Most of them were killed and there were only a few left.)

■ **Why are bison still alive today?** (People started the American Buffalo Society to help save the bison.)

Mention that the real name for the "buffalo" is bison. Also show children an old nickel with the bison on its back.

Amazing Stories

The Return of the
American Bison

Once there were many American bison. But people hunted bison for food and for their skins. Many people hunted them just for sport. By 1900, very few bison were left.

Piles of bison skins

Bison killed for its skin

D 54

Science Background

Saving the Bison
In 1872, President Ulysses S. Grant created the first national park (Yellowstone Valley) in Montana to preserve some of America's natural beauty and be a safe haven for wildlife. Living in the park was a small herd of American bison – the last wild herd. But bison were poached in the park, and in 1894, strict laws forbidding the poaching of bison were passed. Still, the Yellowstone herd remained very small.

In 1902, ranched bison were released into the Yellowstone herd to boost its size. In 1905, William Hornaday, Bronx Zoo director, sent a dozen bison from the zoo's herd to establish a herd in Kansas. In 1906, the American Buffalo Society was founded to help recreate wild bison herds.

lliam Hornaday wanted to help the
on. In 1905, he helped start the
nerican Buffalo Society. (Buffalo is
other name for bison.) They worked
bring back bison. Today bison again
e in the wild.
ople still work
save them.

ny did the
nerican bison
nost die out?

FRED MATTHEWS BUFFALO CORRALS
CUSTER STATE PARK

**A buffalo
ranch today**

**AT THE
COMPUTER**
Visit **www.mhscience02.com**
for more amazing stories and facts.

D 55

Cultural Perspectives

The History of Bison
The bison was an important
natural resource to Native
Americans and the early
settlers of the west. People ate
its meat and used its hide for
leather goods. Native
Americans wasted no part of
the bison. Even the horns and
tail hairs were used.

Thinking Further: *Inferring*

■ **What could the American Buffalo Society do
to help save the bison?** (They could put bison
in a protected area where people would not be
allowed to hunt them.)

Answer to Question
The bison was hunted for skins, food, and sport.

Retelling
Check children's understanding by asking them to
discuss why bison are still alive today.

SCIENCE
Workshop

Unit D Performance Assessment

1. Make a Poster (Chapter 7)

Materials: posterboard; crayons, markers, or paints; old magazines; safety scissors; glue sticks

Teaching Tips: Ask children to recall the natural resources they read about in this unit and list them on the board (air, water, soil, plants, animals, minerals, rocks). Then ask what other natural resources children can think of. (metals, fuels) Children can draw pictures of people using natural resources for their posters and/or cut pictures from magazines.

2. Make a Mobile (Chapter 8)

Materials: drawing paper, crayons, yarn, plastic hangers, safety scissors, hole punch

Teaching Tips: Help children brainstorm a list of examples for each category before they make their drawings. Use a hole-punch to make a hole in the top of children's drawings so they can easily thread the yarn through. Suggest that they use different lengths of yarn so their pictures don't overlap when they tie them to the hanger. Alternatively, children can cut pictures from magazines of items for each category.

SCIENCE
Workshop

1. **Make a poster.** Think of five natural resources. How do people use them? Use words and pictures to show.

2. **Make a mobile** of drawings. Be sure to show a drawing for each of these:

- air pollution
- land pollution
- water pollution
- something that can be reused
- something that can be recycled

D 56

Rubrics for Science Workshop

1. Make a Poster (5-point rubric)

1 point each = for identifying five natural resources and how people use them.

2. Make a Mobile (5-point rubric)

1 point = for drawing an example of something causing air pollution

1 point = for drawing an example of something that causes land pollution

1 point = for drawing an example of something that causes water pollution

1 point = for drawing an example of reusing something

1 point = for drawing an example of recycling something

Formal Assessment

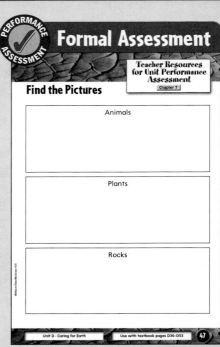

Find the Pictures

Teacher Resources for Unit Performance Assessment
Chapter 7

Animals

Plants

Rocks

Unit D · Caring for Earth | Use with textbook pages D36–D53 | 47

Assessment Book, pp. 45–48

Science Center Card **19**

Caring for Earth
Good for Growing

Objective

- Children observe the growth of bean seeds in two different soils for one week.

What you need

- **Science Center Card 19**
- Activity Resources, Science Center Card 19, p. 108
- 2 kinds of soil, sandy and dark; 2 beans; 2 cups; spray bottle; ruler

What to do

- Gather together two different kinds of soil, enough for each small group of children.
- Place beans in water the night before you do the activity. This speeds up germination.
- Label cups and soils **A** and **B**. This way the children will have the same soil in the same cups.
- Locate a sunny spot to place plants for a week.
- Put all materials in the Science Center.
- Be sure children understand the activity before they begin. Go through each step so they will know what to do.
- Allow children time to observe differences in the soils. Have them look at color and consistency.
- Remind children to clean up the activity area.

Informal Assessment

- Show children the two different types of soil they used in the activity. **If you were a farmer, which of these would you use for planting beans?** (should be the soil that grew the largest plant)
- Check children's filled-in worksheets.

Follow-Up

- Have children compare the two soil samples. Provide children with a simple two-column chart with the headings: *living* and *nonliving*. Ask children to list what they see in the soils.

Science Center Card

Activity Resources, Page 108

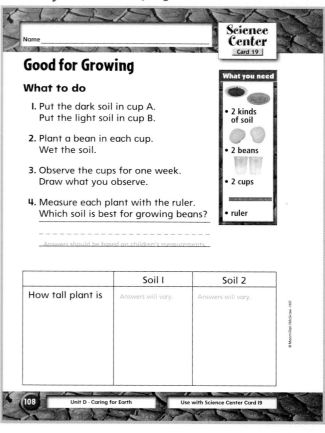

Science Center Card 20

Caring for Earth
Predict

Objectives

- Children pour water onto two different kinds of soil to observe which soil holds water better.

What you need

- **Science Center Card 20**
- Activity Resources, Science Center Card 20, p. 109
- 2 cups with different soils in them; measuring cup; water

What to do

- Label cups and soil **A** and **B** so all children will have the same soils in the same cups. Fill each cup with the same amount of a different soil.
- Place the materials in the Science Center for children to use.
- Use cool water from the faucet.
- Be sure children understand the activity before they begin.
- Model for children how to measure the water. Allow them time to practice measuring before they do the activity. Both cups must get the same amount of water.
- Keep sponges and paper towels handy for any water spills.
- Point out the charts on the worksheet and show children where to record their predictions and observations.
- Remind children to clean up the Science Center.

Informal Assessment

- Ask children why they made the predictions they did. Accept all reasonable explanations. Have children compare the results. Were they far off or close in their predictions?
- Check children's filled-in worksheets.

Follow-Up

- Based on the activity, ask children to predict what kind of soil would be found in hot desert-like places and what kind of soil would be found in cooler climates.

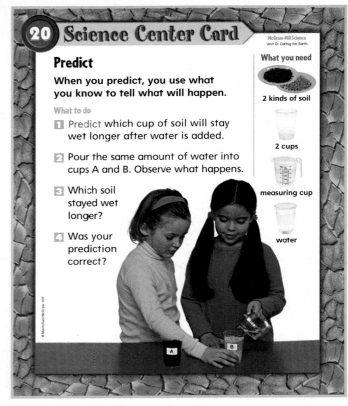

Science Center Card

Activity Resources, Page 109

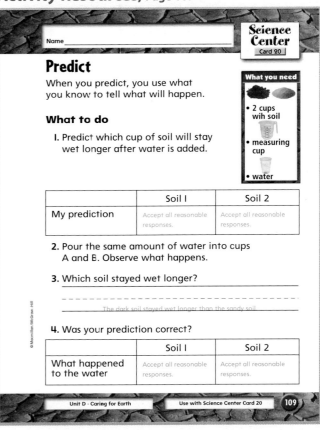

Science Center Card ⌈21⌉

Caring for Earth
Make a Model

Objectives

- Children make a model to show how much salt water, frozen water, and fresh water is on Earth.

What you need

- **Science Center Card 21**
- Activity Resources, Science Center Card 21, p. 110-111
- dark blue crayon; white crayon; light blue crayon

What to do

- Place all materials in the Science Center.
- Be sure children understand the activity before they begin. Read through each step.
- Point out the grid on the worksheet. Ask children to identify one square on the grid so they know what they will be coloring in.
- Be sure children understand that the colored in grid represents the water found on Earth. You may want to show them a globe and point out where salt, frozen, and fresh water are found.

Informal Assessment

- Using their models, ask children to discuss the kinds of water found on Earth.
- Check children's filled-in worksheets.

Follow-Up

- Give each child a circle divided equally into four sections. Ask children to color three sections blue and one section brown. Tell them that this is a model of Earth and challenge them to tell what the blue stands for (water) and what the brown stands for (land).

21 Science Center Card
McGraw-Hill Science
Unit D: Caring for Earth

Make a Model

You can make a model to find out how much of Earth's water is fresh water.

What to do

1. Color 2 squares white. Color 1 square light blue. Color the rest dark blue.

2. White is frozen water. Light blue is fresh water. Dark blue is salt water.

3. What kind of water does Earth have the most of? The least of?

4. How does your model help you learn about the water on Earth?

What you need

crayons

chart

Activity Resources, Page 110

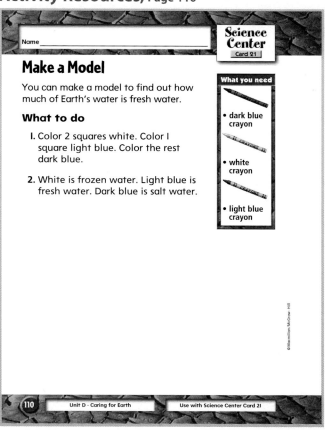

Name

Science Center Card 21

Make a Model

You can make a model to find out how much of Earth's water is fresh water.

What to do

1. Color 2 squares white. Color 1 square light blue. Color the rest dark blue.

2. White is frozen water. Light blue is fresh water. Dark blue is salt water.

What you need

- dark blue crayon
- white crayon
- light blue crayon

110   Unit D · Caring for Earth   Use with Science Center Card 21

Science Center Card 22

Caring for Earth
Make a Pinwheel

Objectives

- Children follow directions to make a pinwheel.

What you need

- **Science Center Card 22**
- Activity Resources, Science Center Card 22, p. 112
- pinwheel pattern; pencil with eraser; straight pin; crayons, optional; scissors, optional

What to do

- Before the activity, cut out pinwheel patterns for each child, or have him or her do it.

- Let children color their pinwheels before assembling them.

- Place all materials in the Science Center.

- Be sure children understand the activity before they begin. Read through each step of the activity together.

- Model for children how to line up the four ends with the center dot. Point out that you are going through the paper first and then pushing the pin into the eraser.

- Explain that children may need to adjust their papers on the pins.

- Take the children outside and watch the wind move the pinwheels if it's a windy day.

Informal Assessment

- Place several items on the table such as a pen, piece of chalk, paper clip, tissue paper, pinwheel pattern, straight pin, and pencil with eraser. **Which parts did you use to make a pinwheel?** (the pencil, pinwheel pattern and the straight pin)

- Check children's filled in worksheets.

Science Center Card

Activity Resources, Page 112

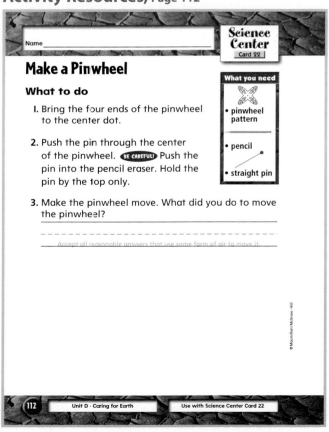

Science Center Card ㉓

Caring for Earth
Thanks for Everything!

Objectives

- Children attach items to a tree branch to show which things come from trees.

What you need

- **Science Center Card 23**
- Activity Resources, Science Center Card 23, p. 113
- large tree branch; can; sand; things made from trees; string; tape

What to do

- Before the activity, ask children to bring in several things that come from trees. Tell them they can cut out pictures of larger things from magazines or newspapers and bring in small items.

- Place all materials in the Science Center.

- Be sure children understand the activity before they begin. Read through each step so children know what to do.

- Fill the cans at least half way with the sand, depending on the heaviness of the objects brought in.

- Model for children how to push the branch into the center of the sand in the can.

- Place each hard to tie item in a sandwich bag and tape the bag to a branch.

Informal Assessment

- Ask children to name all the things on the tree, then sort the objects into these categories: wood, paper, or food.

- Check children's filled in worksheets.

Follow-Up

- Challenge children to think of ways we use plants and animals. Make a two-column chart and have children list different things we get from different plants or animals. For example, jeans come from a cotton plant and eggs come from chickens.

Science Center Card

Activity Resources, Page 113

Science Center Card 24

Caring for Earth
Make a Graph

Objectives

- Children sort and graph objects to show which can be recycled and which can not.

What you need

- **Science Center Card 24**
- Activity Resources, Science Center Card 24, p. 114
- items such as aluminum can, newspaper, white paper, pencil, eraser, chalk, chalk eraser, empty plastic bottle, etc.; crayon

What to do

- Collect items for the children to sort through. Six to 10 of the 12 items per group should be recyclable. You may wish to send a note home asking parents to send in a few recyclable items. Be sure to list options for parents.

- Be sure not to put more than five of one type of recyclable in each grouping because the graph only goes up to five.

- Place all materials in the Science Center.

- Be sure children understand the activity before they begin. Read the steps aloud.

- Point out the graph on the worksheet and explain that children are to color in one square for each recyclable item.

- Have children use their charts to answer the questions.

Informal Assessment

- Show children a filled-in graph with different results than they had. Ask: "Which is the largest group of recyclables? Which is the smallest group?"

- Check children's filled in worksheets.

Follow-Up

- Have children track one week of recycling at home, writing down how many aluminum cans or pieces of plastic they recycle each day. Use the data to make a class recycling graph.

Science Center Card

Activity Resources, Page 114

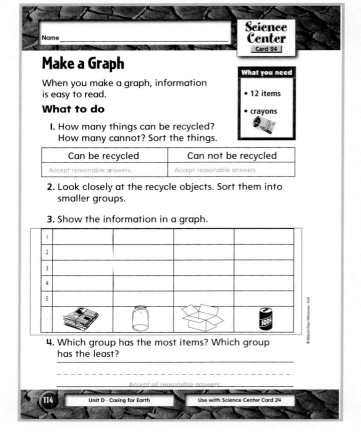

For Your Reference

Skills Handbook

Science Handbook

Health Handbook

Glossary

R 1

Science Skill
BUILDER

Science Process Skill *observe*

Pacing 15–20 minutes

Grouping pairs

What to do

Start by reading and discussing the activity. Caution children never to taste something without permission from a trusted adult—a parent or teacher.

2 You might prompt observations by asking: What color is it? Is it large? Is it small? What shape is it? Is it smooth? Is it fluffy? Is it heavy? Is it light? How does it smell? Is it hard? Is it soft?

3 Encourage children to share their observations.

4 Children can trade objects with a partner. Do they make the same observations?

Going Further

Have children find two objects that have a similar property, such as color or texture.

 ## Technology

■ Skills and Handbook Transparencies R2–R12: *Skills Handbook*

Science Skill Builder 1

Observe

You **observe** with your senses. You see, hear, touch, smell, and taste.

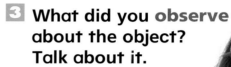

What to do

1 Pick an object in your classroom.

2 Look at it. Touch it. Smell it. Does it make sound?

3 What did you **observe** about the object? Talk about it.

4 Observe other objects.

R 2

Process Skills
MiniLesson

Observe

Develop Observing involves using the senses to determine the properties of an object or event. Children may directly observe something to determine its physical properties. They may manipulate an object to discover some of its properties. They may observe something such as the Sun over time to observe how it seems to change position.

Practice Provide children with a marble, a small rubber or plastic ball, and a ball of clay. Ask questions such as the following: What shape is each object? What happens when you drop each object? Do they all roll? As children answer the questions, have them tell which sense or senses they are using.

Compare

You **compare** when you observe how things are alike and different.

What to do

1 **Compare** the orange and apple.

2 Name two ways they are alike.

3 Name two ways they are different.

4 Compare other things in your classroom.

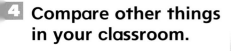

SKILLS HANDBOOK

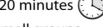

Science Skill
BUILDER

Science Process Skill *compare*

Pacing 15–20 minutes 🕐

Grouping small groups

What to do
Start by reading and discussing the activity.

1 Suggest that children identify the kinds of things they can compare, such as shape, color, size, and texture. Children may also suggest taste using past experiences.

2 Draw two large overlapping circles on the board. Label the space to the left *Apple* and the space to the right *Orange*. As children tell how the two fruits are alike, list their observations in the overlapping space. (Both are fruits, are round shaped, have seeds inside, and taste sweet.)

3 As children identify how the orange and apple are different, list their observations in the corresponding spaces to the left or right. (The orange has bumpy skin, is orange in color, very juicy and soft on the inside. The apple has smooth skin, is red in color, hard and crunchy.)

Going Further
Have children choose another fruit to compare with the apple or orange—a banana, for example.

Process Skills
MiniLesson

Compare

Develop Comparing involves observing the properties of two or more things, to tell how they are alike and different. Children may measure to compare the weight, temperature, dimensions, volume, and mass of objects.

Practice Provide small groups of children with a tape measure, a balance, and an apple and an orange. Have them use the tape measure and the balance to compare the two fruits to find out how they are alike and different. Prompt children with questions such as the following: Does one fruit have more mass than the other fruit? Is one fruit longer around than the other fruit? Cut the fruits into halves so children can directly observe other differences between them.

Science Skill
BUILDER

Science Process Skill *measure*

Pacing 15–20 minutes

Grouping pairs

Plan Ahead Have on hand rulers and/or measuring tapes, crayons, connecting cubes, and other objects children can use to measure length.

What to do
Read and discuss the activity with the class before children begin.

1 and **2** Remind children to place the clips and pencils end to end across their desk, making the line as straight as possible as they measure. The lengths in paper clips and pencils will depend on the length of the clips and pencils children use.

3 List children's suggestions on the board, such as blocks, connecting cubes, counters (math manipulatives) or bingo chips. Have them take turns trying them and reporting the results.

Going Further
Encourage children to explain why they think that all the paper clips or pencils they use to measure should be the same lengths. Have them examine the units on a ruler or measuring tape as a clue if necessary.

Science Skill Builder 3

Measure
You **measure** to find out the size or amount of something.

What you nee

same-size paper clips

same-size pencils

What to do

1 Place paper clips across your desk like this. How many paper clips wide is your desk?

2 Use pencils to **measure** your desk. How many pencils wide is your desk?

3 What else could you use to measure the desk? Try it.

R 4

Process Skills
MiniLesson

Measure

Develop Measuring involves using appropriate units of measurement to quantitatively describe objects and events, estimating, recording data, and space or time relationships. Measuring requires tools such as a thermometer, scale, balance, ruler, and measuring cups.

Practice Display a balance, thermometer, ruler, a measuring cup, and measuring spoons. Review how they are used to measure mass, temperature, distance, and volume. Display a variety of items such as a textbook, a cup of ice water, a small bag of sand, and a large wooden block. Children can use the tools to measure the objects in different ways.

Classify

You classify when you make groups that are alike.

What to do

1 Look at these buttons.

2 Classify the buttons by color. Draw the groups.

3 Find a new way to classify the buttons. Draw the groups.

SKILLS HANDBOOK

Science Skill
BUILDER

Science Process Skill *classify*

Pacing 15–20 minutes

Grouping small groups

Plan Ahead Have children bring in a variety of old buttons or other common items, such as coins or seashells.

What to do
Read and discuss the activity with the class before children begin.

1 Ask children to observe such things as color, shape, size, texture, and so on.

2 Remind children that when they classify, they put together all the things that are alike in some way. Ask how many groups they can make.

3 Remind children of their earlier observations and to think of new ways to classify, such as by the number of holes in the buttons. Are all the buttons the same size? Do all the buttons have the same number of holes?

Going Further
Have children find other things in the classroom to classify, such as writing utensils or paper clips.

Process Skills
MiniLesson

Classify

Develop Classifying involves grouping objects or events according to their properties on the basis of observations. The observer looks for similarities and differences of whatever properties are selected.

Practice Invite children to form a large circle around the room. Ask all children who wear blue shirts to form a group inside the circle. Then have children rejoin the circle. Then ask all children who have black shoes to form a group inside the circle. Continue the activity by having children suggest other ways they can classify themselves into groups. Record the different classifications to review at the end of the activity.

Science Skill
BUILDER

Science Process Skill *communicate*

Pacing 15–20 minutes

Grouping pairs

What to do
Read and discuss the activity with the class before children begin.

1 Have children count the boys and girls as separate groups.

2 Remind children to give their graph a title. Ask how many rows they should make and to explain why.

3 Encourage children to compare their graphs. Do they all show the same results? Encourage children to explain why the results should be the same for all of the graphs.

Going Further
Have children use the information in their graph to solve problems such as the following: How many children are there in all? How many more (or fewer) boys are there than girls?

Communicate

You **communicate** to share ideas. You can talk, write, or draw to communicate.

What to do

1 How many boys and girls are in class today? Count them.

2 **Communicate** this information. Make a graph like the girl did.

3 Talk about your graph.

What you nee

crayons

drawing paper

R 6

Process Skills
MiniLesson

Communicate

Develop Communicating involves using the written and spoken word as well as graphs, tables, diagrams, and other forms of presentations to convey one's observations and ideas.

Practice Write the following questions on the board: What is the weather like today? How many boys and girls have curly hair? Which do most children like best—pizza, burgers, or peanut butter and jelly sandwiches? Have children choose any one of the questions or come up with one of their own, make observations, and then choose a way to communicate the answer to others.

Put Things in Order

You put things in **order** when you tell what happens first, next, and last.

What to do

1 Think of a favorite story.

2 Draw three pictures to show what happens first, next, and last.

3 Mix up your pictures. Have a friend put them in **order**.

What you need

crayons

drawing paper

SKILLS HANDBOOK

R 7

Science Skill
BUILDER

Science Process Skill *put things in order*

Pacing 15–20 minutes

Grouping pairs

What to do
Read and discuss the activity with the class before children begin.

1 Have children name some of their favorite stories. List them on the board, and have children each choose one.

2 Encourage children to think about the most important events in their favorite story and then draw what happens first, next, and last.

3 After children trade pictures and put them in order, encourage them to tell what happens first, next, and last.

Going Further
Have children write what happens first, next, and last on separate strips of paper and then mix up the strips and pictures. Children can then trade strips and pictures with another friend, match each picture and strip, and then put them in order.

Process Skills
MiniLesson

Put Things in Order

Develop Putting things in order is essential when communicating observations and predicting what can happen next in a new or changed situation.

Practice Display a series of pictures in random order that show the stages of growth of a plant, the seasons of the year, the stages of a storm, or similar events. Encourage children to arrange the pictures in order suggesting the thing that happens first. As they arrange the cards ask them to use words such as first, second, next, then, after that, and last to help tell about the events in order.

Science Skill
BUILDER

Science Process Skill *infer*

Pacing 15–20 minutes

Grouping pairs

What to do
Read and discuss the activity with the class before children begin.

 Ask: Did a person or an animal make the footprints at the left? What did they step in to make the footprints? Are the footprints inside or outside? Can you tell where? (Children should say that the footprints at the left were made by a bird with webbed feet, such as duck or gull and that the bird was walking in sand along a beach. The other photo shows a bear walking.)

2 Encourage children to use what they know to figure out where the animal went and what it may have been doing. (Children may infer from the picture that the bird was walking along the beach near the water's edge, probably to find food.)

Going Further
Have children infer the direction the bird was walking in (top left to bottom right).

Infer

You infer when you use what you know to figure something out.

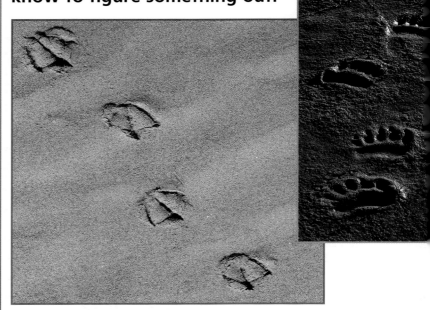

What to do

1 **What do you know about these footprints?**

2 **Use what you know to infer which set of footprints the bird made. Talk about it.**

R 8

Process Skills
MiniLesson

Infer

Develop Inferring involves drawing a conclusion about an event based on observations and data. Inferring also requires evaluation and judgment to determine which observations are relative and which ones are not.

Practice Display an unlabeled container of very warm water and an unlabeled container of very cold water. Place a thermometer in each container. Invite children to observe the containers without touching them and infer which container holds warm water and which container holds cold water.

Make a Model

You make a model to show how a place looks or how a thing works. This model shows what the girl's schoolyard looks like.

What to do

1. Think of a place in your school. Plan a model of that place.

2. Decide how to make the model look real.

3. Make a model. Share it with others.

R 9

Science Skill
BUILDER

Science Process Skill *make a model*

Pacing 30 minutes

Grouping small groups

Plan Ahead Have a variety of art materials on hand, such as shoe-box lids or boxes, construction paper, cardboard, scissors, crayons, chalk, glue, toy furniture, and so on

What to do

Caution children to handle scissors and any other sharp objects with care. Read and discuss the activity with the class before children begin.

1. Have children name places in the school, such as the library, cafeteria, classroom, office, gym, lavatory, hallway, playground. List suggestions on the board and have children choose one they would like to model.

2. Suggest children think about what to include in their models and the materials they will need to make their models. Do they want to draw features? Do they want to make cutouts? Do they want to use toys?

3. Without revealing what the room or place is, have children share their models with others. Can they figure out where it is in the school?

Going Further

Have children make a tabletop model of the classroom.

Process Skills

MiniLesson

Make a Model

Develop Making a model involves representing a place or thing using a physical model. A model can be used to describe and explain a process or phenomenon.

Practice Have children look around the classroom and identify any models you use to teach science or other subjects or models that would be considered toys. Models may include the human skeleton and organs such as the heart, a model dinosaur or other animal, a globe, an airplane or other vehicle. As children identify models, have them tell what they can learn about the real object by studying the model.

Science Skill
BUILDER

Science Process Skill *predict*

Pacing 15–20 minutes

Grouping pairs

What to do
Read and discuss the activity with the class before children begin.

1. Have children identify the objects in the picture, tell what is happening, and where. (The picture shows a beach ball sailing through the air in the direction of a small lamp sitting on a table.)

2. Children's drawings should show the lamp knocked over, possibly onto the floor, with the ball at rest nearby.

Going Further
Have children draw a story based on their observations to explain why the beach ball is sailing across the room toward a lamp in the first place, what happens when the ball hits the lamp, and what happens when the lamp is discovered. Discuss the safety implications of why tossing balls is not to be done indoors.

Predict

You **predict** when you use what you observe to tell what will happen next.

What to do

1. Look at the picture. What do you observe?

2. Draw a picture to show what you **predict** will happen next.

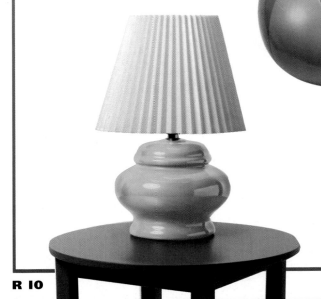

R 10

Process Skills
MiniLesson

Predict

Develop Predicting involves anticipating what will happen in a situation based on one's observations, past experiences, or data.

Practice Use wooden blocks to build two towers about the same height. Some of the blocks should be off center on one of the towers so that it will likely tumble when one or two more blocks are added. The other tower should be constructed so that two or more blocks can be added without the tower tumbling. Have children observe the two towers and predict which one will tumble first when more blocks are added. Then add the blocks and have children tell whether they predicted correctly.

nvestigate

ou investigate when you make a lan and then try it out.

What to do

1. **Investigate** the easiest way to get from your classroom to the cafeteria.

2. **Make a plan to find out which way is easiest. Share your plan with others.**

3. **Try out your plan.**

R II

SKILLS HANDBOOK

Science Skill
BUILDER

Science Process Skill *investigate*

Pacing 30 minutes

Grouping small groups

What to do
Read and discuss the activity with the class before children begin.

1. Encourage children to identify possible routes from the classroom to the cafeteria.

2. Have children consider the different routes and ways to decide which route is easiest. Will they count how many steps it takes to find out the shortest route? Will they use a stopwatch to find out the fastest route?

3. Have children try out their plans and share the results.

Going Further
Have children compare the different routes and then arrange them in order from shortest to longest.

Process Skills
MiniLesson

Investigate

Develop Investigating involves developing a plan, testing it, and then observing the results.

Practice Pass around a magnet and paper clip for children to observe how a magnet will attract certain metallic objects. Then provide children with a variety of nonmetallic and metallic objects such as a safety pin, nail, stainless steel spoon, scissors, washer, bolt, screw, eraser, crayon, wooden clothespin, eraser, connecting cube, pencil. Have children investigate by predicting the objects the magnet will and will not attract and then testing each object to see if they are correct.

Science Skill
BUILDER

Science Process Skill *draw a conclusion*

Pacing 10–15 minutes

Grouping pairs

What to do
Read and discuss the activity with the class before children begin.

1️⃣ As children look at the picture, suggest they observe where the girl is sitting, what is on the table, and what she is holding. Ask what they think she is about to do. (The picture shows a girl sitting at a table with a bowl of soup in front of her and a fork in her hand.)

2️⃣ Children should conclude that the girl cannot eat the soup because she does not have a spoon.

Going Further
Have children look at the girl's expression and draw a conclusion about what she might be thinking.

Draw a Conclusion

You **draw a conclusion** when you use what you observe to explain what happens.

What to do

1️⃣ Look at the picture. What do you observe?

2️⃣ Can you **draw a conclusion** about what's wrong here? Talk about it.

R 12

Process Skills
MiniLesson

Draw a Conclusion

Develop Drawing a conclusion involves using observations to explain what happens in events.

Practice Tell children the following story: *When Max woke up this morning, he was happy to see all the snow. He could hardly wait to go outside to build a snowman. After quickly eating dinner, he put on his sneakers, baseball cap, and sweatshirt. He was ready to go out and play in* *the snow.* Have children draw a conclusion about what is wrong in the story and then retell it correctly.

Save and Recycle

We should not waste things.

...e no more
...an you need.

...n't leave
...e water on.

...cycle as much
...you can.

Use things more than once.

R 13

SCIENCE FOR ALL

Inclusion

Conserving Resources

Explain to children that many of the things we use every day, such as water, paper, and electricity, are limited natural resources. Helping to conserve these kinds of materials can prevent damage to Earth's environment. Have children tell how they can help to conserve water, paper, and electricity at home. **Linguistic**

Save and Recycle

Objective
■ Learn ways to conserve and reuse resources.

Build on Prior Knowledge
Ask:

- **What kinds of things do people recycle?** (paper, glass, metal, cloth)

- **What happens to the things that we recycle?** (The materials are used again to make new objects.)

Using the Illustrations
Ask children to tell how each picture shows a way to save materials.

Exploring the Main Idea
Write "Save and Recycle Tips" on a sheet of chart paper. Ask children to think about specific things they do to save or recycle and share their ideas. Record their ideas as tips. For example: use one tissue to blow your nose if you can; use one paper towel sheet to dry your hands if you can; use up colored paper scraps first; don't let the water run when you brush your teeth; report any leaky faucets; take a quick shower; use plastic milk jugs to make bird feeders; and cut two-liter plastic soda containers in half and use as planters.

Informal Assessment
Ask:

- **What are two things you can do to avoid wasting materials?** (Possible responses: Turn off running water, use up small pieces of paper and scraps first, make sure the water isn't running, reuse plastic containers, reuse paper bags.)

Children can draw, write about, or discuss their ideas about ways to avoid wasting materials.

Technology

- Skills and Handbook Transparencies R13–R26: *Science Handbook*

Science Handbook **R13**

Care of Animals

Care of Animals

Objective

- Learn appropriate ways to care for and observe animals.

Build on Prior Knowledge
Ask:

- **How do you help take care of your pet?** (by providing it food, water, and exercise, and by taking it to the vet)

Using the Illustrations
Ask:

- **How can you tell that the animals are cared for?** (The dog has food and the frog is being handled gently.)

Developing the Main Idea
Ask:

- **Why must you feed and give water to classroom pets?** (They cannot get the food or water they need on their own.)

- **Why must you handle classroom animals very carefully?** (If handled roughly, classroom animals may be hurt or may bite.)

- **When might a wild animal be dangerous?** (when they are surprised, threatened, or if they are protecting their young)

Informal Assessment
Ask:

- **Why should you treat wild animals with more caution than classroom pets?** (Many pets are tame and are used to being touched or handled, but wild animals are not and may bite or attack if you try to touch them or come near them.)

Children can draw, write about, or discuss their experiences in taking care of animals at home or in the classroom.

Here are ways to care for animals.

- Give pets food and water. Give them a safe place to live, too.

- Be kind to pets. Handle them with care.

- Don't touch wild animals. They may bite, sting, or scratch you.

- Do not touch things in places where wild animals live.

R 14

 English Language Learners

Wild Animals
Explain to children that most animals that live outdoors in and around their hometowns are not dangerous to people unless the animals are threatened. However, animals can carry disease or parasites that are dangerous to people. Have children discuss what they would or would not do if they were to see a raccoon or strange dog in their backyard during the day. **Linguistic; Logical**

Care of Plants

Here are ways to care for plants.

- Give plants water and sunlight.

- Ask the teacher before you touch or eat a plant. Some plants can make you very sick!

- Do not dig up plants or pick flowers. Let plants grow where they are.

R 15

Science Background

Plant Needs

Discuss with children that plants need food, soil, water, sunlight, and space in order to live. Soil provides the nutrients for the plant. During daylight, leaves manufacture food from water that is taken in by the roots and carbon dioxide in the air taken in by the leaves. Sunlight provides the energy for this process. Have children discuss whether they think outdoor plants need to be watered like indoor plants. (Most outdoor plants get enough water from rain.) **Logical**

Care of Plants

Objective

- Learn appropriate ways to care for and observe plants.

Build on Prior Knowledge
Ask:

- **How do you care for plants?** (Water them, pull weeds, place plants in bigger pots as they grow, pick off dead leaves.)

Using the Illustrations
Ask:

- **How can you tell that the plant near the window has been cared for?** (It looks big and healthy.)

Developing the Main Idea
Ask:

- **What can happen if you forget to water a plant?** (The leaves may start to wilt and it may die.)

- **What should you do if someone eats a plant and gets sick?** (Tell a responsible adult right away, if one is around. Call 911.)

- **Why shouldn't you dig up wild plants or pick flowers?** (They could be rare and protected by law. You may also be taking away food and homes for animals.)

Informal Assessment
Ask:

- **What can you do if a plant starts to look unhealthy?** (Possible responses: move it to a spot where it can get more sunlight, check to see if the plant needs water or if it has too much water)

Children can draw, write about, or discuss their experiences in taking care of plants at home or in the classroom.

Clean Up

Objective
■ Learn clean-up procedures to use during and after science activities.

Build on Prior Knowledge

Invite children to share their experiences helping adults clean up a work space after a project. Ask:

■ **Why is it important to clean up after a project?** (to prevent accidents and so that the work space is clean for next time)

Using the Illustrations

Have children tell how each picture shows a way to keep themselves or the classroom clean and safe.

Developing the Main Idea

Ask:

■ **What can happen if broken glass is not cleaned up?** (Someone could fall or step on the glass and get cut.)

■ **Why shouldn't you pour water in the trash can?** (Everything in the can would get soggy and the water may leak onto the floor.)

■ **What can you wear so you don't get paint on your clothing?** (an apron, smock, or old shirt)

■ **After wrapping certain foods, why might you put them in the refrigerator?** (to keep them from spoiling) **What should you do with old food? Why?** (throw it away because it could attract bugs, mice, or rats)

Informal Assessment

Ask:

■ **What should you do if a glass bottle breaks in the classroom?** (Tell the teacher so the glass can be safely cleaned up.)

Children can draw, write about, or discuss ways of keeping themselves or their work areas clean.

Clean Up

We need to keep work places clean.

Let an adult clean up broken glass.

Pour water into a sink not into a trash can.

Put food in plastic bag. This keeps bugs away.

Don't get paint or food on you.

R 16

 SCIENCE FOR ALL

Inclusion

What Should You Do? Why?

Present scenarios such as the following: Ann knocked over a big jar of paint on the table; Max left the scissors, tape, string, glue, and ruler on the floor; Al over-watered the plants and water is dripping onto the floor; Jeb poked a hole in the bag of potting soil. Have children show or tell what they would do to help clean up.
Linguistic; Social

How to Measure

You can use many things to measure.

This string is about 8 paper clips long.

This string is about 3 pencils long.

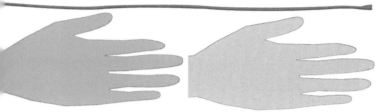

This string is about 2 hands long.

Try This!

- **Measure some string. Tell how you did it.**

- **Can you measure string with these paper clips? Why or why not?**

R 17

Science Background

Ancient Units of Measurement
In ancient times, body parts were used as units of measurement. A cubit was the length of the arm from an adult elbow to the tip of the middle finger. A foot was about the length of a foot, and a yard was the distance from the tip of a nose to the tip of the person's middle finger when the arm was extended.

How to Measure

Objective

- Measure lengths in nonstandard units.

Materials: paper clips, unsharpened pencils, string

Build on Prior Knowledge
Display a ruler and a pencil that are obviously different lengths. Ask:

- **Which is longer, the pencil or the ruler?** (ruler)

- **How can you prove that the ruler is longer than the pencil?** (put them side by side and compare)

Using the Illustrations
Ask:

- **What unit of measurement is used to measure the first string?** (paper clips) **the second string?** (pencils) **the third string?** (hands)

Developing the Main Idea
After you read the sentences under the pictures, have children count the paper clips, pencils, and hands to verify the lengths. Ask:

- **What do you notice about the 8 clips, the 3 pencils, and the 2 hands?** (All the clips are the same length, all the pencils are the same length, and the two hands are the same length.) Point out that you can use any object to measure something, but the same object must be used over and over.

Exploring the Main Idea
Have children do the Try This! activity.

Answer to Try This!
Yes; the clips are all the same length.

Informal Assessment
Ask:

- **What is the length of your science book in paper clips?** (Children should lay paper clips end-to-end.) Have children measure the length and width of their desk top by using unshaved pencils.

Units of Measurement

Objective

- Recognize centimeter as a standard unit of length.

Materials: metric rulers

Build on Prior Knowledge
Ask:

- **What tool do you use to measure length?**
  (a ruler)

Using the Illustrations
Ask:

- **What do the numbers on the ruler show?**
  (how many centimeters there are on the ruler)

- **How many centimeters apart are 0 and 1, 1 and 2, 2 and 3, and so on?** (one centimeter)

Exploring the Main Idea
Ask:

- **Where does the end of the crayon line up on the ruler?** (with the 0) **Where does the end of the insect line up on the ruler?** (with the 0)

Help children count the centimeters on the rulers to find the lengths. Make sure children count the centimeter marks and not the millimeter marks of the ruler.

Answer to Try This!
about 15 centimeters

Informal Assessment
Distribute drawing paper and metric rulers. Say:

- **Draw a line 6 centimeters long. Draw another line 11 centimeters long.** (Check children's work.)

Units of Measurement

There are other ways to measure. You can use centimeters (cm) or meters (m). These are called units of measurement.

The crayon is about 8 centimeters long. We write this as 8 cm

The insect is about 4 centimeters long. We write this as 4 cm.

Try This!

- **How long is this pencil?**

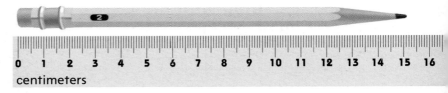

R 18

Science Background

Measurement Systems
There are two measurement systems commonly used, the customary system (English system) and the metric system (SI). Metric units are used in science and throughout most of the world today.

Use a Ruler

You can use a ruler to measure this leaf. Line up the end of the leaf with the 0 on the ruler. The leaf is about 11 centimeters, or 11 cm.

Try This!

Estimate how long each object is. Use a ruler to measure.

Object	Estimate	Measure
scissors	about ____ cm	about ____ cm
penny	about ____ cm	about ____ cm
toy car	about ____ cm	about ____ cm

R 19

Inclusion

SCIENCE FOR ALL

Estimating and Measuring
Children work in pairs. Each partner chooses three different objects and measures the length, width, or height of each. A partner displays one of his or her objects and has the other partner estimate how long, wide, or high it is. Both partners decide if the estimate is accurate. They repeat the estimating procedure, reversing roles as necessary.
Logical; Social

Use a Ruler

Objective
- Use a centimeter ruler to measure length.

Materials: metric rulers, scissors, toy car, penny

Build on Prior Knowledge
Have children look at a metric ruler. Ask:

- **How many centimeters are on the ruler? How do we write that?** (Record the ruler's length on the board.)

Using the Illustrations
Ask:

- **Where does the stem of the leaf line up on the ruler?** (with 0)

- **What can happen if it does not line up with the 0?** (You don't get the correct measurement.)

Have children use their rulers to measure the leaf.

Exploring the Main Idea
Hold up a pencil that is about 10 centimeters long. Ask:

- **About how many centimeters long do you think this pencil is?** (Accept reasonable estimates.)

- **How can you find out if your guess is correct?** (Use a metric ruler to measure it.)

Demonstrate how to measure the pencil. Then ask children to find something that is less than 10 cm long, such as chalk, a crayon, or a paper clip.

Have children do the Try This! activity.

Answers to Try This!
Estimates and actual lengths depend on the objects available in the classroom.

Informal Assessment
Have children find the length of something that is longer than 10 centimeters and demonstrate how they measured the object. (Check children's measurements.)

Children may write about or discuss measuring objects in centimeters.

Use a Thermometer

Objective

- Use a thermometer to compare and read temperatures.

Material: primary thermometers (optional)

Build on Prior Knowledge
Ask:

- **What tool do we use to measure the air temperature outside?** (thermometer)

- **Why is it helpful to know the temperature?** (Possible response: so you can decide what clothing to wear or what activities to do)

Using the Illustrations
Ask:

- **Which thermometer shows a higher or warmer temperature? How can you tell?** (Thermometer B on the right; the red line is higher.)

Exploring the Main Idea
You may wish to use adapted primary thermometers to show children how to compare temperatures. Directions for making primary thermometers can be found on page TR6 in this Teacher Edition.

Have children take a close look at a primary thermometer that has been stored in a cool place. Point out where the liquid is, and have children tell if the thermometer shows a cold, cool, warm, or hot temperature. Call on volunteers to each put a finger on the bulb of the remaining thermometers and to observe what happens. Ask:

- **Does the liquid move up or down?** (up)

- **Is the temperature getting warmer or cooler?** (warmer) Help children read the thermometers, noting whether the temperatures are cold, cool, warm, or hot.

Use a Thermometer

A thermometer measures temperature.

It gets warmer. The liquid in a thermometer moves up.

It gets cooler. The liquid in a thermometer moves down.

Which thermometer shows a warmer temperature? How can you tell?

R 20

Inclusion

Cold, Cool, Warm, Hot
Have children fold a sheet of drawing paper into four quarters and label each quarter *cold, cool, warm, hot*. Have children draw or write the names of things that fit each label.

Use this key:

cold	0°C and below
cool	1°C to 15°C
warm	15°C to 30°C
hot	above 30°C

Logical; Spatial

thermometer has marks with numbers.

degrees
Celsius

degrees
Fahrenheit

Read this thermometer in degrees Celsius. Find the number just below the place where the liquid ends.

The number is 20. Count on 2 degrees for each mark after 20 as: 22, 24, 26. The thermometer shows 26 degrees Celsius, or 26°C.

 Try This!

What temperatures are shown on page R20?

Developing the Main Idea

Remind children that there are different units of measurement. A centimeter is a unit of length. Degrees Celsius and degrees Fahrenheit are units of temperature.

Using the Illustrations

Have children place their finger on the 20 degree Celsius mark and count by twos as they move their finger up each mark of the thermometer. Ask:

■ **What is the temperature on the Celsius scale?** (26 degrees)

Explain that children are now to find the Celsius temperatures shown on the two thermometers on page R20.

Answers to Try This!

Thermometer A: 10 degrees Celsius (50 degrees Fahrenheit)

Thermometer B: 22 degrees Celsius (72 degrees Fahrenheit)

Informal Assessment

Display or draw two thermometers, one with a lower temperature. Ask:

■ **How do you know which thermometer shows the lower temperature?** (Look for the thermometer that has the red line on the lower number.)

Children may write or discuss their experiences in finding temperatures using thermometers.

Science Background

Scale Names

You may wish to point out that the names of the two temperature scales, Fahrenheit and Celsius, were the last names of actual people. Gabriel Daniel Fahrenheit was a German scientist, who lived from 1686 to 1736. He improved the already existing alcohol thermometers by replacing the alcohol with mercury, which gave more accurate readings. The zero degree reading on this scale is the freezing point of a mixture of liquid water, salt, and ice. In 1742, a Swedish scientist, Anders Celsius, based the zero-degree his scale on the freezing point of pure water.

Use a Measuring Cup

Volume is the amount of space something takes up. You can use a measuring cup to find volume.

The marks on this cup show the number of milliliters. There are 500 milliliters (500 mL) of water in this cup.

measuring cup

Objective

- Use a measuring cup to compare the volumes of containers.

Materials per group: metric measuring cup, 3 containers of different sizes, water

Build on Prior Knowledge
Hold up a metric measuring cup. Ask:

- **Why do people use measuring cups like this when they cook or bake?** (to make sure they put in the right amounts)

Developing the Main Idea
Pass around a metric measuring cup for children to examine. Point out the marks and numbers. Help children understand what each line of the measuring cup stands for. You may mention that liters and milliliters are standard units used for measuring volume in the metric system and that milliliters are used to measure small volumes.

Exploring the Main Idea
Have children do the Try This! activity. Ask:

- **How can you use a measuring cup to find how many milliliters of water a small drinking cup holds?** (Pour the water into the measuring cup and then read the line next to the water line.)

Demonstrate for children and then help them to read the mark next to the water line.

Answers to Try This!
Answers will depend on the containers used.

Informal Assessment
Write *800 mL* and *300 mL* on the board. Ask:

- **Which holds more water, a glass that holds 800 mL or a cup that holds 300 mL? How do you know?** (The glass; 800 mL is greater than 300 mL.)

Children can draw, write about, or discuss their experiences with using measuring cups to compare the volumes of containers.

Try This!

- Get 3 different small containers.

- Which holds the most? Which holds the least?

- Fill each container with water. Pour the water into the measuring cup. Find the volumes.

R 22

Advanced Learners

Least to the Greatest
Have children form small groups. Provide each with 4–5 containers of varying shapes and capacities filled with water, a measuring cup, a large container to collect the water, and paper to record how much water each one contains. Challenge children to arrange the containers in order from the least volume to the greatest volume. **Logical; Social**

Use a Balance

balance compares mass.

ace one object on each
e of the balance. The
ject that has more mass will
ake that side of the balance go down.
e object that has less mass will make
at side of the balance go up.

Try This!

Place 2 objects on a balance.
Which has more mass?

Put 3 objects in order from least mass
to most mass. Use the balance to check.

Before you compare mass, make
sure the arrow points to the line.

R 23

English Language Learners

More or Less? Most or Least?
Have children write *more, less,*
most, and *least* on index cards.
Call on volunteers to use a
balance to compare the mass
of two or three objects while
the rest of the children
observe. Have observers then
hold up the correct card as you
point to the block that has
more or less mass or the block
that has the most or least mass.
Logical

Use a Balance

Objective

- Use a balance to compare the
  masses of objects.

Materials per group: pan balance, 3 or more objects
with different masses

Build on Prior Knowledge
Display a pan balance and ask:

- **How is this balance different from a scale?**
  (A scale does not have two pans like a balance.
  A scale measures weight, a balance does not.)

Using the Illustrations
Ask:

- **What is different in the two pictures?** (In the
  top one, there are no objects in the pans of the
  balance. In the bottom one, there is an object in
  each pan.)

- **In the second picture, why is the pan with the
  feather higher than the pan with the other
  object?** (The other object has more mass than
  the feather, so that side of the balance goes
  lower and the pan with the feather goes higher.)

Exploring the Main Idea
Let children examine a balance, noting the arrow,
the line, and how the pans go up and down. Ask:

- **Where does the arrow point when both pans
  are empty?** (to the line)

- **What do you think happens to the line when
  you put something heavy in one pan and
  something lighter in the other pan?** (The pans
  move up or down and make the center line
  move away from the arrow.)

Have children do the Try This! activity.

Answers to Try This!
Answers will depend on the objects used.

Informal Assessment
Provide children with a pair of objects and a balance
scale. Ask:

- **Which object has less mass?** (The one in the pan
  that is higher when both objects are placed in the
  balance.)

Children can draw, write about, or discuss their
experiences with using balances to compare the masses
of objects.

Use a Clock

- Use a clock to measure elapsed time.

Materials connecting cubes, classroom clock

Build on Prior Knowledge
Have children describe clocks and watches they have seen.

Using the Illustrations
Ask:

- **How is the top clock pictured like our classroom clock?** (It has two hands, numbers 1–12, and marks to show minutes.)

- **How are the two hands of the clock different?** (The hour hand is shorter than the minute hand.)

Using the Illustrations
Ask:

- **What time is it on the top clock?** (10 o'clock) **How can you tell?** (The hour hand is on 10 and the minute hand is on 12.)

- **Where is the hour hand on the left clock at the bottom of the page?** (half way between 1 and 2) **Where is the minute hand?** (on 6) Have children count by 5s to 30 as you point to the numbers 1 to 6.

- **How can you tell that it is 9:05 on the right clock?** (The minute hand is on 1, which means that it is 5 minutes after the hour.)

Have children do the Try This! activity.

Answer to Try This!
Answers will vary.

Informal Assessment
Have children estimate how long it will take them to snap together 15 connecting cubes, one at a time, and then take them apart, one at a time. Have children record their estimates and then have a partner time them. Ask:

- **About how many minutes did it take?** (Answers will depend on how quickly children snap together and take apart the cubes.)

Children may write about or discuss time estimates for other kinds of activities.

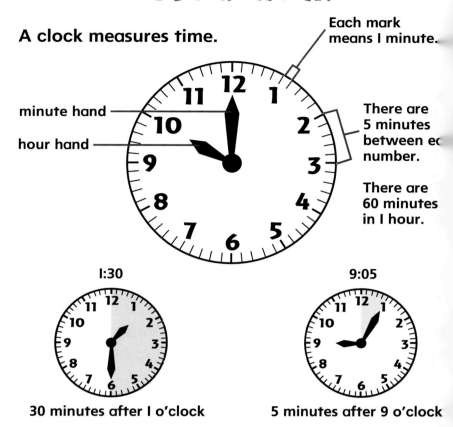

Use a Clock

A clock measures time.

Each mark means 1 minute.

minute hand

hour hand

There are 5 minutes between each number.

There are 60 minutes in 1 hour.

1:30
30 minutes after 1 o'clock

9:05
5 minutes after 9 o'clock

Try This!

How long do you think it takes to write your name 5 times? Have a friend time you.

R 24

Advanced Learners

What Time Is It Now?
Provide pairs of children with two clock faces that have movable hands. Tell them it is 9:15. Have one partner show this time on a clock face. Have the other partner show what the time would be ten minutes later on the second clock face. Ask:

- **What time is it now?** (9:25) Repeat so each partner has a chance to show the start and finish times at least twice.
Logical; Social

Use a Hand Lens

hand lens makes objects
em larger.

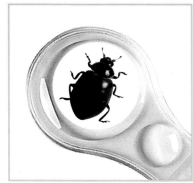

rst, move the lens
way from the object.
op when the object
oks fuzzy.

Next, move the lens a
little closer to the
object. Stop when the
object looks clear.

Try This!

Observe each bug here. Use a hand lens.

How many legs do you see on the bugs?

What else can you see?

R 25

Science Background

Microscopes

In the 17th century, Antonie van Leeuwenhoek built microscopes in which he mounted a single lens. The most powerful of his microscopes magnified objects about 275 times. He was the first person to see one-celled animals with a microscope. Today, optical microscopes can magnify objects 2,000 times, transmission electron microscopes can magnify objects 7,200 times, and the scanning tunneling microscope can produce an image of a single atom.

Use a Hand Lens

Objective
■ Use a hand lens to magnify objects.

Materials hand lens per child or group

Build on Prior Knowledge
Ask:

■ **What do scientists use to observe things that are far away like the planets or very tiny like germs?** (telescopes and microscopes)

Using the Illustrations
Have children compare the two pictures of the insect under the hand lens. Ask:

■ **Why does the insect on the left look fuzzy?** (The hand lens is too far away from the object.)

■ **Should the hand lens be moved closer to the insect in the picture on the right? Why or why not?** (No; the insect looks clear, so the hand lens is in just the right spot.)

Developing the Main Idea
Ask:

■ **How can learning to use a hand lens help you observe?** (Since a hand lens makes an object look larger, you can see more details of what you are observing.)

Exploring the Main Idea
Have children do the Try This! activity.

Answers to Try This!
The spider has 8 legs. The fly has 6 legs. Another observation may include that the spider does not have wings, but the fly does.

Informal Assessment
Ask:

■ **How do you get a clear picture when you use a hand lens?** (Move the lens closer to the object until small details are clear.)

Science Handbook **R25**

Use a Computer

- Recognize that a computer can be used to gather information.

Materials computer with Internet access

Build on Prior Knowledge
Invite children to share their experiences with using computers.

Using the illustrations
Ask:

- **What do the pictures show?** (CD-ROMs and a home page on a computer screen)

Developing the Main Idea
Discuss a computer mouse and how to use it. Ask:

- **Suppose you need help with your math or science. What can you do?** (Go to the Internet and click on Homework Wizard.)

- **How do you get to another window?** (Move the mouse and click on the box or circle you want.)

If available, show children a CD–ROM and how to access the information on it.

Exploring the Main Idea
Have children do the Try This! activity. Have them discuss and write about the areas researched.

Informal Assessment
Ask:

- **What kinds of information can you get from the Internet? Name at least three kinds.** (Accept all reasonable answers.)

Children can write about or discuss their experiences with using the Internet.

Use a Computer

A computer is a tool that can get information.

You can use CD-ROMs. They have a lot of information. You can fit many books on one CD-ROM!

You can also use the Internet. The Internet links your computer to ones far away.

Try This!

- Use the Internet. Visit **www.mhscience02.com** and learn more about science in your world.

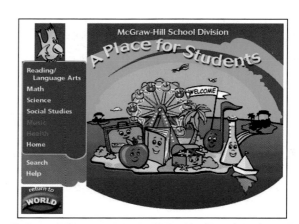

R 26

Science Background

Computer Safety

A computer linked to the Internet is a great source of information, but there are important safety practices that children should follow to avoid possibly being victimized or exposed to inappropriate material. Remind children not to access the Internet without adult supervision or ever tell anyone their name, home address, telephone number, or school name.

Your Body Parts

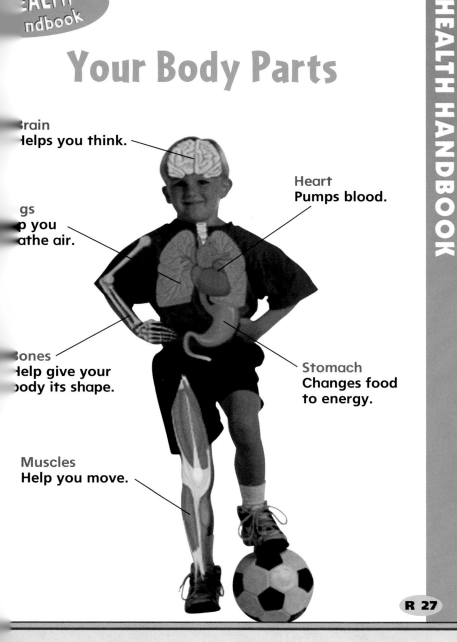

Brain
Helps you think.

Heart
Pumps blood.

Lungs
Help you breathe the air.

Bones
Help give your body its shape.

Stomach
Changes food to energy.

Muscles
Help you move.

R 27

Science Background

Facts about Body Parts

You might want to share these facts about the body parts highlighted on page R27 with children: There are about 700 skeletal muscles and 206 bones in the human body. The brain contains about 10 billion nerve cells. The right lung has three lobes. The left lung has two. Stomach cells live about two days before they are replaced. With every beat, the heart squeezes out about 2.5 ounces of blood.

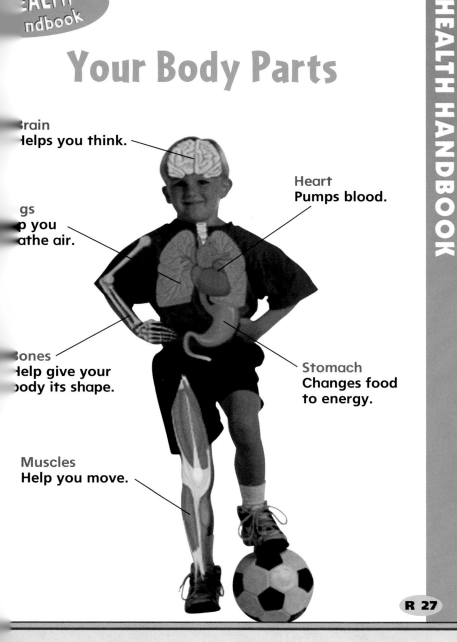

Your Body Parts

Objective

- Recognize basic body parts and what they do.

Build on Prior Knowledge

Ask children to imagine that they can look inside their bodies. Ask:

- **What body parts can you see?** (Possible responses may include the heart, brain, lungs, stomach bones, muscles.)

Using the Illustrations

Ask:

- **How are you like this boy?** (We have the same body parts inside.)

- **How are you different?** (Children may note physical differences such as eye, hair, and skin color, body shape, and sex.)

Exploring the Main Idea

As you read about each body part, pause to have children do the following: 1. Place a hand over their heart to feel it beat. 2. Place their hands on their ribs to feel how they move up and out as they inhale and down and in as they exhale. 3. Feel the skull that protects their brain. 4. Feel how their arm muscles tighten as they make a fist and flex their arm. 5. Listen to stomach noises with a stethoscope, if available.

Informal Assessment

Provide children with body part riddles such as the following: *I am a body part. I pump your blood. What am I?* Have children answer the riddle by pointing to the place where it is found inside their body and naming the body part.

Technology

- Skills and Handbook Transparencies R27–R34

  Health Handbook

- **Science Newsroom CD-ROM**
  Skeleton Key
  Blood Flow

Look Your Best

Objective

- Recognize ways to look your best.

Build on Prior Knowledge
Ask children to think about everything they did before coming to school.

- **What did you do to look and feel your best today?** (Children may mention that they washed, brushed their teeth, combed their hair, put on clean clothes, and ate breakfast.)

Using the Illustrations
Ask:

- **What are these children doing to look their best?** (The girl is brushing her hair; one boy is taking a bath; the other boy is brushing his teeth.)

Developing the Main Idea
Read aloud the tips for looking your best on page R28 with children. Pause to discuss each one. Ask:

- **How can you keep your body clean?** (by bathing or showering, by washing my hands when they get dirty, by washing my hands after going to the washroom, by washing and brushing my hair, by cleaning under my fingernails when they get dirty and keeping them short)

- **What do you think can happen if you cut or scrape your skin?** (Germs can get inside.)

Explain that germs that get into cuts or scrapes can cause infections. Point out that it is important to clean injuries carefully with soap and water.

- **Why should you brush your teeth?** (to help prevent cavities and gum disease) **What else can you do to keep your teeth healthy?** (floss, go to the dentist, eat the right kinds of foods)

Informal Assessment
Ask:

- **How do you feel when you look your best?** (good, happy) **Why?** (Possible responses: because I look good; I am clean and neat; my teeth are brushed.)

Children can write about, draw, or discuss looking and feeling their best.

Keep your body clean.

Brush your teeth.

Sit and stand up tall.

R 28

SCIENCE FOR ALL — Inclusion

Standing Tall
Invite children to demonstrate how to stand tall by holding their head up, chest up and a little forward, shoulders back, arms hanging by their sides, and abdomen flat. Have children then walk around the room as they maintain their posture. **Kinesthetic**

Science Background

Observing Results of a Skin Injury
Show children a fresh, smooth apple. Then make a cut in the skin of the apple and let it sit in the classroom for a few days until the apple shows signs of rotting. Let children observe how the apple has changed, noting how injuries to the skin should be treated to avoid infections. Dispose of the apple after your discussion.

Be Active and Rest

active every day.

sure to get enough
ep and rest, too.

ese things help
u grow!

R 29

Science Background

Sleep Needs

Not everyone needs the same amount of sleep. Many adults sleep from 7 to 8½ hours at night. Newborn babies sleep for short periods throughout the day until they are about 2 to 3 months old, when they learn to sleep through the night. Babies do continue to nap during the day. Four year olds sleep from 10 to 14 hours, while ten year olds sleep from 9 to 12 hours.

Be Active and Rest

Objective

- Recognize the importance of rest and exercise.

Build on Prior Knowledge

Write the words *active* and *rest* on the board. Then call on volunteers to demonstrate what they think each word means. Children may run, skip, hop, or jump to demonstrate *active* and put their heads down on their desks or lie down on the floor and close their eyes to demonstrate *rest*.

Using the Illustrations
Ask:

- **Who is active?** (the children who are running and playing)
- **Who is resting?** (the girl who is asleep)

Developing the Main Idea
Ask:

- **What can you do to be active everyday?** (Children may suggest participating in activities such as soccer, tag, baseball, football, bike-riding, walking, swimming, skating, and jumping rope.)

Emphasize how important it is to be active every day. Point out that being active keeps the heart healthy and the bones and muscles strong.

- **What else does your body need to help you grow?** (rest) Explain that during sleep, energy is restored to the body.

- **What happens when you don't get enough sleep?** (Children may say they feel grumpy, sleepy, and have no energy.)

Informal Assessment

Have children draw a picture to show how they are active, a picture to show how they rest, and then write or dictate a sentence about each healthful behavior.

Eat Healthful Foods

Objective

- Recognize the importance of eating healthful foods.

Build on Prior Knowledge

Invite children to suggest some healthful snacks. List their suggestions on the board. Then ask:

- **What makes a snack healthful?** (Foods that are rich in vitamins and minerals that are low in salt, sugar, and fat make healthful snacks.)

Using the Illustrations

Ask

- **What is the girl eating?** (an apple) **What is an apple?** (a kind of fruit)

Developing the Main Idea

Ask:

- **Why is it important to eat healthful foods?** (They help you to grow.) Explain that food is the source of energy for everything they do and for what their bodies need to work. Have children tell how they feel when they have not eaten and are hungry.
- **What are some healthful foods?** (milk, fruit, bread, vegetables)

Informal Assessment

Provide children with drawing paper and crayons.

- **Plan a healthful meal. Draw a picture to show your choices.** (Children's choices may include a milk product, fruit, bread, and vegetables, as well as meat, poultry, fish, eggs, or nuts.)

Eat Healthful Foods

Choose healthful foods.

Milk and fruit are healthful foods.

So are bread and vegetables.

Healthful foods help you grow, too.

R 30

Inclusion

The Food Pyramid

Display a copy of the Food Pyramid as a guide to making healthful food choices. Point out the food groups and the suggested servings. Then make an empty food pyramid on the bulletin board. Label each food group. Have children sort pictures of foods cut from magazines and tape or pin them in the correct group to complete the pyramid. **Spatial; Social**

Getting Along

...ork and play well with others.

...spect one another's feelings.

...ow others that you care.

R 31

English Language Learners

Showing Feelings

Have small groups of children make a list of feelings they know about. Feelings listed could include scared, surprised, worried, angry, upset, proud, and lonely. Then have children take turns using first their face and then their whole body to show these feelings. **Social; Intrapersonal**

Getting Along

Getting Along

Objective

- Recognize ways to get along with others.

Build on Prior Knowledge
Ask children to think about the people they work and play with. Ask:

- **Do you think you get along well with others most of the time?** (Children will likely say yes.)

- **Is it always easy to get along with others? Why or why not?** (No; people don't always agree on things or give in a little; sometimes people are unfriendly.)

Using the Illustrations
Ask children to tell how these children are alike and different. Children should mention observable physical similarities and differences, but may mention unobservable ways, such as that they may or may not like the same foods, games, and music, or that they may speak different languages and celebrate different holidays.

Developing the Main Idea
Ask:

- **How can you show respect for another's feelings?** (Possible responses: by not making fun of a person who is different; by being willing to learn and try new things; by listening to new ideas; by compromising)

- **How can you show others that you care?** (Possible responses: by offering help, by being friendly and polite, by listening to others when they have a problem they want to talk about)

Informal Assessment
Ask:

- **How would you show a new classmate from another country that you care?** (Possible responses: Introduce myself, introduce the new classmate to others, invite the new classmate to eat lunch with me or play with me, offer to help the new classmate with classwork.)

Be Safe Indoors

Be Safe Indoors

Objective

- Recognize that some things in and around a home are dangerous and should not be touched.

Some things are dangerous.

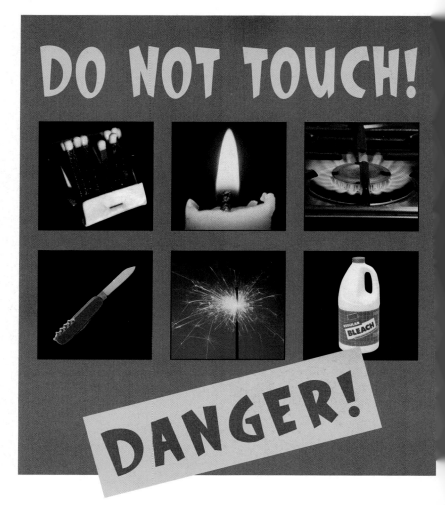

Build on Prior Knowledge
Ask:

- **What would you do if your little sister was about to grab a pair of sharp, pointy scissors that someone forgot to put away?** (Possible responses: stop her; try to get the scissors before she does and put them away.) **Why?** (Scissors are sharp and she could hurt herself.)

Using the Illustrations
Have children look at the pictures. Ask them to identify the items and tell how people use each one.

Explain that although matches, candles, stoves, firecrackers, bleach, and knives have special uses, they can also be dangerous, if someone is careless or doesn't know how to use them.

Developing the Main Idea
Ask:

- **Why are each of these things dangerous, if not used correctly?** (If not used correctly, candles, stoves, and matches could cause burns or start fires. Firecrackers can explode in your hand or face. The fumes of bleach can harm your lungs and the liquid can harm your skin. The blade of a knife is sharp and may cut you.)

Discuss the "Mr. Yuck" and crossbones symbols on products that are dangerous. Children should stay away from cleaning products, plumbing products, and car products.

Informal Assessment
Ask:

- **What would you do if you were to find something dangerous like a broken glass, a bottle of pills, a gun, or a bottle with the poison symbol on it?** (Do not touch it; tell an adult about it right away.)

Have children discuss or act out what they would say and do.

R 32

Inclusion

Don't Touch!
Have small groups of children list things normally found at home that can be dangerous and should not be touched. Have groups share their lists to make a class list. Responses may include medicines, tools, cleaning products, curling iron, detergent, nails, and so on.
Linguistic

Be Safe Outdoors

Follow safety rules.

Wear a helmet.

Buckle up!

STOP

Cross at the corner.

Play safely.

R 33

Be Safe Outdoors

Be Safe Outdoors

Objectives

- Recognize rules for staying safe outdoors.
- Understand the importance of safety rules.

Build on Prior Knowledge
Ask:

- **What is a safety rule?** (a statement that tells what to do or what not to do so you can be safe when you do something)
- **What can happen if you don't follow a safety rule?** (You can get hurt or hurt someone else.)

Using the Illustrations
Ask:

- **Which children do you think are following safety rules?** (all the children)

Developing the Main Idea
Read each rule aloud. Ask:

- **Why is it important to wear a helmet when you ride a bike?** (A helmet can protect your skull and brain from serious injury if you fall.)
- **How can a seatbelt help if you are in an accident?** (It can keep you from being thrown inside the car and becoming badly injured)
- **Why should you cross the street at a corner?** (A driver may not see you coming from between parked cars and you could be hit.)
- **What are some rules you can follow to stay safe at the playground?** (Take turns; don't push or shove; don't run in front of the swings; don't stand on swings.)

Informal Assessment
Ask:

- **What rules can you think of that would help keep you safe on roller blades?** (Possible answers: Wear a helmet, wear knee and elbow guards, cross streets at the corner, obey traffic signs, skate safely.)

Inclusion

Safety at Play
Have children suggest and illustrate safety rules that help keep them safe when they are doing the following outdoor activities: jumping rope, riding a bike, swinging, and swimming in a pool. **Logical**

Advanced Learners

Sport Safety
Have children research and then illustrate or write safety rules that help keep you safe when you are participating in the following outdoor sports: softball, flag football, soccer, and field hockey. **Linguistic; Kinesthetic**

Stay Healthy

Objectives

- Identify ways to stay healthy.

Build on Prior Knowledge
Ask:

- **When do people usually go to the doctor?**
  (When they are ill or hurt or need vaccinations, for a yearly checkup.)

Using the Illustrations
Ask:

- **How is the doctor helping each child to stay healthy?** (The doctor is checking the child's eyes; the doctor is checking the child's teeth.)

Developing the Main Idea
Ask:

- **Why do you think yearly checkups are important for you?** (Possible answer: So the doctor can tell how much I have grown and changed, if I am healthy, and if I am growing normally.)

- **What else might the doctor check?** (Possible answers: height, ears, nose, throat, glands, spine, heart, lungs, and reflexes)

  Mention that children often receive vaccinations or booster shots at the time of a yearly checkup.

- **Why is it important to have your eyes checked each year?** (to find out if glasses are needed to see better)

- **Why is it important to visit the dentist?** (Possible answers: to check for cavities, to make sure gums are healthy, to have teeth cleaned)

Informal Assessment
Ask:

- **Who are the people who help you stay healthy as you grow? How do they help you?** (A doctor checks to make sure my body is growing as it should. A dentist checks my teeth for cavities and to see if they are coming in normally. A nurse gives me shots. My parents make sure I eat the right foods and take me to the doctor for checkups and when I am sick or hurt.)

Stay Healthy

Some people can help you stay healthy as you grow.

Get a checkup every year!

R 34

Reading Strategy

Sequence of Events

Developing Reading Skills
Doctors, nurses, dentists, and other people who help keep people healthy can be grouped under the title of health-care workers. Encourage children who have experienced the care of a health worker to tell or write in order what the worker did to help them. **Linguistic**

Glossary

A

amphibians animals that live in water and on land *(page B18)* **A frog is an amphibian.**

attract A magnet can attract some things to it. *(page F28)* **Iron is a metal that magnets attract.**

B

balance a tool that measures mass *(page E15)* **The side of the balance with more mass will go down.**

C

classify group things by how they are alike *(page B14)* **You can classify these animals.**

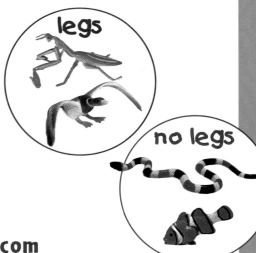

legs

no legs

AT THE COMPUTER Visit **www.mhscience02.com** to find out more about these words.

R 35

clouds made from lots of tiny drops of water that are in the air *(page C30)* **Rain or snow falls from clouds.**

communicate write, draw, or tell your ideas *(page A30)* **The boy draws to communicate what he observes.**

compare observe how things are alike or different *(page A10)* **The child compares the sponge and the ball.**

constellation a group of stars that makes a picture *(page C15)* **This constellation looks like a spoon.**

D

desert a place that gets very little rain *(page B40)* **A desert is very dry.**

draw a conclusion use what you observe to explain what happens *(page E16)* **You can draw a conclusion about what happened to this milk.**

R 36

F

fall the season after summer *(page C46)* **In some places, leaves change color in the fall.**

float to stay on top of water *(page E41)* **Some solids float.**

flowers the plant part that makes seeds *(page A48)* **Flowers make seeds.**

food chain shows what animals eat *(page B35)* **The mouse is part of a food chain.**

force a push or a pull *(page F7)* **It takes a force to move something.**

forest a place with many trees and other plants *(page B41)* **The trees in this forest are very tall.**

R 37

freeze to change from a liquid to a solid *(page E49)* **When it gets very cold, water will freeze.**

fruit the plant part that grows around the seeds *(page A48)* **There are seeds inside this fruit.**

G

gas matter that spreads out to fill all the space of what it is in *(page E24)* **Bubbles have gas inside them.**

gills body parts used to breathe *(page B17)* **All fish have gills.**

gills

grassland a place with many grasses *(page B41)* **Many animals find food in a grassland.**

H

hatch to break out of an egg *(page B23)* **Ducks hatch out of eggs.**

R 38

I

infer use what you know to figure something out *(page A34)* **When a baby cries, you can infer that it needs something.**

insects animals with three body parts and six legs *(page B19)* **This animal is an insect.**

investigate make a plan and try it out *(page D44)* **The boy investigates what happens to water in stems.**

L

leaves plant part that makes food *(page A38)* **Leaves make food for a plant.**

liquid matter that flows and takes the shape of what you pour it in *(page E18)* **Water is a liquid.**

R 39

living thing something that grows, changes, and makes other living things like itself *(page A 12)* **A plant is a living thing.**

lungs body parts used to breathe *(page B16)* **All birds breathe with lungs.**

M

make a model make something to show how something looks *(page B38)* **You can make a model to show where a polar bear lives.**

mammals a group of animals with hair or fur that feed milk to their young *(page B12)* **This animal is a mammal.**

mass how much matter is in an object *(page E9)* **The metal ball has more mass.**

matter what makes up all things *(page E6)* **The block is made of matter.**

R 40

measure find out how far something moves, or how long, how much, or how warm something is *(page F10)* **You can measure how long the toy car is.**

measuring cup measures how much space a liquid takes up *(page E20)* **This is a measuring cup.**

melt to change from a solid to a liquid *(page E46)* **Heat makes the butter melt.**

minerals the building blocks of rocks *(page D6)* **Minerals are a natural resource.**

mixture two or more different things put together *(page E36)* **This mixture is made of solids.**

R 41

N

natural resource something from Earth that people use *(page D8)* **Rock is a natural resource.**

nonliving things things that do not grow, eat, drink, or make more things like themselves *(page A13)* **Cars are nonliving things.**

O

observe see, hear, taste, touch, or smell *(page A4)* **You observe when you touch.**

ocean a very large body of salt water *(page B42)* **The ocean stretches out as far as you can see.**

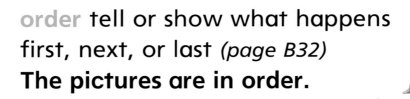

order tell or show what happens first, next, or last *(page B32)* **The pictures are in order.**

oxygen a part of air that people need to live *(page D25)* **We breathe in oxygen from air.**

R 42

P

planet Earth is a planet that moves around the Sun. *(page C18)* **Earth is sometimes called the blue planet.**

poles where a magnet's pull is strongest *(page F34)* **A magnet has two poles.**

pollution harmful things in the air, water, or land *(page D40)* **Pollution happens when air, water, or land get dirty.**

pond a small body of fresh water *(page B43)* **The bird lives in a pond.**

position the place where something is *(page F8)* **The cat's position is inside the box.**

R 43

predict use what you know to tell what will happen *(page A44)* **You predict that the seed will grow.**

properties how something feels, looks, smells, tastes, or sounds *(page E8)* **These things have different properties.**

pull moves something closer to you *(page F6)* **You can move something with a pull.**

push moves something away from you *(page F6)* **You can move something with a push.**

R

recycle to turn old things into new things *(page D47)* **You can recycle old paper to make new paper.**

reduce to use less of something *(page D48)* **The girl reduces the use of paper towels.**

R 44

repel to push away *(page F35)*
These magnets repel each other.

reptiles animals with dry skin that
is covered with scales *(page BI8)*
A turtle is a reptile.

reuse to use something again
(page D46) **The milk carton is
being reused as a bird feeder.**

rocks nonliving things from Earth
(page D6) **These rocks are different.**

roots plant parts that take in
water *(page A32)* **This plant has
many roots.**

ruler measures how long, how
tall, or how big around something
is *(page EI4)* **You can use a ruler
to measure things.**

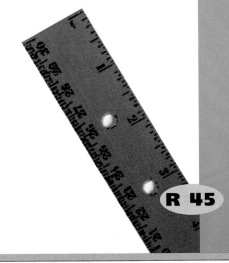

R 45

season a time of the year *(page C40)*
Spring is the season after winter.

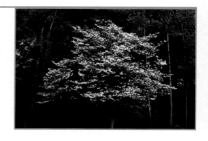

seed the part of a plant that can
grow into new plants *(page A42)*
These seeds look different.

seedling a young plant *(page A46)*
This is a bean seedling.

senses what you use to find
out about the world around you
(page A6) **The girls use the sense
of touch.**

shelter a place where animals
can live and be safe *(page B7)*
This animal uses a tree for shelter.

sink to fall to the bottom *(page E41)*
Some solids sink in water.

R 46

soil Soil has tiny bits of rock and dead plants and animals in it. *(page D12)* **Soil has living and nonliving things in it.**

solid matter that has a shape of its own *(page E12)* **An apple is a solid.**

spring the season after winter *(page C40)* **People plant gardens in spring.**

star objects in the sky that glow and make their own light *(page C6)* **The Sun is a star.**

stem plant part through which water and food move *(page A36)* **This stem has thorns.**

stem

summer the season after spring *(page C42)* **It can be very hot in summer.**

R 47

T

tadpoles young frogs *(page B24)*
This is a tadpole.

temperature how warm or cool something is *(page C7)*
The temperature here is hot.

trunk the stem of a tree *(page A37)*
This trunk is thick and rough.

V

vibrate to move back and forth quickly *(page F42)* **The strings vibrate.**

W

weather what the air is like outside *(page C28)* **The weather here is sunny and hot.**

wind moving air *(page C28)*
The wind blows here.

winter the season after fall *(page C48)* **It is winter here.**

R 48

Contents

Correlated to
National Science Education Content Standards
(Grades K–4)

National Science Education Content Standards	Units of *McGraw-Hill Science*: Grade 1					
	UNIT A Plants are Living Things	UNIT B Animals Are Living Things	UNIT C The Sky and Weather	UNIT D Caring for Earth	UNIT E Matter Everywhere	UNIT F On the Move
Science as Inquiry						
Abilities necessary to do scientific inquiry	✔	✔	✔	✔	✔	✔
Understanding about scientific inquiry	✔	✔	✔	✔	✔	✔
Physical Science						
Properties of objects and material	✔	✔	✔	✔	✔	✔
Position and motion of objects		✔	✔	✔		✔
Light, heat, electricity, and magnetism	✔		✔		✔	✔
Life Science						
The characteristics of organisms	✔	✔				
Life cycles of organisms	✔	✔				
Organisms and environments	✔	✔				
Earth and Space Science						
Properties of Earth materials	✔		✔	✔	✔	
Objects in the sky			✔	✔		
Changes in Earth and sky		✔	✔	✔		
Science and Technology						
Abilities of technological design	✔	✔	✔	✔	✔	✔
Understanding about science and technology	✔	✔	✔	✔	✔	✔
Abilities to distinguish between natural objects and objects made by humans	✔		✔	✔	✔	✔
Science in Personal and Social Perspectives						
Personal health	✔	✔		✔		
Characteristics and changes in populations		✔				
Types of resources	✔	✔		✔	✔	
Changes in environments	✔	✔	✔	✔		
Science and technology in local challenges	✔	✔		✔	✔	✔
Nature and History of Science						
Science as a human endeavor	✔	✔	✔		✔	✔
Unifying concepts and Processes						
Systems, order, and organization	✔	✔	✔	✔		✔
Evidence, models, and explanation			✔		✔	✔
Change, constancy, measurement		✔	✔	✔	✔	✔
Evolution and equilibrium		✔		✔		
Form and function	✔	✔				✔

Correlated to
Benchmarks for Science Literacy
(Grades K–2)

	Units of *McGraw-Hill Science:* Grade 1					
	UNIT A Plants are Living Things	**UNIT B** Animals Are Living Things	**UNIT C** The Sky and Weather	**UNIT D** Caring for Earth	**UNIT E** Matter Everywhere	**UNIT F** On the Move
The Nature of Science						
Scientific view of the world	✔	✔	✔	✔	✔	✔
Scientific inquiry	✔	✔	✔	✔	✔	✔
The scientific enterprise	✔	✔	✔			
The Nature of Technology						
Technology and science	✔	✔	✔	✔	✔	✔
Design and systems		✔	✔	✔	✔	✔
Issues in technology	✔	✔	✔			
The Physical Setting						
The universe			✔			
Earth	✔		✔	✔		
Processes that shape Earth	✔	✔	✔	✔		
Structure of matter				✔	✔	
Energy transformations	✔	✔		✔	✔	✔
Motion		✔		✔	✔	✔
Forces of nature			✔	✔	✔	✔
The Living Environment						
Diversity of life	✔	✔			✔	
Heredity	✔	✔	✔			
Cells	✔	✔				
Interdependence of life	✔	✔				
Flow of matter and energy	✔	✔	✔	✔		✔
Evolution of life	✔	✔				
The Human Organism						
Human identity	✔	✔		✔	✔	
Basic functions	✔	✔			✔	
Physical health	✔	✔		✔		
Common Themes						
Systems	✔	✔	✔	✔		✔
Models			✔			✔
Constancy and change	✔	✔	✔	✔	✔	
Scale	✔	✔	✔	✔	✔	✔

McGraw-Hill Curriculum Integration: Science and Reading

Correlation of *McGraw-Hill Science* with:
- *Spotlight on Literacy* • *McGraw-Hill Reading*

McGraw-Hill Science correlates with these reading programs by means of its content as well as of the Reading Skills highlighted in each unit.

McGraw-Hill Science Grade 1	Spotlight on Literacy selections with corresponding content or skills	McGraw-Hill Reading selections with corresponding content or skills
UNIT A PLANTS ARE LIVING THINGS **Topic Focus** • the senses • plants (living things) • seeds and growth • change • plants and people **Chapter Reading Skills** • Draw conclusions • Compare and contrast	**Content** • Jasper's Beanstalk (seeds, plant growth) • An Egg Is an Egg (growth, change) • Whose Baby? (growth) • The Surprise Family (nests) **Skills** *Draw conclusions* • A Birthday Basket for Tía *Compare and contrast* • The Surprise Family	**Content** • You Can't Smell a Flower with Your Ear • Johnny Appleseed (seeds, growth) • Let's Camp Out! **Skills** *Draw conclusions* • Owl and the Moon • You Can't Smell a Flower with Your Ear * *Compare and Contrast* • Greg's Mask *
UNIT B ANIMALS ARE LIVING THINGS **Topic Focus** • habitats, parts of a pond • growth • animals • food • survival **Chapter Reading Skills** • Summarize • Draw conclusions	**Content** • Five Little Ducks • I Went Walking • Whose Baby • The Chick and the Duckling • Everything Grows • Guinea Pigs Don't Read Books • The Elephant's Trunk • Any Kind of Dog • Imaginary Zoo **Skills** *Draw conclusions* • A Birthday Basket for Tía	**Content** • Snakes (animals) • Let's Camp Out (habitat) • Yasmin's Ducks (animals) • The Night Animals • What Bug Is It? • A Vet • A Year later (growth) • Baby Chick (growth) **Skills** *Draw conclusions* • You Can't Smell a Flower with Your Ear! * • Owl and the Moon
UNIT C THE SKY AND WEATHER **Topic Focus** • the Sun • the Moon • stars • weather changes • seasons **Chapter Reading Skills** • Cause and effect • Sequence of events	**Content** • Rain (weather, sky) • A Letter to Amy (weather) • First Snow (snow) * The Cloud **Skills** *Cause and effect* • The Story of Chicken Licken • One Monday Morning *Sequence of events* • I Went Walking • Jasper's Beanstalk • Just a Little Bit	**Content** • Put Out the Fire (heat) • Owl and the Moon • Splash • To the Top • Raindrops (weather) **Skills** *Cause and effect* • The Knee-High Man * • Put Out the Fire *Sequence of events* • Quack * • The Path on the Map • Ships

*Skill is introduced in McGraw-Hill Reading with a two-page lesson that accompanies the selection.

McGraw-Hill Science
Grade 1

Spotlight on Literacy
Grade 1 selections with corresponding content or skills

Spotlight on Literacy
Grade 1 selections with corresponding content or skills

UNIT D CARING FOR EARTH

Topic Focus
- rocks, minerals, soil
- water
- air
- living resources
- pollution

Chapter Reading Skills
- Compare and contrast
- Summarize

Content
- Rain
- Everything Grows (growth)
- You'll Soon Grow into Them, Titch (growth)

Skills

Compare and contrast
- White Rabbit's Color Book

Content
- Put Out the Fire
- A Vet
- Let's Camp Out!
- Pets

Skills

Compare and contrast
- Greg's Mask *
- Sam's Song

UNIT E MATTER, MATTER EVERYWHERE

Topic Focus
- use of senses
- properties (shape/color)
- solids, liquids, gases
- change

Chapter Reading Skills
- Find the main idea
- Compare and contrast

Content
- White Rabbit's Color Book (properties, color)
- Seven Blind Mice (properties, senses)
- Guinea Pigs Don't Read Books (properties)
- Julieta and Her Paintbox (color)
- Seven Sillies (liquids, solids)

Skills

Find the main idea
- Rain
- Everything Grows

Compare and contrast
- White Rabbit's Color Book

Content
- You Can't Smell a Flower with Your Ear! (senses)

Skills

Find the main idea
- Splash *
- What Bug Is It
- A Vet

Compare and contrast
- Greg's Mask *
- Sam's Song

UNIT F ON THE MOVE

Topic Focus
- position, movement
- pushes and pulls
- how parts work together
- how and why living things move

Chapter Reading Skills
- Cause and effect
- Sequence of events

Content
- Bet You Can't (lifting)
- Coco Can't Wait (moving, position)
- The Folk Who Live in Backward Town (position)
- Just a Little Bit (motion)

Skills

Cause and effect
- The Chick and the Duckling
- Hattie and the Fox

Sequence of events
- I Went Walking
- Jasper's Beanstalk
- Just a Little Bit

Content
- Ships
- On the Go! (transportation)
- Young Amelia Earhart: A Dream to Fly
- Shrinking Mouse (position)

Skills

Cause and effect
- The Shopping List *
- Yasmin's Ducks

Sequence of events
- Quack *
- The Path on the Map
- Ships

---

*Skill is introduced in McGraw-Hill Reading with a two-page lesson that accompanies the selection.

Primary Thermometer

Hot	Hot	Hot	Hot	Hot
Warm	Warm	Warm	Warm	Warm
Cool	Cool	Cool	Cool	Cool
Cold	Cold	Cold	Cold	Cold

To Teacher: Directions to make a primary thermometer:

1. Cut out the 5 strips.

2. Color each cold section blue.

3. Color each cool section green.

4. Color each warm section yellow.

5. Color each hot section orange.

6. Align the strip on the thermometer as follows:
> Cold (below 0°C)
> Cool (1°C–15°C)
> Warm (15°C–30°C)
> Hot (above 30°C)

7. Once aligned, tape the entire strip to the °F side of the thermometer using clear tape. This will help to make it waterproof.

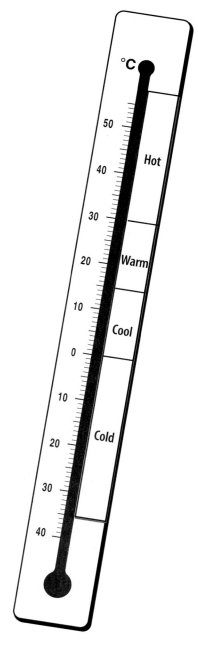

Macmillan/McGraw-Hill

Calendar

Sunday	Monday	Tuesday	Wednesday	Thursday	Friday	Saturday

Macmillan/McGraw-Hill

Inch Graph Paper

Macmillan/McGraw-Hill

Inch Ruler and Centimeter Ruler

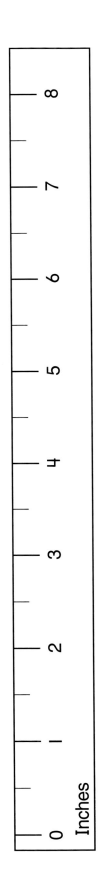

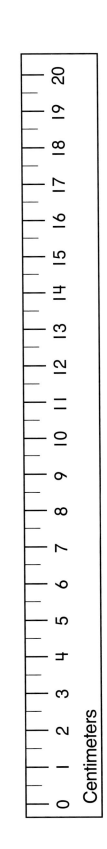

Macmillan/McGraw-Hill

* Indicates an activity related to this topic. • Boldfaced entries are features found exclusively in the Teacher's Edition.

* Indicates an activity related to this topic. • Boldfaced entries are features found exclusively in the Teacher's Edition.

* Indicates an activity related to this topic. • Boldfaced entries are features found exclusively in the Teacher's Edition.

* Indicates an activity related to this topic. • Boldfaced entries are features found exclusively in the Teacher's Edition.

Credits for Teacher's Edition

Cover Design and Illustration: Robert Brook Allen

Cover Photos: bear cub: W. Perry Conway/Corbis; bkgrd: honeycomb Ralph Clevenger/Corbis

Title Page: honeycomb Ralph Clevenger/Corbis

Honeycomb Borders: Ralph Clevenger/Corbis

Contents: iv: l. Orion Press, Index Stock Imagery; b. Dominque Brud/Dembinsky Photo Assoc. v: l. Carl Purcell, Words and Pictures; l. inset Pictor; b. James Carmichael/Image Bank. vi: l. Stephen Simpson, FPG International; b. Photo Library International/Photo Researchers, Inc. vii: l. J. A. Kraulis, Masterfile; b. Diane J. Ali/Bruce Coleman, Inc. viii: l. Dave Starrett, Masterfile; ix: l. Stone/Cosmo Condina

Tvi: t.l. Siede Preis/ PhotoDisc; m.l. Clement Mok/ PhotoDisc; b.l. Siede Preis/ PhotoDisc.

Process Skills in Macmillan/McGraw-Hill: Tviii: t.l. Dan Howell for MHSD; (1/4) David Waitz for MHSD.

National Geographic Tab A: Orion Press, Index Stock Imagery; **Unit A:** p. A1•a: Jim Battles, Dembinky Photo Associates; p. A1•d: t.r. CMCD/PhotoDisc; p. A1: bkgrd Stone/Jake Rajs ; inset Stone/Davies & Starr Inc.

National Geographic Tab B: © Charlie Heidecker/Visuals Unlimited. **Unit B:** p. B1•a: Andy Rouse; p. B1•d: t.r. CMCD/ PhotoDisc; p. B1: bkgrd Carl Purcell, Words and Pictures; inset Pictor

National Geographic Tab C: Bozeman, Montana Stephen Simpson, FPG International. **Unit C:** p. C1•a: E.R. Degginger, Bruce Coleman, Inc.; p. C1•d: t.r. Siede Preis/ PhotoDisc; p. C1: Stone/Jack Dykinga

National Geographic Tab D: Stuart Dee, Image Bank; **Unit D:** p. D1•a: Nancy Sefton, Photo Researchers, Inc.; p. D1•d: t.r. Siede Preis/ PhotoDisc; p. D1: J. A. Kraulis, Masterfile

National Geographic Tab E: © Philip Gould/CORBIS. **Unit E:** p.E1•a: David Sams, Stock • Boston; p. E1•d: t.r. CMCD/ PhotoDisc; p. E1: Dave Starrett, Masterfile

National Geographic Tab F: Stone/Cosmo Condina; **Unit F:** p. F1•a: Junichi Takahashi, Stomp; p. F1•d: t.r. CMCD/ PhotoDisc; p. F1: Stone/Cosmo Condina

Credits for Pupil's Edition

Cover Design and Illustration: Robert Brook Allen
Cover Photos: bear cub: W. Perry Conway/Corbis; bkgrd: honeycomb Ralph Clevenger/Corbis

Design & Production: MKR Design, Inc.

Illustrations: Batelman: p. R19; Rachel Geswaldo: p. R33; Wallace Keller: p. F9; Rob Schuster: pp. R20, R21; Wendy Wax: pp. Who's a Scientist cover, E06-E07; Ted Williams: pp. R17, R18; Josie Yee: pp. S4, C18-C19, C30-C31, D19. Rachel Geswaldo: p. R33;

Photography Credits: All photographs are by MacMillan/McGraw-Hill School Division (MMSD) David Mager for MMSD, Ken Karp for MMSD, Michael Groen for MMSD, and John Serafin for MMSD, except as noted below:

Contents: iv: l. Orion Press, Index Stock Imagery; b. Dominque Brud/Dembinsky Photo Assoc. v: l. Carl Purcell, Words and Pictures; l. inset Pictor; b. James Carmichael/Image Bank. vi: l. Stephen Simpson, FPG International; b. Photo Library International/Photo Researchers, Inc. vii: l. J. A. Kraulis, Masterfile; b. Diane J. Ali/Bruce Coleman, Inc. viii: l. Dave Starrett, Masterfile; ix: l. Stone/Cosmo Condina

Who's a Scientist: cover: m. David Coleman/Stock Boston; b.l. Jim Cummins/FPG International; t.l. Bob Daemmrich/Bob Daemmrich Photo, Inc.; b.r. Lawrence Migdale/Stock Boston. S1: b. Patrice Ceisel/Stock Boston; Tim Flach/Tony Stone Images. S4: inset Bill Aron/Photo Edit; bkgrd Rex Butcher/Bruce Coleman, Inc.. S5: Corbis. S7: bkgrd Don Mason/The Stock Market. S8: b.r. Tom Brakefield/Bruce Coleman, Inc.

National Geographic Unit Opener A: A0: Orion Press, Index Stock Imagery; A1: bkgrd Stone/Jake Rajs ; inset Stone/Davies & Starr Inc.;. **Unit A:** A2-A3: Jim Battles/Dembinsky Photo Assoc.. A4: inset, Howard L. Garrett/Dembinsky Photo Assoc.; b. Lawrence Migdale. A4-A5: bkgrd Michelle Burgess/Stock Boston. A6: Dan Dempster/Dembinsky Photo Assoc. A8: t.r. Mark E. Gibson/Dembinsky Photo Assoc.; b.l. Phyllis Picardi/Stock Boston. A9: Bob Daemmrich/Stock Boston. A10-A11: bkgrd, John Cancalosi/DRK Photo. A12: t.r. Bob Daemmrich/Stock Boston; inset, DPA/Dembinsky Photo Assoc.; b. Pascal Quittemelle/Stock Boston. A13: b.r. Stephen Frisch/Stock Boston; m.l. Felicia Martinez/PhotoEdit; t.r. Mark A. Schneider/Dembinsky Photo Assoc. A15: m.l. Robert P. Falls/Bruce Coleman, Inc. A18-A19: Kitney & Carmen Miller/Liaison. A20-A21: bkgrd Frans Lemmens/Image Bank. A22: t.l. Mark C. Burnett/Stock Boston; b.r. Bob Daemmrich/Stock Boston. A22-A23: bkgrd Lee Foster/Bruce Coleman, Inc. A24: b.l. Dominique Braud/Dembinsky Photo Assoc.; l. Darrell Gulin/DRK Photo.; m. William Johnson/Stock Boston. A25: t.r. Jeff Foott/DRK Photo; b.l. Bob Gurr/DRK Photo; m.r. Bill Lea/Dembinsky Photo Assoc.. A26-A27: bkgrd, Michael Newman/PhotoEdit. A28 : t. Bob Gibbons/Photo Researchers, Inc.; bkgrd Susanna Price/DK. A30-A31: G. R. Roberts/Photo Researchers, Inc.. A32: Dwight Kuhn. A32-A33: bkgrd, Maximillian Stock Ltd/Photo Researchers, Inc.. A33: inset, Rosenfeld Images /Photo Researchers, Inc.. A34-A35: Dwight Kuhn. A36: l. Dwight Kuhn. A36-A37: bkgrd, Bill Lea/Dembinsky Photo Assoc. A37: t.l. David R. Frazier/Photo Researchers, Inc.; b. Bill Gallery/Stock Boston. A38: l. Andrew McRobb/DK. A39: inset, Tom Bean/DRK Photo; m.l. William Johnson/Stock Boston; b.l. Breck P. Kent/Earth Scenes; t.l. Felicia Martinez/PhotoEdit; t.r. Felicia Martinez/PhotoEdit. A40-A41: E. R. Degginger/Dembinsky Photo Assoc. A41: r. Spencer Grant/PhotoEdit; inset, Lynn M. Stone/DRK Photo. A43: m., inset, E. R. Degginger/Dembinsky Photo Assoc.; inset, Jeff Dunn/Stock Boston; b.l. Dwight Kuhn. A44: m. Patricia Lanza/Bruce Coleman, Inc.. A46: l. Kim Taylor/DK. A46-A47: Kim Taylor/DK. A48: m.r. E. R. Degginger/Dembinsky Photo Assoc.; inset Marcia Griffen/Earth Scenes. A49: inset R. J. Erwin/Photo Researchers, Inc.; r. Scott T. Smith/Dembinsky Photo Assoc. A54: Bettman/CORBIS. A55: Bettman/CORBIS.

National Geographic Unit Opener B: B0: © Charlie Heidecker/Visuals Unlimited; B1: bkgrd Carl Purcell, Words and Pictures; inset Pictor; **Unit B:** B2 - B3: Andy Rouse. B4-B5: Ron Croucher/Nature Photographers Ltd. B6: b. Tony Stone Images; t.l. U. & J. Schimmelpfen/Natural Selection. B7: b.r. Brian Kenney/Brian Kenney; t.r. Kim Taylor, Jane Burton/DK. B8: Mark Newman/Stock Connection. B9: t. DK; m.l. Karl Shone/DK; m.r. Ron Spomer/Visuals Unlimited, Inc. B10: Brian Kenney; inset, Fritz Prenzel/Animals Animals. B11: m. PhotoDisc; t.r. Gerry Ellis/ENP Images; m.l. Robert Maier/Animals Animals; b.l. Ken Usami/PhotoDisc; b.r. J. & P. Wegner/Animals Animals. B12: t.r. S. Dalton/Animals Anim m.l. Lynn Stone/Animals Animals. B12-B13: m. M. Harvey/DRK Photo. B13: t.r. The Cou Society/Image Bank. B14: m. PhotoDisc; b.r. Tim Flach/Tony Stone Images; bkgrd, Mich Fogden/DRK Photo; t.r. Allen Blake Sheldon/Animals Animals. B16: b.l. Mary Clay/Maste t.l. Gordon & Cathy Illg/Animals Animals; t.r. Frank Oberia/Tony Stone Images; m.r. Jerry Young/DK. B17: b. M. Gibbs/Animals Animals. B18: b.r. James Carmichael/Image Bank; Grant Heilman/Grant Heilman Photography; t.r. Robert Maier/Animals Animals. B19: m. Grant Heilman/Grant Heilman Photography; t.r. Kim Taylor/DK; b.r. Kim Taylor/DK. B20: Superstock. B22-B23: Jane Burton/DK; t. Jane Burton/DK; b.r. John Daniels/DK; b.l., b.m. b.r.m. Barrie Watts/DK. B24-B25: b.r. George Bernard/Animals Animals; b.l., b.m., m. Jan Burton/Bruce Coleman, Inc.; bkgrd, George Grall/National Geographic Society; t.r. Zig Leszczynski/Animals Animals; b.l. O. S. F. /Animals Animals. B26: m.l. Superstock; t.l. Ala Carruthers/Photo Researchers, Inc.; m.r. Murray Wilson/Omni-Photo Communications. B3 B31: David Dennis/Animals Animals. B32: Betty K. Bruce/Animals Animals; inset J. C. Carton/Bruce Coleman, Inc.; m.l. Gary Meszaros/Bruce Coleman, Inc. B34: b.r. Stanley Breeden/DRK Photo; M.R.J. Erwin/DRK Photo; b.l. Stephen J. Krasemann/DRK Photo. B34 B35: Michael Gadomski/Earth Scenes. B35: Tom Brakefield/DRK Photo. B36: m.r. John Cancalosi/Peter Arnold, Inc.; t.r. Jerry L. Ferrara/Photo Researchers, Inc.; t.l. Belinda Wright/DRK Photo; m. Belinda Wright/DRK Photo. B36-B37: Alan G. Nelson/Animals Animals. B37: t.l. Stephen J. Krasemann/DRK Photo; t.r. Richard La Val/Animals Animals; J. H. Robinson/Photo Researchers, Inc. B38: E. R. Degginger/Animals Animals. B40-B41: b Tom Brakefield/Bruce Coleman, Inc.; m. Ken Cole/Animals Animals; t.l. Eastcott/Momatiuk/Animals Animals; b. Darrell Gulin/DRK Photo; m. Doug Wechsler/Earth Science. B42: b. David Hall; t. Robert C. Hermed/Photo Researchers, Inc.. B43: b.l. William Leonard/DRK Photo; inset, Maslowski/Photo Researchers, Inc.; t. Terry Whittaker/Photo Researchers, Inc.. B44: Leonard Lee Rue III/DRK Photo. B45: m. Wayne Lankinen/DRK Pho t.l. Wayne Lynch/DRK Photo; b. Joe McDonald/DRK Photo. B47: t.r. Michael Fogden/DRK Photo; b.r. David Hall. B48-B49: b. Tim Davis/Photo Researchers, Inc.; m.l. Bill Lea/Dembins Photo Assoc.; t.r. Bill Lea/Dembinsky Photo Assoc.; b.r. George Schaller/Bruce Coleman, Inc B50: m. Rapho-DeSazo/Photo Researchers, Inc. B54: Reuters/ Weinstein/Field Museum /Archive Photos. B55: Bob Burch/Bruce Coleman, Inc.

National Geographic Unit Opener C: C0: Stephen Simpson, FPG International; C1: Stone/Ja Dykinga; **Unit C:** C2: E. R. Degginger/Bruce Coleman, Inc.. C4: Stan Osolinski/Dembinsky Photo Assoc.. C5: tr Tom Salyer/Silver Image. C5: bl Tom

Salyer/Silver Image. C5: br Tom Salyer/Silver Image. C6-C7: b.r. David R. Frazier/Photo Researchers, Inc.; b. Darrell Gulin/DRK Photo; Sakura/Black Sheep. C8: b.l. Sakura/Black Sheep. C8-C9: Tony Stone Images. C9: b.r. Warren Bolster/Tony Stone Images. C10: David Nunuk/Photo Researchers, Inc. C12: m. S. Nielsen/DRK Photo; r. S. Nielsen/DRK Photo; l. S. Nielsen/DRK Photo. C13: m. S. Nielsen/DRK Photo; b.l. S. Nielsen/DRK Photo. C14-C15: Jerr Schad/Photo Researchers, Inc. C16: r. WorldSat International /Photo Researchers, Inc. C18: Photo Library International /Photo Researchers, Inc.. C20: m. Spencer Grant/Photo Edit. C2 Tom Salyer/Silver Image. C24-C25: Jeremy Woodhouse/DRK Photo. C26: Tom McCarthy/PhotoEdit. C28: b. Mark E. Gibson/DRK Photo; t.l. Malcolm Hanes/Bruce Colemar Inc.. C29: m. Frank Krahmer/Bruce Coleman, Inc.; l. Jeremy Woodhouse/DRK Photo. C32-C3 Larry Mishkar/Dembinsky Photo Assoc. C34: Kim Heacox/DRK Photo. C35: t.r. American Re Cross/Photo Researchers, Inc.; m. Tom Bean/DRK Photo; bkgrd Howard Bluestein/Photo Researchers, Inc. C36: l. Christian Grzimek/Photo Researchers, Inc.; m. Jeff Lepore/Photo Researchers, Inc. C37: t.l. Melinda Berge/Bruce Coleman, Inc. t. Bonnie Sue/Photo Researchers, Inc. C38: Susan Smetana/Dembinsky Photo Assoc.. C40: t.r. E. R. Degginger/Photo Researchers, Inc.; b.l. Frank Krahmer/Bruce Coleman, Inc.. C40-C41: t. Michael P. Gadomski/Photo Researchers, Inc. C41: b. Mark E. Gibson/DRK Photo; m. Darrell Gulin/DRK Photo. C42: inset, Johnny's Selected Seeds, Albion, ME; t. David Madison/Bruce Coleman, Inc. C42-C43: b.l. Yva/John Momatiuk/Eastcott/Photo Researchers, Inc. C44: Davi Falconer/DRK Photo. C46: b. Mark E. Gibson/DRK Photo. C46-C47: m. Stephen G. Maka/DRI Photo. C47: t.r. Tom & Pat Leeson/Photo Researchers, Inc.; b. Tom & Pat Leeson/DRK Photo. C48: m. D. Cavagnaro/DRK Photo; b.l. John Gerlach/DRK Photo. C49: m. Gerard Fuehrer/DR Photo; t. Norman Owen Tomalin/Bruce Coleman, Inc.; t.l. Norman Owen Tomalin/Bruce Coleman, Inc. C50-C51: m. Jeff Greenberg/Stock Boston. C54-C55: Warren Faidley/Weatherstock.

National Geographic Unit Opener D: D0: Stuart Dee, Image Bank; D1: J. A. Kraulis, Masterfile; **Unit D:** D2-D3: Nancy Sefton/Photo Researchers, Inc. D4: Lawrence Migdale. D D7: b. Jay Lurie/Bruce Coleman, Inc. D7: (from top) Joyce Photography/Photo Researchers, Inc.; Mark A. Schneider/Dembinsky Photo Assoc.; Ed Degginger/Brian Kenney; Biophoto Assoc./Photo Researchers, Inc.; Mark A. Schneider/Dembinsky Photo Assoc.. D8: bkgrd Bruc Esbin/Omni-Photo Comm.; b. Timothy O'Keefe/Bruce Coleman, Inc. D9: m.r. John D. Cunningham/Visuals Unlimited, Inc.; t.l. Richard Hutchings/PhotoEdit; t.r. Stephen McBrady/PhotoEdit; m. Tom McCarthy/PhotoEdit; b.r. S. McCutcheon/Visuals Unlimited, Inc. b.l. David Young-Wolff/PhotoEdit. D10-D11: bkgrd George H. Harrison/Bruce Coleman, Inc. D12: Photo Researchers, Inc. D13: t.l. Michael Black/Bruce Coleman, Inc.; t.l. inset Phil Degginger/Bruce Coleman, Inc.; m.l. Ron Sherman/Ron Sherman; m.l. inset Glenn M. Oliver/Visuals Unlimited, Inc.; b.r. M. Timothy O'Keefe/Bruce Coleman, Inc.; b.r. inset Deborah Davis/Photo Edit. D14: t.r. Bob Daemmrich/Bob Daemmrich Photo, Inc.. D14-D15: Willard Clay/Dembinsky Photo Assoc.. D15: inset E. R. Degginger/Photo Researchers, Inc.; T Hans Reinhard/Bruce Coleman, Inc. D16: inset Nicholas Devore/Bruce Coleman, Inc. D16-D1 bkgrd Alan Kearney/FPG International. D18: l. Janis Burger/Bruce Coleman, Inc. D18-D19: r Larry Blank/Visuals Unlimited, Inc. D19: Michael James/Photo Researchers, Inc. D20: m.l. Dennis McDonald/Photo Edit; t.r. David Young-Wolff/PhotoEdit. D20-D21: bkgrd Janine Pestel/Visuals Unlimited, Inc. D21: inset D. Pearson/Visuals Unlimited, Inc. D22-D23: bkgrd Myrleen Cate/Photo Edit. D24: t.r. PhotoDisc; b.l. Bonnioe Kamin/Photo Edit; m. Mike Welsch/Photo Edit. D24-D25: bkgrd Jack W. Dykinga/Bruce Coleman, Inc. D25: inset Mary Kate Denny/Photo Edit; t.r. Richard Smith/Dembinsky Photo Assoc.. D26-D27: bkgrd Lawrence Migdale. D28: t.l. Diane J. Ali/Bruce Coleman, Inc.; m.l. M. W. Black/Bruce Coleman, Inc.; t.r. Tony Freeman/PhotoEdit; b. Michael Newman/Photo Edit. D29: b.r. Bruce Coleman, Inc.; m.l. E. R. Degginger/Dembinsky Photo Assoc.; m. Michael Newman/Photo Edit; b. Mary M. Steinbacher/Photo Edit. D30: b.l. D. Cavagnaro/Visuals Unlimited, Inc.; t. Simon Fraser Science Photo Library/Photo Researchers, Inc.; b. David Young-Wolff/Photo Edit. D30-D31: Jock Montgomery/Bruce Coleman, Inc.. D31: t.l. Andrew Dalsimer/Bruce Coleman, Inc.; b. John Elk III/Bruce Coleman, Inc.; t.r. Mark Richards/Photo Edit. D32: Culver Pictures. D36-D37: Bruce M. Herman/Photo Researchers, Inc.. D38-D39: bkgrd Steve McCutcheon/Visuals Unlimited, Inc.. D40: inset Phil Degginger/Phil Degginger. D40-D41: Georg Gerster/Photo Researchers, Inc.. D42: l. John Mielcarek/Dembinsky Photo Assoc.; r. Dick Thomas/Visuals Unlimited, Inc.. D43: Eunice Harris/Photo Researchers, Inc.. D44-d45: John Elk/Stock Boston. D46: t. Jeff Greenberg/Visuals Unlimited, Inc.. D47: t. Myrleen Ferguson/Photo Edit. D49: m. Bill Bachman/Photo Researchers, Inc.. D54: m. The Granger Collection; b.l. The Granger Collection, New York; bkgrd Layne Kennedy/Corbis. D55: m.r.

e Kennedy/Corbis.

nal Geographic Unit Opener E: E0: © Philip Gould/CORBIS; E1: Dave Starrett,
erfile; **Unit E:** E2 - E3: David Sams/Stock Boston. E4-E5: Jeff Greenberg/Stock Boston. E8:
nne White/Photo Researchers, Inc.. E16: t.r. Barbara Alper/Stock Boston; b. Robert
r/Animals Animals. E22-E23: bkgrd, Superstock. E30-E31: Craig Tuttle/The Stock Market.
39: bkgrd, Henryk Kaiser/Leo de Wye Stock Photo Agency. E44-E45: bkgrd, Tom
rt/The Stock Market. E46: t.l. The Stock Market. E46-E47: m. Robert Essel/The Stock
et. E47: t.l. George Kamper/Tony Stone Images; r. Charles D. Winters/Photo
rchers, Inc. E48: l. Superstock; b.l. Bill Bonoszewski/Visuals Unlimited, Inc. E48-E49: t.r.
n Oppermans/Tony Stone Images.

nal Geographic Unit Opener F: F0: Stone/Cosmo Condina; F1: Stone/Cosmo Condina;
F: F2-F3: Lori Adamski Peek/Tony Stone Images. F4-F5: Myrleen Cate/Photo Edit; bkgrd
Press/Natural Selection. F10-F11: bkgrd Dennis O'Clair/Tony Stone Images. F14-F15:
d /Superstock. F16 : b. Spencer Grant/Photo Edit; inset ,MichaelNewman/Photo Edit.
F17: bkgrd David R. Frazier/David R. Frazier Photolibrary. F17: t.l. Robert E.
nmrich/Tony Stone Images. F18: l. David Madison/Tony Stone Images. F18-F19: m.
rstock; t.r. Margaret Kois/The Stock Market. F19: t.l. Lori Adamski Peek/Tony Stone
es. F40-F41: bkgrd Superstock; inset George Disario/The Stock Market. F42: l. Bill
/PhotoEdit; m. Tom McCarthy/Photo Edit. F43: b.r. Laura Dwight/; t. Lawrence Migdale.
Mark Downey/Viesti Associates, Inc.; b.l. Robert Fried/Stock Boston. F46: t. Jeff
nberg/David R. Frazier Photolibrary; b. J. Barry O'Rourke/The Stock Market. F47: b.r.
d R. Frazier Photolibrary; t.r. A. Ramey/Photo Edit. F48: b. Andy Cox/Tony Stone Images;
enis Scott/The Stock Market. F49: David R. Frazier Photolibrary; b.l. John Lamb/Tony
e Images. F54: b.r. Robert Holmgren. F55: Robert Holmgren.

nce and Health Handbook: R8: l. J. C. Carton/Bruce Coleman, Inc.; b.r. E. R.
gginger/Bruce Coleman, Inc.; r. Phil Degginger/Bruce Coleman, Inc.. R14: PhotoDisc. R28:
im Whitmer/FPG International. R29: PhotoDisc; b.l. Laura Dwight/Peter Arnold, Inc..
Myrleen Ferguson/Photo Edit. R32: Jerry Schad/Photo Researchers, Inc. R34: t.r. Adam
th/FPG International; b.l. Ed Wheeler/The Stock Market.

tographs by Roman Sapecki and/or Lew Lause for MMSD: pp. R27; R28:m. & b.; R30: t;
: b.

Teacher's Notes